Berry

Martha Berry

Sketches of Her Schools and College

Edited by
Doyle Mathis and Ouida Dickey
Berry College
Mount Berry, Georgia

Published by
Wings Publishers
1700 Chattahoochee Avenue
Atlanta, Georgia 30318

Book design and composition by Melanie M. McMahon

Manufactured in the United States of America

10 9 8 7 6 5 4 3 2 1
First Edition

ISBN 1-930897-05-7

Dedication

To the memory of Garland Martin Dickey, Berry alumnus (1942), this book is dedicated. Garland will be remembered for his friendly way and for the manner in which he filled a number of roles during his years at Berry: instructor in history and professor of health and physical education, coach, director of athletics, dean of men and others.

Born in 1919 in Tennessee, Garland arrived at Berry College as a student in 1938; and, with the exception of a stint in the Navy during World War II and a year of doctoral residency, he never left. He fit the profile of the ideal student for whom Martha Berry had created her school—a poor farm boy willing to work for his education. Garland worked his way through college on the grounds crew, planting many of the oak trees that still line the streets of the campus today. He and his brothers, Edward and Bob, roomed together, worked together, and played throughout their college years in the positions of pitcher, catcher, and shortstop, respectively, for the Lemley baseball team. Garland joined the faculty at Berry in 1946 and was instrumental in the development of intercollegiate sports at Berry.

He often proudly proclaimed that working at Berry was the only job he ever had. He delighted in the daily walks to his office at Memorial Gymnasium and in the steady stream of students who strolled through to greet or visit with him. He taught a generation of faculty children how to swim. He knew that playing tennis and shooting baskets, activities for which he provided equipment, were thirsty work and always kept a stack of nickels and dimes in the corner of his desk drawer in case any of those children wandered into the gym while he was teaching class and needed a little change to buy a Coke from the machine. He cleverly engaged the faculty children to assist with his special education classes, instilling in them a sense of volunteerism still evident today.

Garland Dickey

Garland and Edward once calculated that they and Bob had influenced over 100 young people to come to Berry College, among them Garland's and Bob's daughters. In 1976, he received the Berry Alumni Association's Distinguished Service Award because his service was far and wide. Among the first faculty members at Berry to receive tenure, Garland remained devoted to the school that had opened a gate of opportunity for him until his death in 1981. A dedicatory plaque at the site of the Garland Dickey Memorial Fitness Trail, gift of the Student Government in October 1982, refers to him as "a devoted teacher and friend."

ACKNOWLEDGMENTS

Many people have made it possible for this book to be available. Especially helpful were the following persons associated with Berry College:

Ruth Ash, archivist, and Amy Summerlin, technical assistant in the archives, gave guidance and time in the location of information among the Martha Berry letters and other collections there. Evelyn Hoge Pendley, associate professor of English emerita, shared valuable recollections and granted permission for the use of her works, as did John Lipscomb, vice president for development emeritus.

Lending assistance through inquiries and interviews were Susan Asbury, curator of Oak Hill and The Martha Berry Museum; Joseph Walton, vice president for finance; Alan Storey, executive assistant to the president and director of public relations; Randolph Green and Virginia Green Matheny, Berry graduates, son and daughter of G. Leland Green, Berry's first president; J. Donald Jones, Berry graduate and former employee; and John R. Bertrand, president emeritus of Berry. Scott Breithaupt, director of historic Berry and special events, guided us in the selection of photographs and helped gather, identify, and digitize historic pictures. Herman Higgins, associate professor of history emeritus, assisted in selecting and gathering historic photographs; Mark Drummond, director of media production, public relations, produced new photographs; and Kevin Kleine, advisor to Student Publications, scanned the photographs and signatures.

Providing capable skills in the scanning of documents and preparation of manuscript were Alan Storey, secretary to the board of trustees; Alisa Ray, office manager, faculty research and sponsored programs; Susan Burr, secretary, rhetoric and writing; and Laquieda Joiner, secretary, Memorial Library. Shannon Biggers, director of creative services, public relations, and Sybil Parker, typesetter in printing services, were especially helpful in preparing materials for the publisher. Pat Millican, president of

Northwest Georgia Genealogical Society, assisted Amy Summerlin in establishing on the archives computer the pedigree chart of the Berry family. Berry graduates Jennifer and Angela Dickey contributed to the dedication. Rheba Mathis read the manuscript and made valuable suggestions.

Scott Colley, president of Berry College, lent encouragement and support from inception to completion of this project. To Dr. Colley, our colleagues and friends mentioned above, and to numerous others not named here who exhibited interest in the progress of our efforts and thus spurred us on, we extend wholehearted thanks.

Doyle Mathis and Ouida Dickey

Introduction

The editors became somewhat familiar with and interested in Berry history while students in the college in the 1940s and 1950s. This project had its origin in the early 1980s when Doyle Mathis, then the chief academic officer of the college, began a search for and encouraged the collection and preservation of documents related to the history of the early decades of the Berry Schools and the founder, Martha Berry. This effort led to the collection of Martha Berry papers and eventually to the creation of the Berry College Archives, a unit of the college's Memorial Library, where most of the historical materials possessed by the institution are now housed.

When the editors retired from their administrative duties at the college in 1999 and 2000, they gave priority to the selection of documents and the preparation for publication of this volume, commemorating the first one hundred years of the institution. A centennial celebration is planned throughout the year 2002. The editors expect to author a second volume which is planned as a combined biography of Martha Berry and a history of the Berry Schools and College.

The documents included in this volume were selected to provide sketches of the life of Martha Berry and the history of the institution she founded. Part One gives Highlights of Martha Berry's Life, including the numerous honors and recognitions received during her lifetime and since. Part Two contains Sketches of the Berry Schools and College's history, including some significant anniversary celebrations. Part Three provides Selected Writings and Speeches by Martha Berry or about her and the schools. Part Four includes Selected Letters chosen to show something of the range of friendships and connections developed by the founder. Part Five contains Additional Reading about Martha Berry and Her Schools.

The reading list was prepared by the Berry College Archives and the editors. The editors prepared the lists concerning the life of Martha Berry, the history of the schools, the presiding officers of the Board of' Trustees and the Board of Visitors, the chief administrative officers of the institution, and the chief academic officers of the college. Other materials presented in this volume were selected from the papers of the Berry College Archives unless another source is cited at the end of a document. Editing has been minimal in an effort to retain the style of each writer.

Berry College

Main Campus

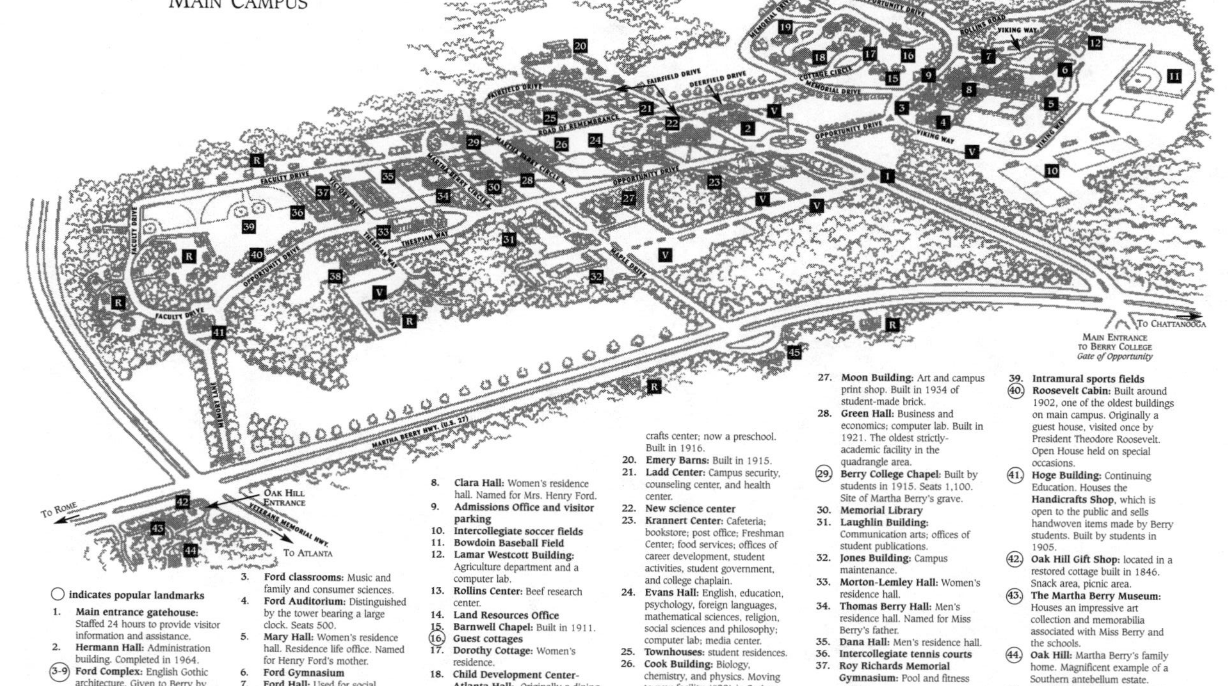

◯ **indicates popular landmarks**

1. **Main entrance gatehouse:** Staffed 24 hours to provide visitor information and assistance.
2. **Hermann Hall:** Administration building. Completed in 1964.

(3-9) **Ford Complex:** English Gothic architecture. Given to Berry by Mr. and Mrs. Henry Ford of Dearborn, Mich. Constructed in phases beginning in 1925.

3. **Ford classrooms:** Music and family and consumer sciences.
4. **Ford Auditorium:** Distinguished by the tower bearing a large clock. Seats 500.
5. **Mary Hall:** Women's residence hall. Residence life office. Named for Henry Ford's mother.
6. **Ford Gymnasium**
7. **Ford Hall:** Used for social events, band hall. Modeled after the dining hall at Christ College of Oxford, England.
8. **Clara Hall:** Women's residence hall. Named for Mrs. Henry Ford.
9. **Admissions Office and visitor parking**
10. **Intercollegiate soccer fields**
11. **Bowdoin Baseball Field**
12. **Lamar Westcott Building:** Agriculture department and a computer lab.
13. **Rollins Center:** Beef research center.
14. **Land Resources Office**
15. **Barnwell Chapel:** Built in 1911.

(16) **Guest cottages**

17. **Dorothy Cottage:** Women's residence.
18. **Child Development Center-Atlanta Hall:** Originally a dining hall; now a preschool. Built in 1910.
19. **Child Development Center-Sunshine Cottage:** Originally a crafts center; now a preschool. Built in 1916.
20. **Emery Barns:** Built in 1915.
21. **Ladd Center:** Campus security, counseling center, and health center.
22. **New science center**
23. **Krannert Center:** Cafeteria; bookstore; post office; Freshman Center; food services; offices of career development, student activities, student government, and college chaplain.
24. **Evans Hall:** English, education, psychology, foreign languages, mathematical sciences, religion, social sciences and philosophy; computer lab; media center.
25. **Townhouses:** student residences.
26. **Cook Building:** Biology, chemistry, and physics. Moving to new facility (#22) in Spring 2001. Built by students in 1937 with Berry-produced brick and timber.
27. **Moon Building:** Art and campus print shop. Built in 1934 of student-made brick.
28. **Green Hall:** Business and economics; computer lab. Built in 1921. The oldest strictly-academic facility in the quadrangle area.

(29) **Berry College Chapel:** Built by students in 1915. Seats 1,100. Site of Martha Berry's grave.

30. **Memorial Library**
31. **Laughlin Building:** Communication arts; offices of student publications.
32. **Jones Building:** Campus maintenance.
33. **Morton-Lemley Hall:** Women's residence hall.
34. **Thomas Berry Hall:** Men's residence hall. Named for Miss Berry's father.
35. **Dana Hall:** Men's residence hall.
36. **Intercollegiate tennis courts**
37. **Roy Richards Memorial Gymnasium:** Pool and fitness center.
38. **Blackstone Hall:** Houses the E.H. Young Theatre.
39. **Intramural sports fields**

(40) **Roosevelt Cabin:** Built around 1902, one of the oldest buildings on main campus. Originally a guest house, visited once by President Theodore Roosevelt. Open House held on special occasions.

(41) **Hoge Building:** Continuing Education. Houses the **Handicrafts Shop**, which is open to the public and sells handwoven items made by Berry students. Built by students in 1905.

(42) **Oak Hill Gift Shop:** located in a restored cottage built in 1846. Snack area, picnic area.

(43) **The Martha Berry Museum:** Houses an impressive art collection and memorabilia associated with Miss Berry and the schools.

(44) **Oak Hill:** Martha Berry's family home. Magnificent example of a Southern antebellum estate.

45. **Berry College president's home**

R. **Faculty and staff residences**

V. **Visitor parking**

Berry College

Mountain Campus

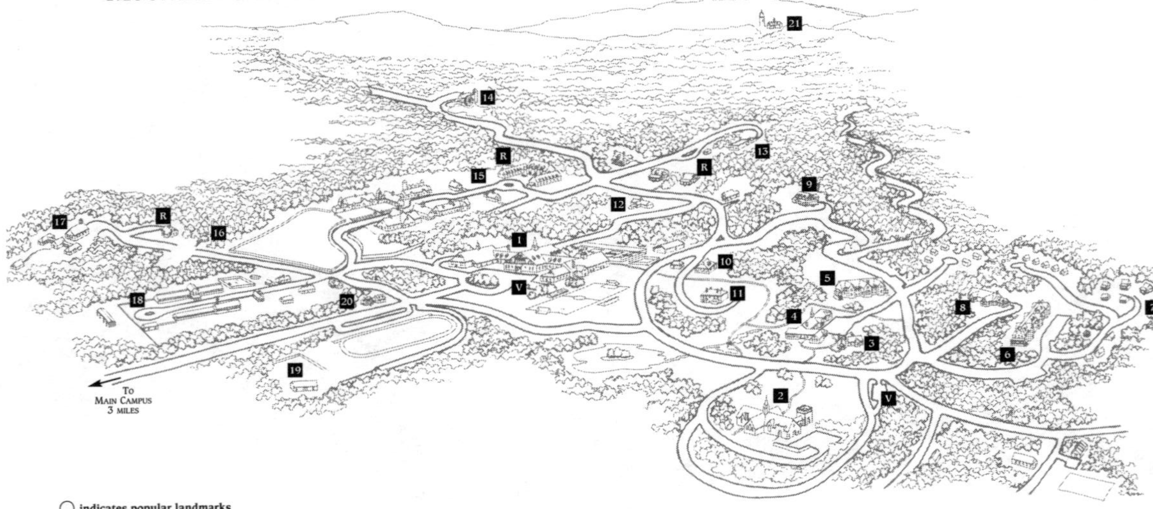

◯ **indicates popular landmarks**

1. **WinShape Centre:** Established in 1984 by Chick-fil-A founder Truett Cathy to provide college scholarships and special opportunities for personal growth for young people. Also utilized in summer for Camp WinShape. Previously a high school campus.
(2.) **Frost Memorial Chapel:** Constructed by students and staff in 1936-37. Features wooden beamed ceiling, flagstone floor, leaded glass windows, slate roof, and three beautiful stained glass windows.
3. **Barstow Memorial Library:** Presently used as study area.
4. **Berry College Elementary School** (Hamrick Hall): A private school for grades K-6.
5. **Friendship Hall:** Women's residence hall.
6. **Pilgrim Hall:** Men's residence hall.
7. **Log cabins:** Constructed in recent years for summer campers attending Camp WinShape.
8. **Hill Dining Hall:** Built in 1923, originally served as a bakery. Now used for special occasions, summer camp, WinShape students.
9. **Meacham Hall:** Guest housing for WinShape Centre. Built in 1921.
10. **Cherokee Lodge:** Home for WinShape Centre Director. Built in 1920.
11. **Pine Lodge:** Guest housing for WinShape Centre. Built in 1916, oldest building on Mountain Campus. The original Foundation School for Boys.
12. **Kimbell Cottage:** WinShape Centre facility.
13. **Water filtration plant**
(14.) **Old Mill Wheel:** Built in 1930. One of the largest operational wooden overshot waterwheels anywhere at 42 feet in diameter.
(15.) **Normandy Apartments and Dairy Barn:** Built between 1931 and 1937. Originally housing students who worked at the dairy, the apartments are now faculty/staff residences. The dairy is fully operational and houses the college's registered Jersey and Holstein herds.
16. **Pew Observatory:** Used for labs and classroom instruction.
(17.) **Possum Trot:** Built in 1850 and considered the "cradle of Berry College." Martha Berry began the Possum Trot Sunday School in 1900. It was the needs of the mountain people she met here that inspired her to build her schools.
(18.) **Gunby Equine Center:** 77-acre equestrian center.
19. **Freemantown Barn:** WinShape Centre facility.
20. **Woodbury Cottage:** WinShape Centre facility.
(21.) **House o' Dreams:** Built in 1926 by staff and students as a mountain retreat for Miss Berry. Seen by appointment. Call The Martha Berry Museum at (706) 291-1883.

R. **Faculty and staff residences**
V. **Visitor parking**

Contents

Part I

Highlights of Martha Berry's Life

Martha Berry, Founder

Ancestors of Martha McChesney BERRY

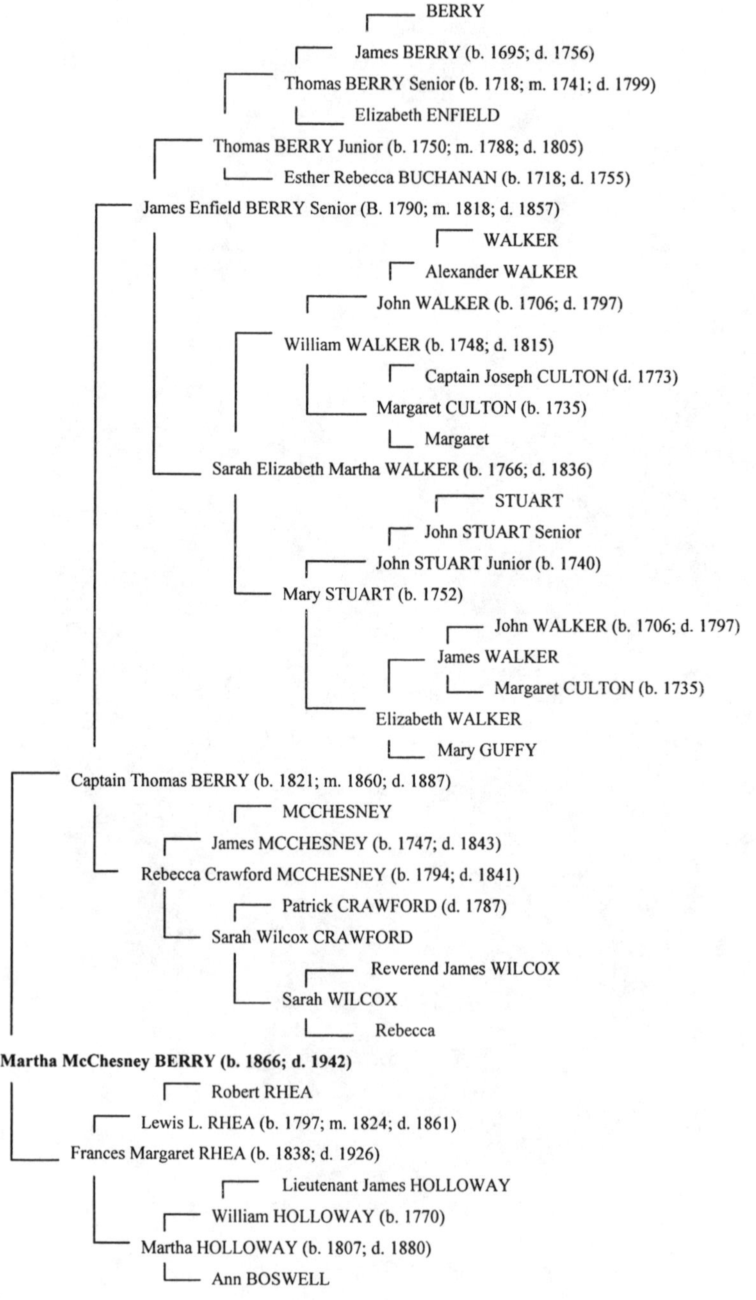

Important Dates in Martha Berry's Life

1790 (April 5)

James Enfield Berry (paternal grandfather) born in Virginia.

1794 (April 11)

Rebecca Crawford McChesney (paternal grandmother) born in Virginia.

1797 (April 16)

Lewis L. Rhea (maternal grandfather) born in Tennessee.

1807 (October 10)

Martha Holloway (maternal grandmother) born in South Carolina.

1818 (August 20)

James Enfield Berry and Rebecca Crawford McChesney married in Tennessee.

1821 (September 21)

Thomas Berry (father) born in Tennessee.

1824 (December 8)

Lewis L. Rhea and Martha Holloway married in Alabama.

1838 (July 30)

Frances Margaret Rhea (mother) born in Alabama.

1840 (January)

James Enfield Berry chosen as first mayor of Chattanooga, Tennessee.

1846-48

Thomas Berry served in Mexican War as a First Lieutenant of Co. D, Mounted Battalion, Georgia Volunteers.

1860 (April 10)

Thomas Berry and Frances Margaret Rhea married in Alabama and lived in Turkeytown area of Cherokee County (now in Etowah County), Alabama.

1862-1865

Thomas Berry served as a Confederate officer in the Civil War. He began as a First Lieutenant in Captain Moragne's Company, Alabama Volunteers (subsequently known as Company A, 31st Regiment, Alabama Infantry), on March 3, 1862. He was promoted to Captain and Quartermaster of the same company on October 14, 1862. He was captured at Vicksburg, Mississippi, on July 4, 1863, and paroled on July 9, 1863. The last military record of his service was on November 14, 1864; but his widow claimed in a pension application that he served until the end of the war. She placed him at Greensboro, North Carolina, when his company's troops surrendered in 1865.

1866 (October 7)

Martha McChesney Berry was born in Alabama.
Other records indicate she may have been born in an earlier year. The U.S. Census of 1870, Floyd County, Georgia, lists her as Mattie, age 5. Since all accounts agree that she was born on October 7 and the census was taken in June, the 1870 census suggests that she became 5 on October 7, 1869. If this information is correct, she would have been born in 1864. The U.S. Census of 1880, Floyd County, Georgia, also taken in June, lists her as Mattie, age 14, suggesting she was born in 1865. The record of her baptism on April 2, 1881, in St. Peter's Episcopal Church, Rome, Georgia, lists her birth date as October 7, 1865.

1866

Her confirmation in St. Peter's Church occurred on October 29, 1882. Her age was listed as 17, indicating she was born in 1865. Martha Berry, herself, gave her birth date as October 7, 1866.

(July 23)

Thomas Berry bought first real estate in Floyd County, Georgia, on Howard Street, now Second Avenue.

1871 (July 7)

Thomas Berry purchased property which included original part of house now known as Oak Hill.

1881 (April 2)

Baptized, St. Peter's Episcopal Church, Rome, Georgia.

1882 (October 29)

Confirmed, St. Peter's Episcopal Church.

Entered Madame LeFevre's Edgeworth School in Baltimore, Maryland, about this time.

1887 (January 18)

Father died.

1900

Began Sunday schools and day schools in the Rome area about this time.

1902 (January 13)

Opened boarding school for boys.

1909 (Thanksgiving Day)

Opened boarding school for girls.

1920

Received honorary Doctor of Pedagogy degree, University of Georgia.

1924

Voted Distinguished Citizen of the State, by the Georgia General Assembly.

Elected to the National Institute of Social Sciences.

1925

Received Roosevelt Medal, Roosevelt Memorial Association, presented by President Calvin Coolidge.

1926

Opened Junior College.

(December 30)

Mother died.

1927

Obtained remaining ownership of Oak Hill.

Deeded Oak Hill to The Berry Schools.

Received *Pictorial Review* Annual Achievement Award.

1927-1928

Remodeled Oak Hill extensively.

1930

Opened Senior College.

Received Doctor of Laws degree, University of North Carolina.

Included in Ida Tarbell's list of America's 50 greatest women.

1931

Voted one of America's Twelve Greatest Women, *Good Housekeeping* magazine contest.

Received Town Hall Medal as member of club doing most to bring honor to organization during that year.

1932

Appointed to Board of Regents, University System of Georgia.

Tracy Byars' *Martha Berry, the Sunday Lady of Possum Trot* (first book-length biography of Martha Berry) published.

1933

Received Eleanor van Renssalaer Biennial Medal for patriotic service to America, Colonial Dames of America.

Received Doctor of Laws degree, Bates College.

Received Doctor of Humanities degree, Berry College.

1934

Received at the Court of St. James by King George V and Queen Mary.

1935

Received Doctor of Public Service degree, Oglethorpe University.

Received Doctor of Laws degree, Duke University.

Appointed to national committee for observance of 400th anniversary of the English Bible.

1936

Received Doctor of Letters degree, Oberlin College.

1937

Received Doctor of Laws degree, University of Wisconsin.

Appointed member of Georgia State Planning Board.

1938

School named Martha Berry School, Thomaston, Georgia.

1939

Received American Institute of Social Sciences Medal (see presentation and her response later in this section).

1940

Received annual Humanitarian Award, Variety Clubs of America.

Received key to City of Chattanooga, Tennessee, at annual Cotton Ball.

1942 (February 27)

Died in Saint Joseph Hospital, Atlanta.

1966

Received first posthumous Shining Light Award from Atlanta Gas Light Company. The plaque at her grave site reads: *"She lighted the flame of learning with a distinctive educational program and that flame of knowledge continues to burn brightly."*

1981

Portrait hung in Georgia State Capitol's Gallery of Distinguished Georgians.

1992

Inducted into Georgia Women of Achievement (Hall of Fame established through efforts of Mrs. Jimmy Carter).

2000

Named one of "100 Georgians of the [20th] Century" by *Georgia Trend* magazine.

"The Vision Victorious"

By Evelyn Hoge Pendley

Introduction

We need not seek out distant lands or days
To find true greatness and to learn its ways.
Here in these Georgia hills a spirit grew,
A mind developed, and a brave soul knew

That life was more than breath—that those who live
Life to its fullness look and love and give
Their best to others, so that all might share
The blessings and the beauties that are here.

No miracle or sudden wonder came
To pave a way of wisdom and of fame,
But Martha Berry learned from day to day
The deepest truths of life's abundant way.

Scene I
The Child

Child among children, yet a child apart
She caught the feeling in her father's heart
While sitting on his knee, hearing him tell
The stories of the folks he knew so well—

The men and boys who came to him in need,
Knowing somehow that he would help them feed
And clothe their children and their women-folk.
He gave with kindness, and with wisdom spoke

Some cheering word, so that they went away
Not with poor beggars' hearts, but feeling they

Had found a friend and could take heart again
And show the world that they were truly men.

The father counseled, "Help the poor, my child.
Be kind to them and keep your judgment mild,
For often those who need the greatest aid
Are trying hardest, but they are dismayed.
Help them to face the future unafraid.
Become that blessing for which they have prayed."

Scene II
Girlhood

Girlhood is full of dreams of gay romance
Of dashing youths who cast a charming glance
Of admiration. Then it is the time
That social consciousness reaches its prime,

That etiquette and words of gay Paris
Taught in exclusive schools are made to be
Of some vague value. Martha knew that she
Was much like other girls, still young and free.

She sat outside her little cabin door.
It seemed that only a short while before
This spot had been her playhouse. Now she came
To think and dream, rather than play some game.

She had been "finished" like all proper girls,
Of speaking, dancing, life in other worlds,
She had been taught. She knew each rule
Madame LeFevre set forth in her school.

She thought of this. She knew also that there
Were handsome youths to whom she had seemed fair.

She dreamed of them and felt strange, wondrous thrills.
But even then she looked up to the hills.

Up to the hills, because before her passed
Some mountain boys. Impulsively she asked
If they would like to stop and rest awhile
Before continuing each dusty mile

They had to tread in order to reach home.
"Have you boys been to Sunday school in Rome?"
"No ma'am," they grinned, "No country boys like us
Could mix with all the town folk and their fuss.

Our shirts is dirty and our britches tore.
Don't guess we'll get to meeting much before
The summer comes. Trap Holler's church fell in.
When it gits warm then preachin' can begin."

"Do you like Bible stories? Do you read
The Scriptures?" she asked, trying hard to lead
The conversation on to things they knew.
"Is stories in the Bible? Is that true?

No, ma'am, we'uns can't read nary a word.
Our folks can't neither or I guess we'd heard
Them tales. We're kinda wonderin' if you
Could tell us some." She did, and the group grew.

Sunday by Sunday till there were a score
Of families. And there were even more
Who wished that they might hear Miss Mattie talk.
But it was far for them to have to walk.

In hand with opportunity there stood
Trials and problems, but she knew she would

Find ways of solving them. She played a game
Of soap and water with the boys who came

With dirty hands. Among the group she'd pass
To take a look. With magnifying glass
They first would gaze upon their fingers. Then
They made some bubbles and they looked again.
They really didn't look at all the same.
Truly, that must have been a magic game!

The hungry lads Aunt Martha always fed
With goodies from her kitchen—gingerbread
And milk, or fancy cakes and lemonade
Or other tempting sweets that she had made.

Miss Berry's nurse Aunt Martha once had been,
But now her child was grown. A big white grin
Shone forth against her cheeks of ebony.
"That Martha Berry—Right now Ah can see

She's gwine to need my help and dat Ah'll give
As long as our good Lawd does let me live.
Miss Martha, she am always doin' good—
De kind of doins Ah would if Ah could.
But she can be de boss and Ah will try
To keep her workin' for de Lawd on high."

The bigger problems called for greater skill
With which to overcome them. All Oak Hill
Was quite upset each Sunday afternoon.
Though coming there was like a blessed boon

Unto the country folk, still they disturbed
Other activities. Miss Mattie was perturbed
Also because the people were so tired
By their long rides each week. Deeply inspired

At last, she found her answer, saying she
Would drive around and meet them if they'd be
At Possum Trot and other places where
They could have services. They could be near

Their homes. She would hitch Roany to her cart
And strap her organ on the back. She'd start
Out early every Sunday and she'd teach
Each eager soul who came within her reach.

And this she did until at last one day
She went along a solitary way.
And unto her a quiet vision came.
Within her mind it seemed an ugly shame

The Sunday school in broken, run-down shacks,
Disturbed by pigs and fleas and leaks and cracks,
Was all that she could give. She must do more.
Yes, she would start a school, open the door
To learning for these youths needing a chance.
Sacrifice, but joy. This was her romance.

Scene III
The Pioneer

The pioneers into a distant land
Deserve great praise, but those who understand
New needs at home, and strive courageously,
Though there be times of great adversity,
To make a better world near their own door
Should merit laud and honor even more.

A pioneer, though just across the road—
Miss Berry squared her shoulders 'neath the load
Of new responsibility. At first
A white-washed school had seemed to quench the thirst

For knowledge in the boys she taught. But then
She thought about their growing into men.
She sensed that there was much they could not learn
Until they lived and worked and did not spurn

Real labor or the laws of cleanliness,
Of order and of love and loftiness.
A boarding school—not like those where she went,
But one of work and good environment

For building future citizens. How great
A plan! How small her start! How blessed her fate!
So in an humble building with some boys
She started struggling, teaching grace and poise

And dignity of labor, living so
These eager lads could work and come to know
All those good things which make a better life,
That lead to happiness and blot out strife.

How many were the trials of those days!
The fellows would not take up women's ways
They said, and cook and clean and scrub. They sought
For larnin' out of books. This they'd be taught.

Miss Berry's heart sank low. "Well, boys," she said,
"This washing must be done. You must be fed.
We have but little money. And you see
I am the woman here. If you want me

To do this work, I shall." She rolled her sleeves
Up to her elbows, as one who believes
In honest toil will do. She caught her skirt
And pinned it back, then started at the dirt.

A little dazed, the boys at first stood by,
But not for long. "Stop ma'am, guess we can try
Our hands at that. Them clothes is ours, and we
Can't have you waitin' on us. We can see

That if you ain't ashamed of doing such,
Guess we can do it and not mind it much."
From that time on the fellows did not shirk
The tasks that came their way. They seemed to work

With joy and pride because they watched her go
About her tasks, her spirit all aglow.
They studied, labored, prayed and struggled through
Those first school days. Proudly they grew.

A spirit had prevailed within their band.
Their school was like none other in the land.
They felt they, too, were helping blaze a trail.
As youthful pioneers, they must not fail!

Scene IV
The Tent Commencement

Commencement times bring mingled tears and joys,
But in those early days, seeing her boys
Go forth from her, to Martha Berry meant
Saying farewell to friends with whom she'd spent

Long hours of labor. Yet her spirit thrilled,
Feeling her vision partially fulfilled,
To know at last her school was sending out
Trained hands into the world, hearts that were stout,

And minds that had adjusted to so much
That they must keep on reaching out and clutch

More truth. All that they did should make her proud.
Inspired with hope, she walked as on a cloud.

The graduation day she talked of most
Was held within a tent set on crude posts.
It had been borrowed from the Baptist Church.
For this great day, the boys had made a search

For all available that might impress
The speaker, families, and other guests.
They had one big bass drum by which they marched
Donned in their best apparel—collars starched,

Shoes shining, and their coats and pants well pressed.
Patched and ill-fitted, still they looked their best.
The governor of Georgia made the speech.
"On this auspicious day, I do beseech

You, from your Alma Mater's massive walls
Go forth. Open your ears and heed the calls
For service of your heart and hands and head."
He spoke, and as they thought on what he said,

The tent began to flop. A heavy shower
Had come to interrupt that honored hour.
Alas, the "massive" hall began to leak!
The celebrated guest was forced to speak

With an umbrella held above his head.
Miss Berry saved the day. She laughed and said
She should have known, having a Baptist tent,
That showers of damp blessings would be sent

To fall upon all those who gathered there.
And thus the school went on from year to year

Because the Founder always found a way
To carry on or to progress each day.

Scene V
The Girls' School Begins

Within the dining room Miss Berry stood.
She looked about with care. Shortly she would
Have all the Trustees as her guests, and she
Had to convince them, let them clearly see

She had been wise, for they had disapproved
Her plan to start a school for girls. She moved
From place to place, and as she did she thought
What she would say to them—how she had caught

This new desire. Yes, she would simply tell
How it all came about. Things must go well.
While waiting there she thought the story through
And dwelt on things she knew the girls could do.

How much the school had meant to all the boys!
They would be men of dignity and poise.
But when she talked to them she found they yearned
To have their sisters study what they'd learned.

Yes, sisters—but at once her mind had caught
A deeper hope than this. Girls should be taught
As they had been because they'd want to find
Good wives—girls, like themselves, who'd be inclined

To have a set of standards like their own,
Who'd master the new ways they might be shown.
Long had she thought it through. The boys were right.
The women set the standards, lit the light

Within the home; they taught the children; they
Would teach as well as live a better way.
The Trustees had not seemed to like the plan
Of adding girls, she knew. But she began

This other school. She had a pile of logs
Stacked up upon a hill. In her old togs
She hired a carpenter and went with him
So that he, too, though aspects still were grim,

Could visualize a school and help her build
And make another vision be fulfilled.
While yet the pile of logs was lying there,
She found another soul able to share

Her dream: a teacher who would help her start
The plan for girls that lay within her heart.
Together they had worked. Students had come,
And, like the boys, they'd had to struggle some.

But now the school was started on its way.
Her mind raced on. These were the things she'd say.
And they would see how well the girls could cook,
How clean they had each spot. Surely they'd look

At them, with all their loveliness and grace,
And realize they added to the place.
The guests arrived. She did as she had planned.
She said she hoped they'd see and understand.

The girls served well, and then they came and sang
Until the rafters in the building rang.
With grace and dignity they entertained
Most willingly. They graciously explained

The things they did and what their training meant,
Their time and energy were aptly spent.
They won the blessings of all there that day.
The Girls' School had its place and it would stay.

Scene VI
An Ambassador of the King

New York could be so cold, so very cold—
But still Miss Berry knew she must take hold,
Combat the icy elements, perhaps
Cold hearts as well. She pulled her borrowed wraps

Closer about her. The fur coat was tight.
No doubt she was not such a striking sight
As far as cuts and fits and fashions went.
But little did she care, her heart intent

Upon one goal: She must obtain some aid
To build on the foundations she had laid.
For all the boys and girls the school must live.
She must find kindly hearts—hearts that would give.

Already she had used her little wealth
And given of her youthful strength and health.
But hers was not enough, and so she must
Find friends of means whose confidence and trust

She could secure—good friends who too could see
The cause for which she labored constantly.
But it was hard—Her noble spirit filled
With pride. She was to speak before a guild

As one who came to beg. How that word stung
The aristocracy from which she'd sprung.

But on she went and found herself inside
Grace Church. Somehow she felt she must confide

In Dr. Huntington, the pastor there.
"I cannot speak," she said, "I just came here
To tell my simple story. How I do hate
To be a beggar and to have to wait

At beggars' entrances and then to plead
For help for those I know who greatly need.
I have to swallow so and hide my pride
Each instance when I find myself inside

Some place of wealth, or when I come to speak
To groups like this, whose help they know I seek."
The pastor looked at her with sympathy,
But then he said to her triumphantly,

"Look up, my daughter. Lift your head above
These clouds. Yours is to be a life of love.
Cast out false pride and let your spirit sing,
Ambassador of our great heavenly King."

Transfigured was her outlook by that word
Ambassador—and for her King. They heard
Her speak that day and many eyes were blurred
And many empty souls were touched and stirred

By the unselfish work, the noble plan
Of this great heart to help her fellow man.
But humble was this heart, for well she knew
That there was still so much for her to do.
The clouds had seemed so dark. But lights of dawn
Had come to spread her vision further on.

Scene VII
The Growth of the Schools and Their Friendships

Days grew to weeks and months and then to years,
And there were hours of sunshine, hours of tears.
But ever did Miss Berry work and pray
To keep her schools along an upward way.

She sought new contacts; thus she traveled much
In hopes of finding hearts that she could touch
With this true story that she had to tell.
She told the story often—told it well.

And as she gathered friends, the schools progressed,
For by these friendships they were greatly blessed.
The friends not only listened graciously,
But many of them said they wished to see

These Berry Schools. So there began to come
To visit Berry men and women from
All sections of our land and other lands
To see these schools of head and heart and hands.

Well trained in southern hospitality,
The students entertained with courtesy
All of the visitors. They let them see
The work they did, the great variety

Of skills they learned. Always they tried to show
The care they took of things they had. And so,
Noting the gracious way that they were served,
The people looked and felt the schools deserved

Better equipment, more supplies and tools
To build still more efficient Berry Schools.

Miss Berry spent much time with all the guests,
Forever showing, giving them the best,

But always pointing out the further needs,
Saying that she had only planted seeds
That must be tended; but with kindly aid
A greater institution could be made.

And many, knowing her, came to believe
It is more blessed to give than to receive.
And once their hearts had come to understand,
They offered her true friendship's helping hand.

Scene VIII
The College Is Begun

"Before one dream of mine had all come true
I always saw some other thing to do,"
Explained Miss Berry, "and it happened so
That in my watching Berry high schools grow,

I talked to students and I heard them yearn
For further training still, so they could learn
To do more work upon a higher plane.
Consolidated schools sprang up to train

A growing portion of the rural South.
I sang their praises with my heart and mouth
As on and on I watched them bravely spread,
For I was thankful for them all," she said.

"Yes, all the world was learning more and more
With training coming closer to each door.
But going off to school and paying board
Was still a luxury few could afford.

And this was just about the only way
To study beyond high school in that day.
Yet, if the southern young folks would keep pace
They needed greater skills to find a place

To be of truest service to their race.
So once again, I knew I had to face
The joys and trials of another school.
It would be hard. I did not try to fool

The Trustees or myself. I could well see
A college education, a degree,
Was much to offer. I knew it would take
Equipment, teachers highly trained, to make

A school of higher education. I
Should have to labor even more and try
To raise more money, win more friends to build
A college—have this later dream fulfilled.

Upon my plank of faith I'd walked before.
The Lord had blessed the Schools, and so once more
I bowed my head and said a word of prayer,
Then looking up, I realized that there

Was added strength within my soul, and now
I must get down to work, discover how
To reach this goal. Thus, step by step I went,
Ever ambitious, never quite content

With what I had for my dear girls and boys.
They are my children—they, my greatest joys.
It is for them I've done what I have done.
But still, I feel these schools are just begun.
We have the college, yes: but it must grow.
Always ahead must Berry standards go."

Scene IX
Her Honors

Hers was a life of love. She worked because
She looked and cared, and saw how much there was
For some kind soul to do; so bravely she
Did all she could to serve humanity.

"For my dear boys and girls,"—how often she
Would say those words with pride, but tenderly.
In truth, it was for them she labored on
Until her strength and energy were gone.

For her devotion, her philanthropy
Great honors came her way. Humility
Was ever in her heart when she expressed
Her gratitude. She felt she had been blessed

In simply seeing her work grow and grow—
In being satisfied that she could know
Her work was not in vain—in looking out
And seeing those she loved go on about

Their work and play—in realizing they
Would be prepared and then go forth one day
To spread the Berry spirit everywhere.
How many times she said she did not care

About the honors for herself. She blushed
When others called her great. Her pale cheeks flushed
At tributes paid to her. "I speak with pride
For my dear boys and girls, who by my side

Have done their share and worked with dignity.
But humbly for myself I solemnly

Accept these honors and these words of praise."
The honors came to her in many ways.

Eight schools of learning each gave a degree—
Doctor of laws from four—pedagogy,
And letters, public service, but of these
The highest one was of humanities.

Organizations—she belonged to six
Of widespread fame. With pride did each affix
Her name unto its roll. Four medals won
Showed gratitude for work that she had done.

Two high awards—and thrice she found a place
Among the greatest women of her race.
Again, three times it was her happy fate
To be awarded honors from her State.

On boards of wisdom she was asked to serve.
A nearby city felt she did deserve
Its key. High on the list of honored names
Was she abroad. In England at St. James

She was presented to the king and queen
And mingled in their honored courtly scene.
Biographers and poets sang her praise;
Frank journalists admired her life and ways.

From far off writers came so they might hear
Her captivating story, so that their
Own pens might echo every charming word
And deed and action they had seen and heard.

But those who knew her closely day by day
Knew best her greatness and her love, for they

Had watched her lift her eyes up to the hills,
Had known her times of trials and of thrills,

Had seen her go about her tasks each day,
Her heart upon a more abundant way
For her dear boys and girls. They knew she meant
Each humble word she spoke and that she spent

Her life for others, though they knew
That she was human. They had seen her do
Her best, and in all truth they could proclaim
That laud and honor should surround her name.

Scene X
The Spirit of Martha Berry

At last our Founder crossed another road
And went unto her heavenly abode.
You who would know her noble spirit, look
Far out across the spaces, in each nook

Where beauty lies. She walks the paths no more.
She speaks not as she did in days of yore;
But there is not a blade of grass or tree
That does not speak of her. No one can see

The loveliness about him and not know
It was a noble spirit made it so.
You who would feel the friendship of her heart,
Look in each face about you, and then start

By doing deeds of service for each one
For whom you feel some kindness could be done.
You who would know the secret of her soul,
Get down upon your knees and bare your whole

Heart unto God. And then humbly arise
And do the task you see before your eyes.
You who would sense her presence hovering
About the earth, still touching everything,

Think on the deeds she did, and then think on
To work that must not cease, though she is gone.
Remember how she labored, how she prayed
That on these sure foundations she had laid

Others would build and work. Keep well in mind
The standards that she set. Go forth and find
Your place to carry on. Never forget
The cabin for simplicity—nor yet

The lamp for learning, spreading greater light—
The plow for labor of the mind and might—
And last, but never least, the Book of God
For guidance in the ways the Master trod.

Choose for your motto, even as she chose
His words of the good life that each heart knows:
"Not to be ministered unto, but to
Go forth and minister." To this be true.

Despise not bowing in humility.
The greatest of you shall your servant be.
And thus was she, and thus it fell her fate
To be among those who are truly great.

Originally presented by The Daughters of Berry as Sketches of the Life of Martha Berry in 1945

Evelyn Hoge Pendley (pictured here with Miss Berry at her graduation), associate professor of English emerita, Berry College, is a 1938 graduate of Berry College. She was married to Dr. Walter Pendley (deceased), also a Berry graduate.

Comments by Martha Berry

The greatest influence in my life was having a father who praised and encouraged me whenever I did anything well and who taught me to love animals, birds, and flowers and take care of every living thing. He never allowed me to waste even an apple peeling, and I had to save the bread crumbs for the birds. He made me feel that if I wasted anything that a living creature could use it was sinful.

I had for ten years a governess who had a strong Christian character and a great love for nature. She knew a great deal about birds and flowers and trees. She always read stories of heroes and heroines and of people whose lives were brave and true, and she had the power of kindling my imagination and making them live again. I felt that I also could and MUST do something worthwhile with my life.

We have trained thousands of students at Berry, from rural and mountainous districts, and all of our success in teaching them has been due to the balanced life we lead here. Our pupils are given certain periods of work, study, devotion, and recreation. Each morning and evening we have prayers. Someone has said that here we teach the aristocracy of work. We teach here that the only true aristocrat is the worker—men and women who are doing something for someone, who are helping others in their daily work—in the shop, on the farm, in the dairy, and in the laundry. The boys and girls are working with happy, smiling faces, doing their work in the very best way and getting joy and pleasure out of their work. Rewards for work well done, praise and encouragement, it seems to me are the things young people need—and they should be taught to love the great out-of-doors. They should be given work and the care and responsibility of some living and growing things.

—Martha Berry

Some of Martha's Activities

Martha had a wonderful sense of humor, but she also had a deep sense of responsibility. She helped my mother in various ways, paying the taxes at the courthouse, doing the shopping, and interesting herself in her younger brothers and sisters.

She loved horseback riding, rode a great deal. Also loved tennis and Martha was quite a good player. There were two tennis courts at Oak Hill and she often had tennis matches with her friends. She was very popular and had many beaux, as we called them. She read a great deal. She took over the old Play Cabin as a retreat where she could read and study.

When she returned from her travels, she always had amusing anecdotes to relate. I remember one. She was in London, going to Scotland to visit some friends. When she entered the second-class carriage, she found an English lady and her son, quite young. Also, an American girl, very pretty, about 19. The English lady never spoke, but the young man became quite interested in the girl's beauty and accent, and entered into their conversation. The young girl was from Mississippi. She was going to Scotland to visit relatives. That afternoon, the young man said they were going to stop and tea baskets could be had. "Would you like one?" The girl's reply—"Yes, my mouth is that dry I could spit cotton." The young man was shocked. "Vulgar Americans!" He joined his mother in cold silence. That phrase could not be translated into "English" English, but to Martha, it was familiar—the call of the cotton pickers for the water boy.

Martha would like to have pictured a plantation scene to those silent travelers, but she dared not. A little boy trudging up one row of cotton, down the other, a cedar bucket full of cool, fresh water and a gourd dipper, all day long under the hot sun. The girl's relatives met her at the station; and when she said goodbye, Martha wondered if she would meet with more success with the Scots.

—Frances Berry Bonnyman
Sister of Martha Berry
May 16, 1956

National Institute of Social Sciences Dinner

Address by Mrs. John Henry Hammond

In awarding Martha Berry the medal from the Roosevelt Memorial Association in 1925, President Coolidge said: "In building out of nothing a great educational institution for the children of the mountains you have contributed to your time one of its most creative achievements."

Theodore Roosevelt, after visiting the Schools, exclaimed, "This is the greatest practical work for American citizenship that has been done within this decade."

In 1902 Martha Berry started her school with a handful of ragged boys in a small log cabin. Eight years later she got them to build a school for the girls while she went to New York to raise funds. Mr. R. Fulton Cutting was the first one to give her a substantial check, and he repeated this gift every subsequent year until his death. One day when Miss Berry expressed her discouragement to Dr. Huntington at Grace Church, he said to her: "Miss Berry, you should never be ashamed to ask for money; remember, you are an Ambassador of the King."

Ever since then Miss Berry has gone forth bravely on her plank of faith realizing that prayer does change things. It requires great faith to raise $150,000 a year to sustain the schools, especially in these times!

From a small beginning Miss Berry's dreams have become realities. Through the Gate of Opportunity over 10,000 boys and girls have passed, and then gone forth into the world equipped to meet their responsibilities. This I know full well as for many years I have had the privilege of taking to Berry each spring about twenty friends who have become Berry Pilgrims.

I have recently returned from my nineteenth visit and I am more than ever impressed with the extraordinary results accomplished by one woman who has dedicated thirty-seven years of her life to bringing light and learning to the boys and girls of the Southland.

Every graduate from the College finds employment. Some 25 industries are taught, and so no wonder there is an ever-growing demand for such fine material. There are now 1200 students enrolled annually. More than 92 percent of them earn their entire way at the Schools. They are drawn from the oldest Anglo-Saxon stock in America who settled in the hills and valleys of the Southern Highlands. They do all the work on the place, and there are no paid workers. The schools cover 25,000 acres of land, and are fifteen miles across at the longest part.

The Mount Berry High School for Boys situated on the hill-side takes care of 300 students whose ages vary from fourteen to thirty. It is touching to see the older men pocket their pride and sit side by side with the younger boys because of their eagerness for an education. The Martha Berry School for Girls is now housed in the beautiful Gothic Quadrangle, the gift of Mr. and Mrs. Henry Ford. The College occupies another unit where 600 boys and girls study together.

Because Miss Berry believes in training head, heart and hand, four days of the week are devoted to academic work, and two days to the industries.

At Possum Trot, five miles from the Girls' School, there is a Grammar School for the younger children, where excellent foundations are laid and where the college students have an opportunity to do practice work. Nearby is a small community house where the poor mothers are taught how to sew and cook and take care of their families.

Miss Berry has not left out anything in her educational scheme.

In 1938 the Berry herd of Jerseys was given second place in the United States in number of test cows producing fifty pounds or more of butterfat. The Berry herd led all college herds, thanks largely to the farm superintendent, a Berry graduate.

The students quarry the stone, make the bricks and tiles, and put up the buildings and furnish them. There are well over one hundred of these. The campus is unbelievably beautiful and all the planting has been done under Miss Berry's supervision.

Hundreds of the alumni are now teachers and helping to build a better educational system for Georgia, Alabama, and neighboring states. Many are principals of schools, some county superintendents, and others supervisors of vocational departments. In other fields one finds Berry graduates leading in law, medicine, the ministry, and all branches of commerce.

Girls have found especial demand as home economics supervisors, and many are teachers and trained nurses.

From the very start Miss Berry determined to stress the religious life because she believed that "character is built by religious faith." Noonday services are held each day in the various chapels, and these are undenominational [sic].

Visiting ministers of all faiths are invited to speak and the Bible is an important feature in the School shield. Miss Berry is a living example of the truth she preaches, and no wonder she is beloved by all her students.

Miss Berry has been awarded many honorary degrees, and in 1931 was voted one of America's Twelve Greatest Women in the *Good Housekeeping* magazine contest.

She said "I want each boy and girl here to have the loving care I would want my own child to have if I had married and had one. I want them to walk down paths lined with violets; to live and feel the beauty of wide lawns and stately buildings. Our lives all need so much more beauty, and beauty has to be lived, not preached alone."

I am indeed glad that the National Institute of Social Sciences is awarding Miss Berry one of its medals, for no woman in this country has done a more outstanding piece of work. Thousands of graduates are already rising throughout the South to call Miss Berry blessed. Her influence is bound to spread as the years go by, and I only hope that many other schools will be established to perpetuate the high educational standards which she has so ably demonstrated.

May 10, 1939
New York

Acceptance Response at National Institute of Social Sciences by Martha Berry

I accept this medal humbly for myself but proudly for my boys and girls.

My life work has been conservation of the country's greatest natural resource, the children of the mountain forests. My life ambition has been to free them and to give them to America, strong of heart, of mind, and of soul.

May the time come when the stream of young men and women, ever increasingly great, may go out from our schools to make the world brighter, and happier, and better. May they take up their life work fired with the zeal of conservative Americanship, and intense loyalty to the Constitution and to the Flag.

May 10, 1939
New York

THE BERRY SCHOOLS
Martha Berry, Founder & Director
Mount Berry, Ga.

October 14, 1941

Mr. I. J. Berry,
P. O. Box 236,
Huntsville, Alabama.

Dear Ike:

I appreciated your letter so much and am glad that you are spending a while with Grace and Frank. Am also happy that you are near the Episcopal Church and can go to the services. I have always heard of that sweet church and have wished, often, that I could go there. I think of our childhood days and remember you as a Choir boy, and how we all went to church with Miss Ida.

As I grow older I realize what the children meant to our parents and what we meant to each other, and I do hope that all of the children of our family will do well.

I am still in the hospital and don't know whether I am getting better or worse, but I know that I have tried hard to get well. Am even willing to take the pills and be stuck with all the needles to try to get out of this hospital. They are enlarging the building and the work goes on day and night.

I am hoping and praying that I shall be able to get out and get home once more to go over the place and to see the school. I have learned to say, "Let go and let God," and I feel that it is best to be patient and just to do the best I can. Bess comes down to see me about every week and Laura and Virginia are good about coming to see me. Laura has been most kind in sending food to me in the hospital, but my one great desire is to get home and see the school again before I pass into the Great Beyond.

I am sending you a book which I hope you will enjoy reading, "The Self You Have to Live With." I have found great comfort in reading it and thought you might like a copy. Please give my love to Grace and Frank.

Just to let you know that I am thinking of you and to send you my love,

Affectionately,

Martha Berry

Ike Berry was Martha Berry's younger brother.

Miss Martha Berry Passed Feb. 27, 1942

Founder and director of
THE BERRY SCHOOLS, MOUNT BERRY, GA.
Born Oct. 7, 1866

Funeral of Martha Berry

MISS BERRY'S LAST HOMECOMING

Just at dawn Friday morning (February 27, 1942) the passing bell was tolled for Miss Berry, one stroke for each year of her life. At nine o'clock the chimes, given by the Alumni on her last birthday, played the school hymn, "O God Our Help in Ages Past"; also "Lead Kindly Light," "O Master Let Me Walk With Thee," "Faith of our Fathers," and "Abide With Me." It was very beautiful and comforting.

Although it seems that we should have been prepared for the end by her serious illness of nearly a year, we had not been able to think of the time when she would not be here; but her gallant spirit will remain with us as long as the school endures.

At noon Saturday all work of every kind on the campus stopped and when the funeral car drove through the gates bringing Miss Berry home for the last time students were standing in line all the way to Barnwell Chapel where she was taken to lie in state with a student guard around her night and day until the funeral Sunday afternoon, March 1st, at the Mount Berry Church. I could not keep from thinking of "Queen Victoria's Last Ride,"

Riding away from the world's unrest
To a mystical goal, on a secret quest,
Bow low your heads—lift your hearts on high—
The Queen in silence is driving by!

All day Sunday old students were arriving. I am told that about a thousand cars came through the gates. Old friends who have helped Miss Berry through the years were here. Mr. and Mrs. Henry Ford came from Dearborn, Michigan, Mr. and Mrs. Lister Carlisle and Miss Elizabeth Billings from New York, Dr. Charles Proctor from Boston. Mrs. Hammond was not well enough to come. The wives of our former Presidents of the Board of Trustees (Mrs. Eagan and Mrs. Alston), members of the Board of Trustees, the Governor of the state, the President of Agnes Scott College, and many, many others were here.

We had expected Bishop Mikell to hold the last service for Miss Berry, but he was taken himself just about a week before. Dr. John Moore Walker of St. Luke's in Atlanta assisted by our Chaplain, Rev. Belton, read the Episcopal service. Senior college boys served as pallbearers, and Miss Berry's eldest sister, Princess Ruspoli, led the procession following the casket down the aisle as the Rector read "I am the resurrection and the life." Following were the other sisters and one brother (her brother Tom having died a few weeks before) and other relatives. When the choir sang "Lead Kindly Light," the entire student body joined in the hymn "Ten Thousand Times Ten Thousand, In Sparkling Raiments Bright" we could feel the very presence of the Choir Invisible. The chancel was filled with flowers sent by many, many friends. Roses, roses, roses of every kind. Violets, lilies and orchids. It seemed that everyone wanted to enfold her in the beauty she so much loved. A group of Alumni had the log cabin reproduced in rows of roses, and the faculty and students sent the blanket of pink roses.

Saturday and Sunday were perfect days of spring sunshine. I have no words with which to tell you of the solemn beauty of the final service at the grave in the grove beside the church at the close of that Sabbath day as the student choir in white vestments sang "Abide With Me, Fast Falls the Eventide."

Monday morning we awoke to find that a heavy snow had fallen, and the grave and whole campus were covered with a silence deep and white. It seemed that heaven had dropped down a garment of beauty upon us.

We are trying to carry on the work as Miss Berry would have wished, and we feel that she is not far away.

—Alice Logan Wingo
Dean of Girls' School

The Flame

A dread wind blew
Against a Flame
And no one knew
From whence it came.

The Flame burned low
For it could not stand
The deadly blow
Of that wind's hand.

It flickered down
To a tiny spark—
And then surrendered
To the dark.

That Flame brought light
For forty years
To mountain homes,
It dried up tears

With gifts of love,
Snatched from despair
Untutored lives
And made them fair;

Taught those who teach,
That learning's goal
Combines the head
With hand and soul;

Taught those with gold,
That serving need
Is after all,
Man's lasting meed.

The Flame is gone
But ere it went,
It touched with fire
A continent

—Dr. G. Leland Green

Berry

Young, fearless dreamer,
Faith so strong,
Working without ceasing
For so long.

Training youth
Into better men
With the help
Which you could lend.

Times of sorrow,
Friends ever near,
God-sent messengers
Of Comfort and cheer.

Through times of joy
And times of tears,
Growth, expansion
Came with the years.

Struggles, trials,
Successfully by,
The spirit of Berry
Will never die.

Dream of old,
Now come true,
I pledge my loyalty
Now, to you.

—Thomas Gandy

G. Leland Green was first president of Berry College. Thomas Gandy, a 1942 graduate of Berry, served as academic dean and Berry's first vice president.

TO MISS BERRY

Authors may pen your story
And artists may paint your face,
But we, as Berry students
Testify to your faith.
These buildings and beautiful campuses
May bring you much praise and fame
Yet the highest tributes are paid you
In the hearts where you've kindled hope's flame.
You spent your life in God's service
Serving with no thought of pay
So youth in the Southland might learn
"That where there's a will, there's a way."
Religion, simplicity, learning,
Labor—your pillars four!
Though you've left us in body,
Miss Berry,
Your spirit shall live evermore.

*—Elizabeth**

**Last name unknown. Elizabeth was a student at the time of Martha Berry's death.*

LADY OF DREAMS MARTHA BERRY

(Written after a pilgrimage to the Berry Schools, Mount Berry, Georgia)

The pilgrims visited the schools with Mrs. Emily Vanderbilt Hammond

Miss Angela Morgan, noted poetess and lecturer, who was here with the pilgrims several years ago has just published a volume of poems by the Pennsylvania Publishing Company of Philadelphia. In the volume are included the following verses dedicated to Miss Martha Berry, founder and director of these schools:

If all the dreams of all the world
Should one day come to pass,
As hers who dreamed this Paradise
For mountain lad and lass;
If all the dreamers of the earth
Should make their longings true—
My Neighbor's noble wish for me,
My happy wish for you;
The dream of love for all mankind,

Of wars forever stilled,
Of want and sorrow swept aside,
Utopia fulfilled—
No sweeter triumph could there be
Than hers who made this place
The very mirror of the Lord,
The rapture of His Face.

Oh, never have I seen such beauty
Bursting from the soil,
Such splendor of activity,
Such miracle of toil,
Such yearning for enlightenment,
Such worship for the good
In holy hearts of mountain lads
Whose dreams she understood.
They build the roads,
They plant the trees,
They fashion houses meet
For any prince to occupy
On any noble street.
For here lie humbler deeds of life
Are glorified because
Perception sees their eloquence
And Knowledge spells their laws.

In wishful hearts of mountain maids
She found the Vision, too,
And nurtured it and brought to birth
As splendid mothers do,
Moulder of future mothers,
Who weave and sew and spin,
And make the home a dwelling
Fit for queens to enter in.

Each lad a living torch of light,
Each girl a golden star,
You'd never find their like again,
Though you should travel far.

Oh, never have I heard such tales
Of want and sacrifice,
Nor have I seen such godliness
Ablaze in human eyes.
And always shall I bear with me
Along the enchanted years
The songs they sang to us who listened
Unashamed of tears.

If all the dreamers of the earth
Should make their longings true—
My neighbor's golden wish for me,
My royal wish for you;
If suddenly like fairy cities
Breathed upon the glass,
Our dearest hope for humankind
Should one day come to pass—
As lovely as a harvest field
Or brave as goldenrod—
What triumph for humanity,
What ecstasy for God!

And yet if here have fruited thus
Like grapes upon the vine,
Like apples out of Paradise—
Then why not yours and mine?

O God, bequeath to all of us
The mighty strength to make
Our Highest dream, reality—
We ask it for Love's sake.

The Berry Alumni Quarterly, October 1930, Vol. 13., No. 4.

Miss Berry's Final Letter to Alumni

The Berry Schools, Mount Berry, Georgia, July 1, 1925

To the Graduates of the Berry Schools:

When I am gone, I want you to always think of me as alive—alive beyond your farthest thoughts, and near and loving you, and growing more like God wants me to become. I want you to love the Berry Schools and stand ready to help them in every emergency. Use all of your influence to hold the Schools to the original plan, simple living, work, prayer, the Bible being taught, Christian teachers; keeping the Schools a separate community, protecting and guarding the property and the good name of the Schools. I feel that I shall not be separated from the Schools which have been my life and work and which I have always loved so dearly. I shall not be separated from any of the boys and girls who are my logical heirs. I shall just be closer to God, and will understand better the way in which prayer and faith can open the ways through which God can keep and guard our beloved Berry Schools.

I would like to leave an especial message to the graduates of the Berry Schools who are giving back in service what you have gotten from the Schools. You who are putting your lives into the work are the real dependence of the Schools and I want to ask you especially to be faithful and guard and protect the Berry Schools. My prayer is that the Schools may stand through the ages, for the honor and glory of God and for the Christian training of poor boys and girls of the mountains and country districts.

I leave with each one of you the motto which I have kept on my desk for years, "Prayer Changes Things".

Faithfully Yours,

Martha Berry

Editor's note—This letter was attached to Miss Berry's will and marked, "To be opened after Miss Berry's death."

Miss Berry's Final Letter to the Trustees of the Berry Schools

July 1, 1925.

To the Trustees of the Berry Schools:

The future of the Berry Schools has always been on my mind and heart. In leaving it, I want to entreat the trustees to carry on the work in the spirit in which it was founded, keeping it always within the means of poor boys and girls; maintaining the industrial work and teaching the dignity of labor, so that in later years the students will have a sympathetic understanding with all who have to work.

The real strength of the school lies in its Christian faith, and it is my prayer that the future of the Berry Schools will be maintained and carried on by Christian men and women who are working, not for salaries only, but for a higher Master and for higher wages. I would advise that Gordon Keown be made the Director of the schools. He has been so closely associated with me in my work and all the work of the Berry Schools for the past twenty years that I feel that he should be the one to succeed me.

My life work has been to help poor boys and girls who are willing to help themselves. There will always be a need to help poor boys and girls of the mountains and rural districts, and I implore the trustees, alumni, and friends of Berry to maintain and carry on the work in the spirit in which it was founded,

Faithfully yours,

Martha Berry

Editor's note—This letter was attached to Miss Berry's will and marked, "To be opened after Miss Berry's death."

Martha Berry
1866–1942

FOREWORD

Doctor Charles Marden Proctor, the author of this beautiful tribute to Miss Berry, many years ago established the Robert Raisbeck Proctor Dental Clinic at the Berry Schools, in memory of his deceased son. Not only did Doctor Proctor donate the Clinic, but since its establishment, he has assumed the responsibility of providing, at his own expense, a dentist and a dental hygienist to carry on the work. Because of the program of dentistry and oral hygiene furnished by this Clinic, thousands of Berry students have enjoyed sounder health and their lives have thereby been made happier and more efficient.

Dr. Proctor possesses the honorary degree of Doctor of Science from Berry College and he has at all times and under all circumstances proved himself a loyal alumnus and a never-failing friend of the Berry Schools. Dr. Proctor is a living testimonial to the genius of Miss Berry for winning and keeping great friends. Upon lives such as his—lives imbued with the spirit of unselfish Christian service for others—she built her Schools on firm and lasting foundations.

—*G. Leland Green,*
President of Berry College

Martha Berry
An Appreciation

By Dr. Charles Marden Proctor

For more than three score years and ten Martha Berry responded to the best suggestions which life held out. From the moment of her existence there was never a time when her character and personality ceased in its development. She was a woman of rare character, devoted not only to the promotion of the good name and well-being of the profession of education she so zealously loved, but by closer human contact she was able to suggest a large method of living, so that the true values of life in their relation to the hereafter were pointed out to all whom she knew.

A colossal spirit reigned in the soul of Martha Berry. There was always something vital, something virile, something so alive about Miss Berry. Courage was a part of her flesh and blood. There were many battles with their scars happily faded through the passing of years. She was like a pine that has long fought wind, rain, snow and hail. Martha Berry spoke in the softest tones of the breeze yet, if need be, with the force of a hurricane.

There were many decisive moments in her life. Many momentous decisions had to be made, and how they were made! When her need was greatest, her strength came through faith and prayer, with an assurance of its answer.

In Martha Berry there was never any deviation once a decision was made. She began her work with no fanfare, no shouts, no blowing of trumpets or beating of drums, but over the threshold of her little cabin, like the opening of a bud to a full bloom, or a blade of grass pushing through the earth, or the morning return of the increasing dawn she came, directing the light to thousands of boys and girls, casting its refulgent glow through the daytime of her natural life to the setting at the eventide, when her eternal life began.

It is of frequent occurrence that the closer one lives to an actuality, the less clear is the perspective. It requires the lapse of time to allow us to see clearly and to clarify an objective or the personality of an individual. This did not apply to Martha Berry. She so lived and unfolded her program to public confidence that the time value of her work struck a trial balance each day, as evidenced by the encomiums and honors heaped upon her during the last two decades of her life. Miss Berry so gave of herself that every favor was full to overflowing out of the richness of her life, a complete measure in itself.

It was a rare privilege to have had Martha Berry as a friend. To have had the value of her words and thoughts was indeed a choice treasure. She possessed, in every essential, traits which, as we look upon them, are the ideals of mankind. Mean and petty jealousies, discontent and unhappy strife, had no place in her life. It was the broad view of the universe into which she looked that makes her memory so rare, so precious to us today.

It is often said that a memorial tribute to a friend is for the living and not for the dead. So far as we know, the dead have passed beyond our reach; they do not answer to our clasp or word. The living can hear us, they can respond to our greeting, and to them we can bring inspiration and sympathy. All this sounds conclusive; it seems to reduce all to the recollection of precious memories. Yet man is not flesh and blood alone.

Our departed friends have a reputation, and we can serve them by giving a fair estimate of their earthly lives and of their character. Even as a living man can serve another living man by a jealous guarding of his name, so a living man can serve his dead friend by setting forth and summing up his career, the issue of his mind and heart, so as to give a just rating of a strong life. In this spirit I shall try to speak of Miss Berry; the terms of general human nature would not suffice; her individuality was distinctive. Our impression of her was that of reality. She was genuine; when she expressed herself, the expression was true.

Those who were closest to her will tell you that she was always real. The primal law of the universe insists upon sincerity, and our friend had that virtue in full degree, which is the very source and formation of character. How strong was the impression of her intellectuality. Her mind lived in high regions. She was born for knowledge; she was ever an inquirer.

There was nothing of the pedant about her; her reality prevented her from being an intellectual pharisee. She was a purist in speech; her language was exact and accurate. Association with her was a process of culture, not because she assumed the air of a teacher but rather because she had ever the mood of the real scholar, and with it all, you must agree that her life had a tone of spirituality with logical thought of the hereafter. Herein, then, is comfort to those whose lives were closely mingled with hers, and to her friends an inspiration for a better well-being.

How appropriate that Martha Berry should have entered into her spiritual adventure in the time of these days of awaking spring. At a time when the wood paths are becoming sweet with the incense of flowers. These days when the ferns begin to curl upward from the ground and the daffodils brighten the fields, amidst the music of bird songs and running waters, while the morning breeze off Lavendar Mountain reminds us of her joy in these things.

In her spiritual life Miss Berry will find her loved ones around her; she will have flowers that never fade; she will have come again into her youth, to live again a greater life than she ever knew here. Thus in these days of her setting sun, there is thankfulness in our hearts for the life God has given to us all. A cloud has come and passed over our lives which in the passing will leave a brighter haven of memory for having known her.

As the stately oak draws nourishment deep where its roots lie, so did Miss Berry receive encouragement, comfort and help from her thousands of friends and workers here and abroad.

Our greatest tribute to the life of Martha Berry is not in assembling here for the moment in honor of her memory, but in accepting for ourselves the rare characteristics which she exemplified by her life; and as we take away these memories, let us not regret that she has gone, but rather feel that we are blest in having known her and rare will be our privilege to carry on where she left off.

February 1942
Mount Berry, Georgia

PART II

SKETCHES OF THE BERRY SCHOOLS AND COLLEGE

Important Dates in Berry's History

Berry College…A Living Legend

The Story of Berry Schools

Charter and Bylaws
Summary 1903 to Present
1982 Charter Excerpt
2001 Charter and Bylaws

Letter to Alumni from Dr. G. Leland Green (1927)
(Intent to Start Four-Year College)

Letter to Boys and Girls from Martha Berry (1930)
(Plan to Start Four-Year Program)

Anniversaries—25th, 30th, 50th, 75th; Plans for 100th

Faculty Tenure and List of First Recipients

S. H. Cook Eulogy

Administrative Reorganization of Academic Areas Into Four Schools
(Memo from Dean Doyle Mathis)

Presiding Officers of the Board of Trustees and the Board of Visitors

Chief Administrative Officers and Chief Academic Officers

Important Dates in Berry's History

1866

October 7, Martha Berry's birthday. Miss Berry gave a picnic for students on the mountain campus each year on the Saturday nearest her birthday. The "Mountain Day" celebration is now held on the first Saturday in October, at which time students and alumni join together in celebrating this traditional day.

1902

January 13, Boy's Industrial School founded on Lower Campus.

1903

April 6, "Boy's Industrial School" incorporated by order of the judge of the Superior Court of Floyd County.

Martha Berry deeded 83 acres of land to Boys Industrial School.

1908

Corporate charter amended with legal name changed to "The Berry School."

1909

Thanksgiving Day, The Martha Berry School for Girls opened on Log Cabin Campus.

1910

President Theodore Roosevelt visited Berry.

1915

First brick buildings, Berry College Chapel and Blackstone Dining Hall, constructed.

1916

School for older boys started on Mountain Campus at foot of Lavendar Mountain.

1917

Corporate charter amended with legal name changed to "The Berry Schools."

1922

The Berry Schools accredited by Southern Association of Colleges and Secondary Schools.

1923

Clara and Henry Ford first visited Berry.

1925-1931

Ford Buildings constructed—Clara Hall, the first, completed 1925.

1926

Berry Junior College established.

G. Leland Green became Berry College's first president.

Memorial Library opened.

1928

Berry Junior College accredited by Southern Association of Colleges and Secondary Schools.

First two-year college class graduated.

1930

Berry College (senior college) established.

1932

First senior-college class received degrees.

1942

February 27, Martha Berry died.

1942

Marcus Gordon Keown became acting director of The Berry Schools.

1944

Dr. William Jesse Baird became Berry's second president.

1946

Dr. James Armour Lindsay became Berry's third president.

1951

Dr. Samuel Henry Cook became acting president of Berry.

1953

Dr. Robert Stanley Lambert became Berry's fourth president.

1955

William McChesney Martin, Jr., became acting president of Berry.

The Martha Berry School for Girls closed.

1956

Dr. John R. Bertrand became Berry's fifth president.

1957

Berry College accredited by Southern Association of Colleges and Schools.

1959

First international student admitted.

1961

Board approved a modification of the two-day work requirement.

Day students allowed to enroll.

1962

Fall term, Berry College changed to quarter-system calendar.

Uniforms abolished.

1964

First African-American students enrolled in Berry College.

Name of Mount Berry School for Boys changed to Berry Academy

1968

Berry College's accreditation reaffirmed by Southern Association of Colleges and Schools.

Berry College Board of Vistors organized.

1969

Chapel attendance requirement abolished.

1971

Girls first enrolled in Berry Academy.

1972

Master of Education degree instituted.

Martha Berry Museum and Art Gallery dedicated.

1973

Master of Business Administration degree instituted.

1978

Berry's accreditation reaffirmed by Southern Association of Colleges and Schools.

1980

Dr. Gloria Shatto became Berry's sixth president.

1982

Corporate charter amended with legal name changed to "Berry College, Inc."

1983

Berry Academy closed.

1984

Chick-fil-A/Berry College partnership established. Winshape Centre established on Mountain Campus as part of this educational partnership.

1985

Berry College listed as one of "America's Best Colleges" by *U.S. News and World Report*. Berry ranked third in the category of "Comprehensive Institutions, South, Border States." Berry was also listed in *New York Times' Best Buys in College Education.*

Alumni Work Week tradition established.

Education Specialist program instituted.

1988

Berry's accreditation reaffirmed by Southern Association of Colleges and Schools.

1989

Fall term, Berry College changed to semester-system calendar.

1991

Berry College reorganized, with 16 departments merged into four schools effective October 1.

The Bonner Scholars program established.

Berry named to *Peterson's Guide to Competitive Colleges.*

1993

December, Berry's first Rhodes Scholar named (for fall of 1994).

Bonner Scholarship Program endowed.

1996

School of Business endowed through the Laura Berry Campbell Trust.

Berry served as site of summer 1996 International Olympic Youth Camp.

1998

Dr. Scott Colley became Berry's seventh president.

Berry's accreditation reaffirmed by Southern Association of Colleges and Schools.

2000

Berry listed 13th time in *U.S. News and World Report* as one of "America's Best Colleges," second in South among regional liberal-arts colleges.

Berry College...A Living Legend

What was it about Berry that caught the interest of Andrew Carnegie, that captured the enthusiasm of Theodore Roosevelt, that appealed to the practical mind of Henry Ford and earned his generous support?

What is it about Berry today that commands an equal measure of enthusiasm among leading Americans and thousands of loyal friends?

The answers to these questions are found in the fascinating story of Martha Berry and the remarkable institution she built from a cabin to a college.

Gate of Opportunity, 1920s

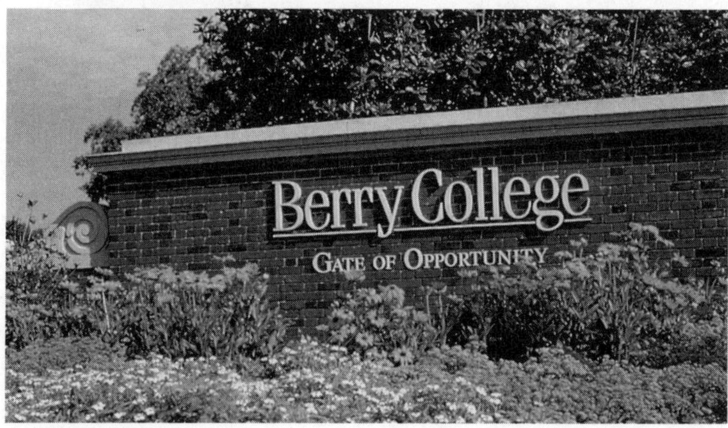

Gate of Opportunity, 2001

Midway between Atlanta and Chattanooga stands an extraordinary institution, Berry College. Each year thousands of visitors come to enjoy the beauty of these fields, forests, mountains, lakes, and streams.

Emphasizing academic excellence, the value of religion in life, and the dignity of worthwhile work well done, the college offers young men and young women opportunities for a rich educational experience leading to the degrees of Bachelor of Arts, Bachelor of Science, Bachelor of Music, Master of Business Administration, Master of Education, and Education Specialist. Students come from all parts of the United States and from several other countries, representing widely varying backgrounds. Some have had every advantage in youth; others, almost none. Most come from the surrounding region, but numbers come from more distant states and countries. At Berry College they share opportunities for improving themselves through Berry's distinctive threefold program of study, work, and worship.

Berry graduates have distinguished themselves in nearly all fields of endeavor from public service worldwide to a broad array of professions and business careers around the globe. They are known for their idealism, scholarship, spirit of service, and eager acceptance of responsibility. Visitors seeing the magnificent

Emily Guest Cottage

and modern educational facilities that grace the Berry campuses can scarcely believe how it all began. Yet there before them—now in the quaint guest-house area—they can see for themselves the early log buildings, and they can hear the story firsthand from members of the faculty and staff. For the first 40 years Berry was the story of a great-hearted lady of high purposes, bold dreams, and indomitable spirit.

Martha Berry as a young woman

Martha Berry was born October 7, 1866, in Northeast Alabama and was nurtured at Oak Hill, her parents' plantation home near Rome, Georgia. When they were not engaged in more active pursuits, she and her five sisters and two brothers were tutored by Miss Ida McCullough, who often held classes in their log-cabin playhouse. When all the children were grown, Martha, who alone chose not to marry, converted the cabin into her personal den and study. A gifted storyteller, she wanted to be a writer.

Sitting in her cabin one Sunday afternoon near the turn of the twentieth century, Martha heard children's voices coming from the woods outside. Then through her window she saw three boys in ragged overalls. Opening the door, she invited them inside to have some apples.

The boys ate apples while Martha told them stories from the Bible—stories to which they listened in awe and wonder until she was silent. Noting their keen interest, Martha was distressed when she learned there was no school the boys could attend.

Then and there she determined to do something about their obvious thirst for knowledge.

In this simple fashion began Martha Berry's lifetime work as an educator of the young people of her region. From the start, she made as her aim the education not only of the head but also of the hands and of the heart.

When the next Sunday arrived, the first boys brought their brothers and sisters to the little cabin, and soon their parents and other relatives began to appear. The Sunday School outgrew the cabin schoolhouse, and Martha moved her pupils to an old church at nearby Possum Trot, center of a small mountain community. As the group continued to grow, she opened other Sunday Schools at Mount Alto and Foster's Bend.

Early Possum Trot church

Although she was delighted with the good-heartedness of the people who came to her Sunday classes, Martha was distressed by their woeful lack of learning. She could not endure the thought that many bright boys and girls would never have the opportunity for real education. To give them some chance, she decided to conduct day classes at each of the Sunday Schools because there were no free rural schools in the area. In fact, there were only five public high schools in Georgia. In 1901, with $1,000 of the money her father had left her, she built a whitewashed schoolhouse across the road (now U.S. 27, the Martha Berry Highway) from her home, persuading the men and boys in her Sunday Schools to contribute most of the carpentry.

But the day classes were not fully satisfactory. The children were kept away too frequently for cotton and corn planting or for harvesting, or because it was raining or snowing. Many of the hill roads were passable only at the mercy of the weather. The following year Martha built a dormitory and opened a boarding school for boys.

Knowing the rural boys of that era could not afford high tuition, Martha declared that every student would work to help meet his expenses. This meant the school needed land for gardens and pastures, and so Martha acted in her characteristic fashion.

She took a property deed to town and told her friend Attorney Moses Wright that she wanted to deed to the school 83 acres of land she had inherited. Mr. Wright and other friends of the family tried to dissuade her. "Let someone else do it," they said. But Martha prevailed and gave the land, and soon Moses Wright became one of her first trustees.

Boys began appearing at the school at all hours of the day and night. The Boys' Industrial School, as the new school chartered in 1903 was called, offered a high-school diploma. In those days a high-school education was less common than a college education is today. For many young men, this school represented their only opportunity for a secondary education. Appropriately, Martha named the entrance to her school the "Gate of Opportunity." It opened upon a truly distinctive program with balanced emphasis on learning, working, and worshiping. During the first year of the school, more than a dozen students enrolled. The first graduate, Clayton Henson, finished his studies in 1904; and Martha held a special graduation ceremony for him.

As more students came from a wider and wider area, the little school grew, and Martha could no longer meet its needs from her own resources. Again this southern gentlewoman shocked her friends—this time by going north to campaign for funds. Andrew Carnegie promised her $50,000 for endowment if she could match it with an equal amount in gifts. She did. President Theodore Roosevelt gave a dinner party for her at the White House and introduced her to many of his wealthy and prominent friends, who began to help her with her work.

By 1908 there were 150 boys in the boarding school, and the name was changed to "The Berry School." In 1909—once more against well-meaning advice but with the encouragement of former President Roosevelt—Martha started a girls' division.

President Theodore Roosevelt with Martha Berry

With two schools in operation, she adopted in 1917 an inclusive corporate name, "The Berry Schools."

Sometimes Martha joked about how she had opened the school with boys because she thought they could do more work than girls. Then she would add, "If I had known how much more boys could eat, I might have begun with girls instead."

Despite an increasing need for funds, the schools continued to grow. From time to time a generous friend would give a building or an electric plant or a herd of cows. By 1915 the first brick buildings—Blackstone Dining Hall and the Berry College Chapel—were in place. Hundreds of acres were added to the fields and forests where many of the boys worked. The forests grew into a significant source of income.

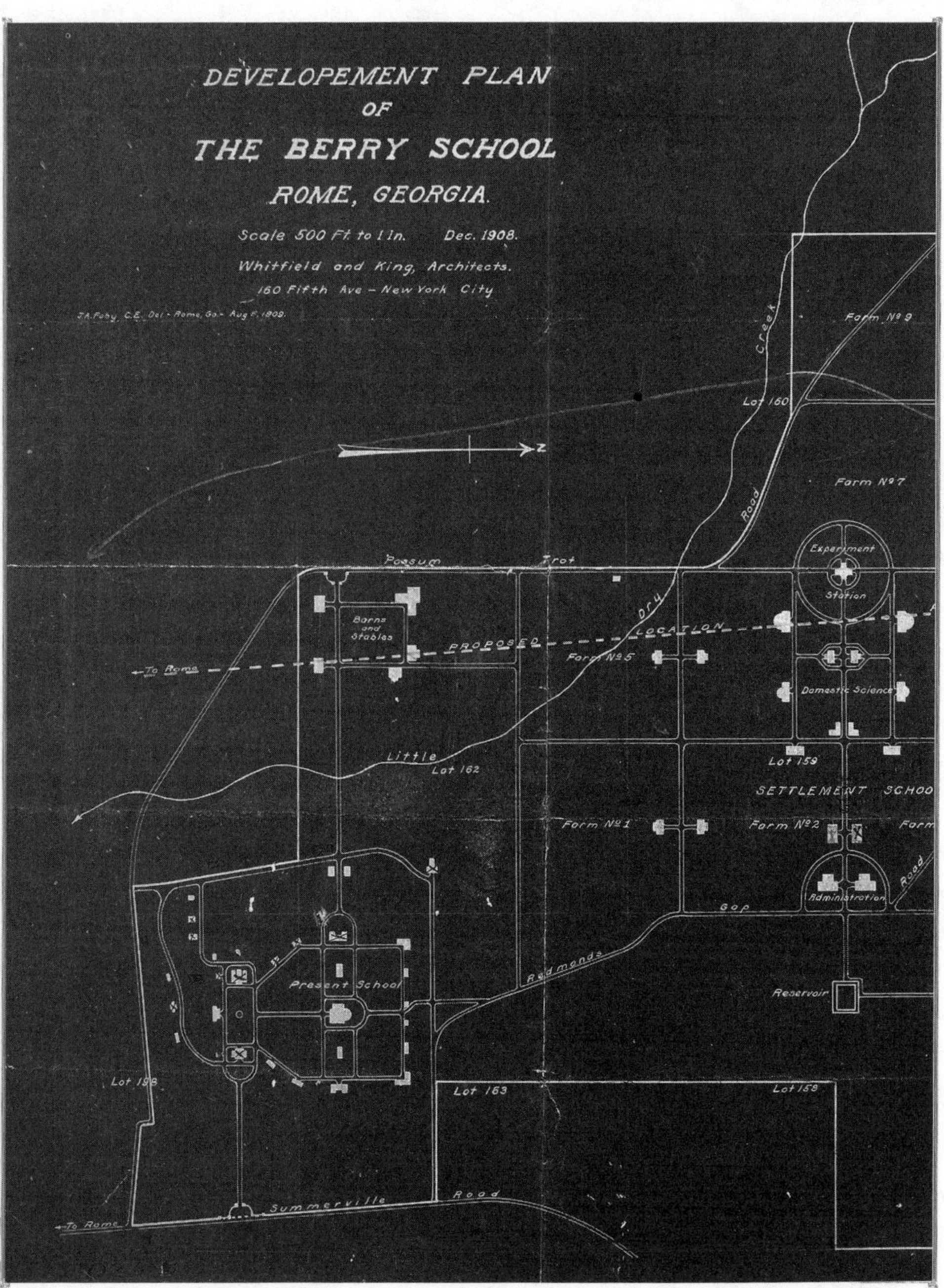

Development Plan map including existing buildings in 1908 (lower left area)

Young men from Berry distinguished themselves in military service during World War I. By the time they returned, young people in the Southeast could attend public high schools in many locations, and there was a critical need for colleges to train teachers for the public schools. In response to this need, Miss Berry opened Berry Junior College in 1926. Dr. G. Leland Green, previously principal of The Berry Schools, became president of the institution. Twelve students comprised the first graduating class of the junior college. Soon courses were added for juniors and seniors; and the founder handed diplomas to 17 graduates, the first class of the four-year college, in May of 1932. Because of the extensive work-study program, it was possible for a student at the schools to work his or her way through high school and college at Berry.

Students' literary skills were developed beyond the classroom through literary societies—the Athenian and the Philomathean Societies at the high school, the Georgian and the Syrreb Societies at the college—whose purpose was to encourage literary attainment in public speaking and debate, dramatics, and music. The societies, each with girls' and boys' divisions, also became competitive in athletics and were active through the 1972-73 academic year, by which time national honor societies had been instituted at Berry.

Sport has also enjoyed a rich tradition throughout Berry's hundred-year history. As soon as 1904, Berry boys had a baseball team. Soon followed the long-standing tradition of inter-dormitory competitions in baseball, basketball, and track. Berry women later played basketball, tennis, and volleyball on courts built for them at the girls' school. Largely through the efforts of Samuel Henry Cook, who joined the faculty in 1910, sport continued to develop as part of campus life; and physical education became part of the curriculum. A varsity club established in 1916 for outstanding athletes aroused interest.

Following a slump in sports development during the 1930s and 1940s, perhaps exacerbated by the Depression and World War II, Berry expanded its intercollegiate program for men under

1914 Girls' Basketball Team

the guidance of Garland and Edward Dickey. In 1962, the Viking became the mascot, and women for the first time played intercollegiate sport. In the 1980s and 1990s sport grew in diversity under the leadership of Bob Pearson.

Berry teams have won several national titles. Successful intercollegiate programs continue for both men and women in basketball, running, cross-country, tennis, soccer, and golf, and in baseball for men. Berry has retained as well the intramural program it began during the first years of its existence, and both men and women are able to compete in a variety of sports.

During the early 1920s, Miss Berry persuaded Mr. and Mrs. Henry Ford to visit her at Berry. The pioneer industrialist, impressed with Berry's practical approach to education, decided to have a part in it. He gave tractors for the farms and helped with the acquisition of more land. He also built at Berry a group of magnificent Gothic structures, the Ford Buildings, to house and educate the young women who had occupied log buildings until that time. The last section of the Ford Buildings was completed in 1931.

Henry and Clara Ford gave more than money and buildings to Berry, however; seeing the need for broadening the social experiences of Berry's students, he introduced dancing. To accomplish his goal, Mr. Ford brought his own dance orchestra

Ford Archway

Henry Ford dances with student

and taught students the dance steps. They looked forward to these visits from Henry and Clara Ford until the late 1940s.

By the time Berry granted its first bachelor's degrees, the land holdings of the schools had increased to 25,000 acres. Today Berry's forests, fields, and campuses include approximately 28,000 acres. Throughout this pastoral academic setting, one of the largest and most beautiful in the world, approximately 2,000 students now pursue their studies in classrooms and natural laboratories that provide a true environment for learning.

By 1932 several marble-pillared Georgian buildings had been added to the original log and frame buildings, and others were being planned. Expertly supervised, the boys themselves made brick and built the handsome three-story Science Building (Cook Hall), Memorial Gymnasium (later named Richards Gymnasium), Thomas Berry residence hall, the industrial shops (Laughlin Building, now used for the communication program), and

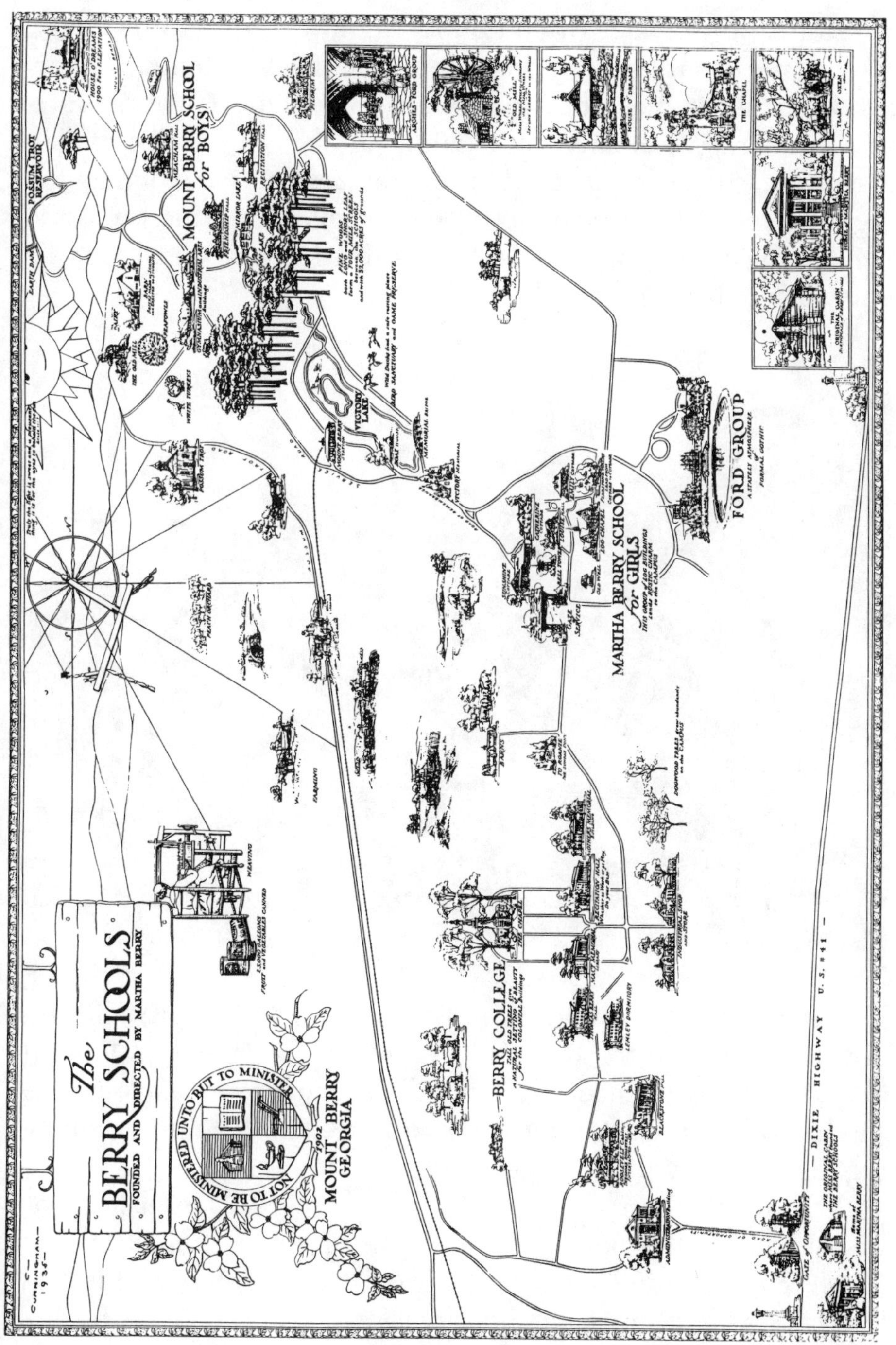

1935 campus map

the store at the college (Moon Building, now used for fine arts).

On the mountain campus (early site of The Mountain Farm School for Boys, then The Mount Berry School for Boys, and, ultimately, Berry Academy until 1983) at the foot of Lavendar Mountain, students constructed several large native-stone buildings. In the 1930s students built the extensive Normandy complex (farm, dairy, and residential) of bricks they had made in Berry's own brick plant.

Normandy barns with Martha Berry's signature steeple

Despite a major depression, Berry continued to grow in the last decade of Martha Berry's life, and she never ceased to give fully of her intelligence and tremendous energy to the institution she had started. Gratefully, she had placed spires on her buildings as visible symbols of her faith.

When Miss Berry died on February 27, 1942, thousands of friends across the nation mourned her passing. *The New York Herald Tribune* noted that she had died "full of years and full of honors." An editor of the *San Francisco Examiner* called her "a true patriot who gave her life for her country." *The Miami Herald* commented, "It is harder to live for one's country than to die for it, and America so needs a few more patriots like Martha Berry to stand by it."

By this time, enrollment had grown to an average of approximately 1,000 young men and women, and more than 10,000 young people had already gone out through the Gate of Opportunity to excel in a wide variety of careers. While building an outstanding physical, spiritual, and educational environment, Martha Berry had also managed to gather for the institution an endowment of nearly two million dollars.

The loss of this dynamic leader was a severe blow. At that time Berry faced another crisis: most male students and many members of the faculty and staff were called into service for World War II, leaving behind a large physical plant as well as hundreds of acres of farmland to be planted, cultivated, and harvested. Women students, already accustomed to useful work, volunteered to drive trucks and tractors and to do what had to be done. Thus, the manpower crisis was met with woman-power; but finding new leadership to guide the institution into a new era was not simple.

In the two years following Miss Berry's death, M. Gordon Keown, one of Berry's first graduates, served as acting director of the schools. A series of presidents then followed over the next 12 years. During this period Dr. Jesse Baird (1944-1946), Dr. James Armour Lindsay (1946-1951), and Dr. Robert Lambert (1953-1955) served as president. Dr. S. H. Cook, long-time dean, was acting president in 1951-1953. William McChesney Martin, chairman of Berry's board of trustees and also chairman of the Federal Reserve Board, filled the role as acting president in 1955-1956.

The challenge facing the succession of presidents was the adaptation of Berry's program to the economic and social changes that swept the region after World War II. To do this, while building upon Berry's heritage and adhering to the basic values for which Berry had become widely known and highly respected, was not an easy task for anyone.

Still, as each year went by, the need to strengthen the academic program became more urgent. Like other colleges, Berry was caught up in a shock wave caused by the so-called "explosion of knowledge." Graduates were expected to exhibit more and more sophistication in their fields of study. In fairness to its students, the college could not fail to provide thorough and up-to-date instruction. Yet, Berry did not have the financial resources required for vital adjustments in faculty salaries, essential improvements in library holdings, and the modernization of classrooms and laboratories. There was danger in the early 1950's that this school, which had earned world-wide recognition, would lose its momentum.

Students in the work-opportunity program

There were problems even in the work-opportunity program, which had become a model for similar programs in a number of other institutions. Some of the student-work projects were requiring a substantial subsidy, which reduced funds for the academic program.

Throughout this difficult time, the spirit of Berry remained strong. This spirit was evident each year in several hundred new and purposeful students, in a dedicated faculty, and in Berry's distinguished governing board, which worked tirelessly throughout this period, making sure that Berry was continuing to offer sound preparation to each new class of students. Opinions varied on how to cope with immediate problems and on how to face the future; yet everyone believed in Berry, and some were confident that a great new era was about to dawn.

In 1956 Board Chairman William McChesney Martin, who had served as acting president for a year, persuaded Dr. John R. Bertrand to accept the presidency of Berry College and the high school. This experienced educator was attracted by Berry's declared mission of providing low-cost educational opportunity to qualified and interested students and by Berry's emphasis on spiritual values. He saw also Berry's great potential as an increasingly vital force in education, and he accepted the challenge these possibilities presented.

D. H. Cook, dean emeritus; John R. Bertrand, president; and G. Leland Green, president emertus, ca. 1960

Upon arrival at Berry, President Bertrand set out to understand every aspect of Berry's program. He consulted with Dr. G. Leland Green, Dr. S. H. Cook, other former associates of Miss Berry, department heads, work supervisors, students, and alumni. He also asked other distinguished educators to examine Berry's program in depth and offer their recommendations. Meanwhile, he studied Berry's history in great detail, and someone observed that he came nearer than anyone else to capturing the essence of Martha Berry's philosophy of education.

Under his leadership began the great new era many had dreamed about and some had approached with apprehension. Student rights and responsibilities were more fully recognized, faculty salaries were increased, a system of promotion and tenure for faculty was instituted, less-productive student-work projects were eliminated or modified, modern business procedures were adopted, and tuition charges were increased for those who could pay. Scholarships and loans were expanded for those who needed extra assistance. Admissions policies were broadened—ultimately to include qualified students without regard to race, creed, area of residence, or economic circumstances. Under Dr. Bertrand's leadership, the college became fully accredited in 1957 by the Southern Association of Colleges and Schools, a mark of recognition of great importance to the college's graduates.

Although an affluent urban student could now gain admission, Berry retained the policy that no qualified student would be denied an education simply for lack of funds. The gates would continue to swing wide for all students willing to work and to help themselves.

As greater emphasis was placed on the academic program, improvements were soon evident. The curriculum was revised, updated, and strengthened. Additional highly competent scholars joined the faculty. Increasing numbers of Berry College graduates went on to advanced studies, and their graduate-school professors were so favorably impressed that they began actively recruiting Berry graduates. By the early 1970s Berry had added its own graduate programs to meet the needs of education and business in Northwest Georgia. Academically, Berry had moved into the space age and was graduating several hundred students each year.

Berry College Graduation

The new era at Berry was marked by the same kind of vitality and excitement that had characterized those earlier days of growth and development under the direction of Martha Berry. There was one major difference. In the earlier days, Miss Berry had built a great institution largely through the force of her own remarkable will and personality. In a way that no one could ever match, she had dramatized her dreams for an expanding program at Berry, and her admirers by the thousands had responded to her invitation to have a part in making her dreams come true. More than 50 years after hearing Miss Berry, some of these early supporters continued to invest regularly in her undying dream for the ongoing development of her school.

In the new era, no one person could do what Miss Berry had done. Fortunately, by this time Berry had assembled a team of exceptional strength. Serving on Berry's board of trustees were men and women of ability, dedication, and influence. The competent staff headed by Dr. Bertrand included persons who had worked closely with Miss Berry. Major benefactors invested not only their funds but also their good will and counsel for Berry's benefit.

In 1962 the board of trustees launched an ambitious development program to enable Berry to expand its services to increasing numbers of students without becoming overgrown or impersonal. Grover M. Hermann, by a gift of more than a million dollars, set the pace for the greatest sustained building expansion in Berry's history. In announcing his gift for a new administration building, Mr. Hermann, then chairman of the board of Martin-Marietta Corporation, described succinctly the special mission of Berry College: "The qualities of

Hermann Hall

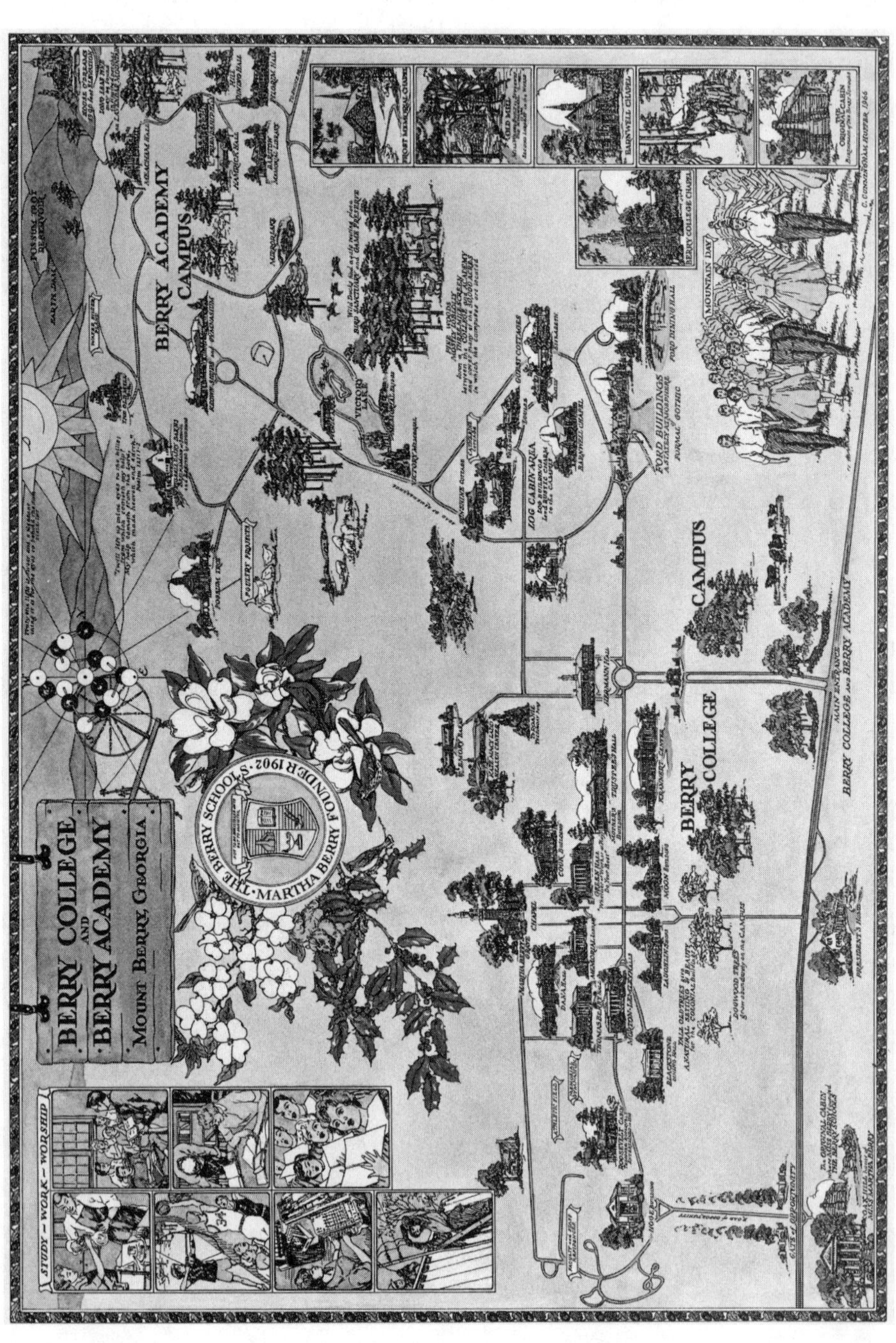

1966 campus map

faith in man and God, individual initiative, hard work, mental discipline, and personal responsibility are fundamental to a free society. Berry College is dedicated to the development of these qualities. This is why I am happy to contribute to its achievement."

Dana Hall

Charles A. Dana, then chairman of the board of Dana Corporation, with a long-time interest in Berry, challenged Berry's board of trustees to match his grant toward a new classroom building; and they met his challenge. Mr. Dana invested extensively in buildings, in scholarships, and in faculty development. He left $1 million to Berry, the only college or university mentioned in his will. A men's residence hall bears his name.

Krannert Student Center

Herman C. Krannert, then chairman of the board of Inland Container Corporation, had for years contributed generously in funds and in professional counsel to the improved management of Berry's agricultural and forest resources. Impressed with Berry's total program and growing promise, Mr. Krannert and his wife, Ellnora, made a gift to Berry for an urgently needed student-activities center.

Other major construction during Dr. Bertrand's 23-year tenure included additional classroom and residence-hall space, a new student-health center, total renovation of both an old classroom building and the school store to provide more classrooms, and a new physical-plant building.

These visible evidences of progress were not necessarily the most vital, however. Berry exists to make educational opportunity available to young people. Thousands of friends and alumni helped to meet the mounting costs of this mission. Their generous gifts helped to pay students for their work on the campus, provide scholarships to qualified students requiring extra assistance, buy books for the libraries, and attract and hold faculty of high quality. By the time of his retirement at the end of 1979, Dr. Bertrand had laid strong groundwork for the college to make giant leaps forward in strength and in recognition.

The presidency of Dr. Gloria Shatto, beginning in January of 1980 and ending in June of 1998, continued this focus on strengthening the college through collaborative and strategic planning. By the mid-1980s several researchers/raters of colleges began to highlight Berry as one of America's best colleges. The year 2000 edition of *America's Best Colleges* by *U. S. News and World Report* carried Berry's thirteenth listing, this time as second in the South among regional liberal-arts institutions.

During Dr. Shatto's presidency and under the guidance of Vice President and Dean of the College Doyle Mathis, the college was reorganized academically into four schools and its emphasis on excellence was continued.

Making improvements in the physical plant was also a focus in the time of Dr. Shatto, as was continuing to build the endowment. Outdated modular units were removed, new town houses were added as student residences, the library was renovated and more than doubled in size, and plans for a new science facility were underway at the time of her retirement.

Early in 2001 this new state-of-the-art science building was occupied by the School of Mathematical and Natural Sciences. Cook Hall, the former science building named for long-time dean

Memorial Library

S. H. Cook, was renovated to serve as the home of the Charter School of Education and Human Sciences. The Campbell School of Business now occupies Green Hall, named for Berry's first president. This hall, completely renovated in the summers of 1997 and 1998, became a state-of-the-art classroom building that stands as a living memorial to John Bulow Campbell, early trustee and brother-in-law of Martha Berry, and Laura Berry Campbell, sister of Martha Berry. A large endowment gift to the school made this transformation possible.

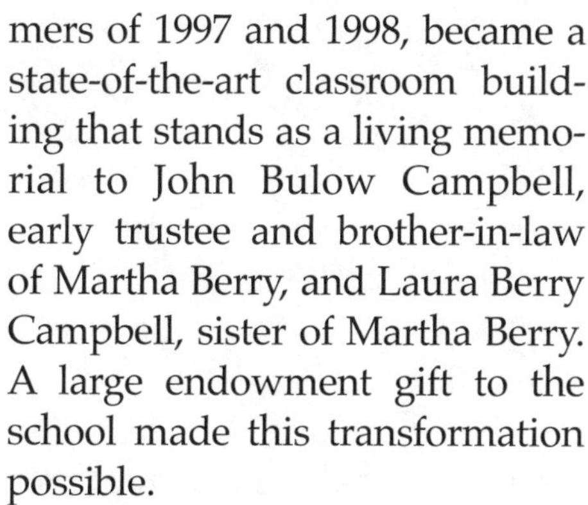

Science Center

Evans Hall, named for Lettie Pate Whitehead Evans, benefactor and long-time friend of Berry's founder, will serve as the home of the School of Humanities and Social Sciences upon the move of the Charter School of Education and Human Sciences into Cook Hall. The south segment of Evans Hall was the Mothers' Building, which had been occupied by students and faculty until its conversion to a classroom building in 1967.

For his inauguration on April 9, 1999, Dr. Scott Colley, seventh president of Berry, chose as his theme "A Heritage of Hope, A Vision for the Future." Dr. Colley stands on the "strong shoulders" of those who preceded him; with his own wisdom and perspective,

Inauguration of Scott Colley as president of Berry College, 1998

supported by a stalwart administration and faculty, his vision can become reality as did that of Martha Berry.

Persons visiting Berry for the first time are awed by the size and beauty of the campuses and are equally impressed by the splendid young people they meet. They note that the campuses are surrounded by extensive Berry-owned fields and forests that permit Berry to preserve in an ideal setting its unique environment for education. The nature lover delights in the abundance of flora and fauna. All are inspired by the harmony they see at Berry between the handiwork of God and the handiwork of man.

A long-time associate of Martha Berry once said, "The secret of Miss Berry's genius lies in her eternal dissatisfaction." Something of that spirit persists at Berry today. While the college has benefited immeasurably from the advancements of previous years, the future makes even greater demands and holds even greater promise.

The Old Mill, 1931

Strengthening Berry in a special role are members of the Berry College Board of Visitors, initially headed by Ben S. Gilmer, president of American Telephone and Telegraph Company. As members of this board, prominent men and women from several states advise and assist the president in many ways and share information about Berry with friends and associates.

Speaking to this group on the college campus, former Board of Trustees Chairman William McChesney Martin said, "In a land parched with problems, I find at Berry an oasis of opportunity—opportunity for young people seeking an education as well as opportunity for those desiring a part in making possible Berry's distinctive program of education." In the years since that comment was made, thousands of students and a multitude of friends have thrived in this oasis. Graduates go out with their degrees representing a broad range of specialities—undergirded by a strong liberal education and the skills and values gained from their threefold program of study, work, and worship—to help make the world a better place for all.

As Berry approached the centennial of its founding, its alumni—11,288 Baccalaureate graduates by spring 2001—were located in 50 states, the District of Columbia, four territories or possessions of the United States, and 47 other countries. Through their careers, their spirit of service, and their influence, these alumni are wielding a positive impact around the globe.

The original article by this title was written in 1974 by John R. Lipscomb, Berry alumnus and now vice president for development (of Berry College) emeritus, and was updated for this publication—Martha Berry, Sketches of Her Schools and College—by Ouida W. Dickey, co-editor.

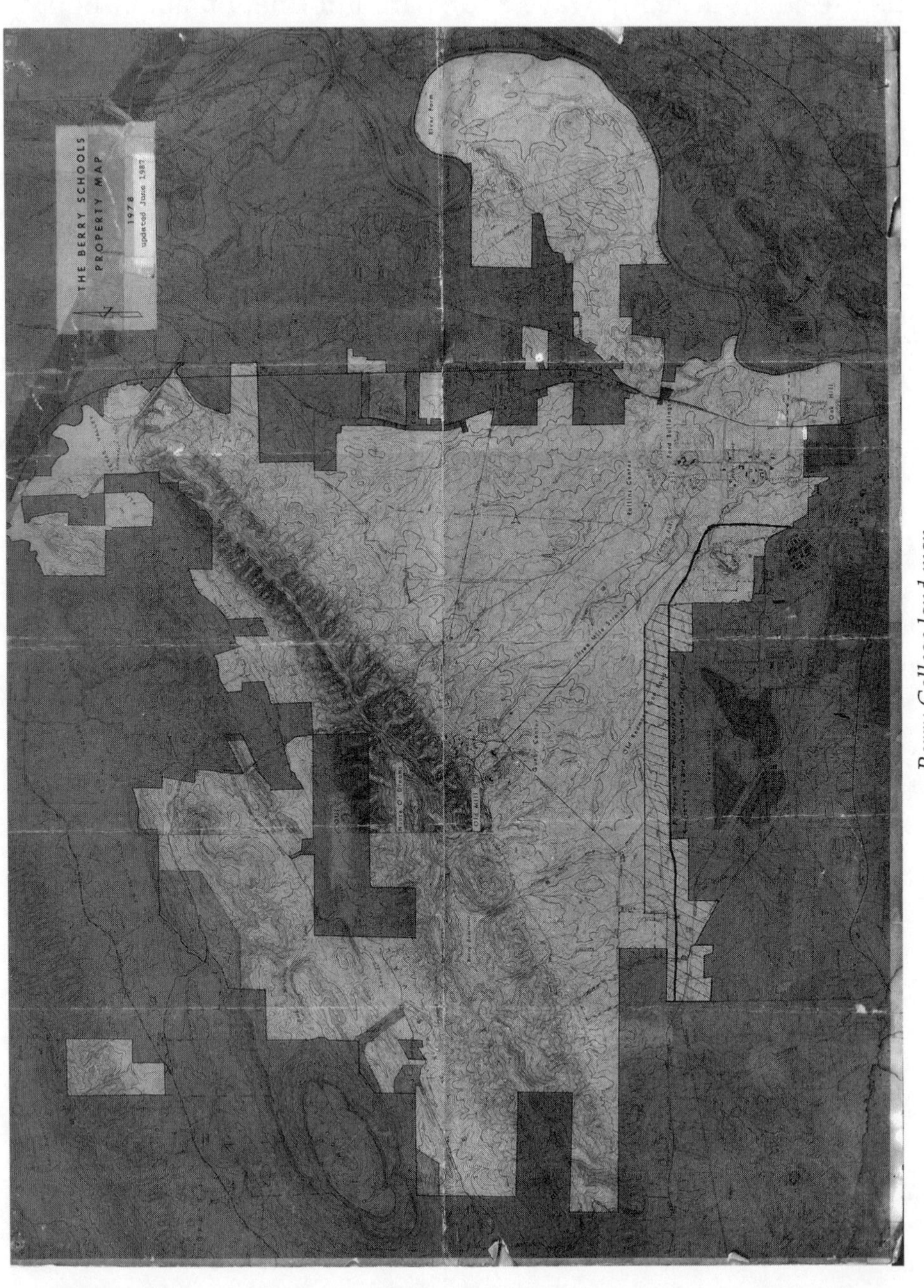

Berry College land map

The Story of Berry Schools
THE ORIGINAL CABIN
MOUNT BERRY, Ga.

The Berry Schools

Incorporated
Mount Berry, Georgia

Miss Martha Berry,
Founder and Director September 16, 1925

TO THE READERS OF THIS BOOKLET:

For twenty-three years I have been telling the story of the Berry Schools—their humble beginnings and their wonderful growth.

Thousands have been educated at Berry by the friends made through the telling of this simple story.

I am sending this booklet on its journey with the earnest prayer that through reading it new friends will help hundreds of boys and girls who are now waiting for their opportunity.

Faithfully yours,

Martha Berry

A similar story appeared under Martha Berry's by-line in The Southern Highlander issues of December 1915, April 1916, and June 1916.

The Story of the Berry Schools

If you go north today from Atlanta, Georgia, to Chattanooga, Tennessee, on the Dixie Highway, it isn't many miles before you will strike a great avenue of trees and glimpse through them a view of fine buildings. On a sign beside the entrance wall is an inscription, "The Berry Schools." You may not know it as you look at that sign, but you are gazing on one of the greatest human achievements of today—or as Emerson might have put it, the shadow of one of the most extraordinary women in America, Martha Berry.

Twenty years ago, there were no such buildings or chapels in sight. Instead, a young girl was sitting in a small log cabin by this same spot, an open book in her lap, returning the stares of three ragged little youngsters in homespun who stood in the doorway.

"What do you all do Sunday afternoons?" she was inquiring.
"Nuthin'," the eldest lad ventured after a silence.
"But don't you go to Sunday school?"
"There ain't any Sunday schools."

More questions brought out the fact that they were poor Cracker children from the farms around her father's plantation, unable to read or write. So to amuse them, she told them Bible stories. They seemed such shy little creatures, so plainly starving for knowledge and so completely shut out from the world of beauty. At the end of an hour, indeed, she had told them all the Bible stories she knew.

"But you all come back next Sunday, and I will tell you some new ones," she suggested.
"We'll be back," they chorused in embarrassed whispers.

The next Sunday they were back, too. And one of the boys had brought his two little sisters. The Sunday after that, the number had increased to ten. And in another week Martha Berry realized, to her astonishment, that she had a kind of Sunday school on her hands.

Now, teaching Sunday school had not been included either in her studies at the finishing school in Baltimore, or in the round of house parties and fox hunts which had made up existence for her since her return home. But there was an old melodeon up in the white-pillared house—well battered up, but still useful—and there was the Bible and the world of nature at the door, which she could use as a curriculum at first. So she began with those. She told the children Bible stories, and played and sang old-fashioned hymns with them, lining out the songs as she had heard mountain preachers do. And she took them on walks through the Georgia woods, unfolding to them all she knew of the romance of the plants and flowers.

And Sunday by Sunday the size of the assemblage grew, as not only brothers and sisters, but soon mothers and babies and dogs came. By fall, indeed, forty youngsters and oldsters were gathering on Sunday in the cabin on the Berry place, sitting on soap boxes, skins, shuck mats, singing the hymns—three children had to hold the old melodeon together or it wouldn't play!—and listening to their youthful teacher. And the bare cabin was bare no longer, but was decorated with a curious collection of colored stones and wasps' nests, flowers and ferns, whatever the fancy of the children fell upon on their walks.

Martha Berry had worked herself into a job. She was the "Sunday Lady." The thing came to her with somewhat of a shock, too, in the Sundays that followed, as she made her children wash their hands in the tin basins outside, and showed them, through an old microscope, the startling difference between clean hands and dirty. What a poignant need there was for education in these mountains, she could not help thinking—for real education of heart and brain and hand! Something more than Sunday schools was needed, indeed, if these children were ever to be released from the bondage in which poverty held them and had held their ancestors. There was some of the best blood of America in these hills—blood that only wanted a chance, an opportunity! She had found evidences of that fact everywhere during her rides—in the old Bibles, in the bare cabins, in the hand-woven counterpanes, the flintlock muskets and old, unused spinning wheels—all evidences of an ancient culture strangled by the poverty of the generations since Colonial days. What could not a real school do, a school which would simply teach the boys and girls of the mountains how to do with their own hands the things their ancestors had been able to do, and would add to that all the ethical training and character which her little Sunday school tried hard to teach now?

It was her first glimpse of her childhood dream. With it, too, came a practical thought. Why couldn't she build a one-room, board schoolhouse, get the County to put in a three months' teacher, and then herself pay for as many months as the children could be held together? She owned a beautiful little piece of woodland down the road, part of the farm given to her by her father when she was a child, and she could buy enough lumber from the sawmill to put up the house. Why couldn't that be done? It wouldn't be a fine, splendid school, but it would be something.

"The Sunday Lady"

By spring it had been done. And in the woods, a half-mile away from her house, stood a little one-room, whitewashed building, ready to do duty as a schoolhouse and as a Sunday school, a school that in six months had so increased in numbers that rooms had been added on either side, pride had demanded a steeple and a bell, and its pupils were coming from as far as eight miles away.

In a year, too, the news of the achievement had traveled far and wide, and from all over the neighborhood requests began to arrive for her to go and start schools in other places. In two years, indeed, she had four Sunday schools and day schools under her direction, going, and going successfully, and she herself was about the busiest young woman in Georgia. And yet Martha Berry felt dimly dissatisfied somehow. Despite all her best efforts, the children could not be kept long enough in these schools, when behind each child, every day, was the drag of poverty and hard work at home. And the teaching itself, it was becoming plainer every day, could never accomplish what she herself had dreamed of in the beginning. Wasn't there some way to make that into a wonderful reality—some way, when the world was so full of wealthy and fine-hearted people and human sympathy?

In the old-fashioned law office of her family's adviser, overlooking the tree-shaded main street of Rome, she put that question to Judge Wright one day.

"If I give my farm to start the thing, and get people to help me, why couldn't we have a school that would be a real school?"

In the quiet office the Judge looked at her humorously. "Aren't you feeling very well today?" he inquired. Why, it would mean giving up forever the social life she had always enjoyed, he pointed out. Day schools were all right, but she couldn't realize the mountainous burden she was so casually offering to shoulder with a thing like this! People's enthusiasm changed; people's loyalty faded. In the end, she would be left with a white elephant.

It was an earnest and sincere talk that the Judge gave that day in the law office. And yet he saw before long, that he was wasting his breath on an impulsive girl.

"All right, Martha," he said at last. "I'll do it. You will be just as poor as you want to be when I get through."

"But I'll be raising a mighty sight better crop than those acres produce just now," she retorted.

She spent the next few weeks, then, living laborious days, selecting a site in the woods, getting lumber from the cheap sawmill, acting as timekeeper over the day labor she got, and constructing finally a two-story, modest frame building, the first home of her girlhood's dream.

And what a home! Hidden behind weeds and broom sedge, surrounded by deep gullies, almost embraced by thick undergrowth and trees, it could hardly be seen as a stranger came up the footpath from the road. Inside it gave even a ruder appearance. Drygoods boxes donated by generous merchants in Rome, turned into shelves and bureaus by the prospective pupils; old odds and ends of ancient furniture from the Berry attic; one small, two-eyed stove, reinforced by two huge pots in the open fireplace! Brewster Hall they called it, without thought of humor.

And yet it was a tangible beginning, a real start. None of the twelve pupils could pay anything, her own resources were very slender and a winter of really hard work lay ahead. But with so many willing helpers, she faced the future with youthful confidence. She had a real school, at last!

She learned a good deal about boys that first winter. She learned, in the first place, that just because you transplanted a boy from a mountain cabin to a clapboard school, he didn't change overnight. As she put it humorously to herself after the first week, he didn't want to be improved too rapidly. Whereas she had supposed that any boy who came would be more than glad to do cooking or washing or scrubbing or dig stumps or make roads or milk the cows—she had absolutely no help of any kind, you must remember!—and would study in between, she found that was by no means the case. She found it out the second Monday morning, indeed, when the need for washday had become apparent.

Brewster Hall

She had some barrels sawed in two for washtubs, and some donated, old-fashioned scrubbing boards. Before these she lined up the boys.

"Now, boys," she said cheerfully, "we're ready. We've got to get these things all clean and white. Take your places."

But a dead silence was the only reply she got.

Then one of the older boys said: "Waal, I ain't never seen no boys or men washin' clothes whar I come from. Wimmen an' gals does the washin', and they ain't ever washed reg'lar."

It was one of the prejudices of the mountains Miss Berry realized instantly. Most things were others' work in these hills! But it was also the first crisis for the Berry School. The very foundation of her school, financially and educationally, would have to be the doing of all the work by the pupils. There could be no exceptions, no work that was considered beneath any one in the school. She might as well fight it out now—or give up!

"All right, boys," she said calmly. "It isn't a question of who you are, or what you do in this school; it's just a question of strength. If you can't do this washing, I will."

And she started in then while the crowd watched her uncertainly. But not for long. She had not finished the first pile, indeed, before one of the boys could stand it no longer. If the "Sunday Lady" could wash clothes, why, he could!

"Miss Berry," he said, "I ain't never seen men doin' washin'—but I'm going to wash them clothes."

In an hour the rest had all followed suit, and the first crisis was over.

She had won the victory.

As soon as she had the school organized on a regular schedule, then with squads for the cooking, baking, and cleaning—all under her direction—she began to drive through the neighboring country, sometimes coming back to the school at night, oftentimes sleeping in some one-room cabin by the road with some family with which she was acquainted, so as to penetrate still farther into the back country. Every place she spread the news of the school and talked to the boys. And every place, too, she found some boy to whom the opportunity came as if from Heaven; some boy who could not wait to trudge the miles that lay between his home cabin and the school where he could work for an education. In less than a month, indeed, as the news really sunk into the slow consciousness of the mountains, from all directions boys clad in rags, or barefooted and in overalls began to drop in at the frame buildings in the woods, begging to be given a chance. And Miss Berry began to realize what a task she had undertaken!

Why, there were more boys waiting in these mountains for a chance than Brewster Hall could ever accommodate, or she herself ever provide for, or Elizabeth Brewster could ever teach. There were only so many cots, for instance, where they could sleep! And the school lacked practically everything else. In actual money, too, it could pay very little for many years. To give even a small number of these hundreds of boys a real chance, she would have to find some way of meeting a deficit every year, and some way of increasing her accommodations for pupils, as well!

It was around the fire in the cabin one night that the solution came. She was drawing, for the tenth time, perhaps, for the boys, that picture of hers that she always drew of what Berry could be some day. And in the silence around the blazing log, one of the boys spoke up:

"Well, they're always giving money to schools and colleges up in New York, Miss Berry. Why couldn't they give you some for here?"

It was the first time the idea had come to her. And yet, why not? Three days later, she set out for New York.

It was in the winter of 1901 when she arrived there. Beyond the names of three girls she had been acquainted with at school she did not know a soul in the snow-swept city. In her excitement, and inexperience, too, she had forgotten to bring any introductions of any kind; she had no photographs of her school or her boys nor any papers of any kind to show. But she put all thoughts of failure from her mind, gulped down her homesickness, sought out a cheap boarding house where she rented a tiny hall bedroom, and sat down to besiege New York.

Her first two assaults were failures. Both her friends advised her to give up all thought of trying to do any such impossible thing. New York was full of people asking for money. There were hundreds of worthy institutions in the city itself. Without influence, she would merely be wasting her time.

In the tiny hall bedroom she almost wept with disappointment. Wasn't there any way she could be heard, she asked her third and last friend one afternoon?

This friend knew a clergyman over in Brooklyn who was very liberal minded and friendly. He might let her speak for a few minutes after prayer meeting Wednesday night. So that was arranged. And in a blinding snowstorm that impeded all traffic she set out for the Brooklyn church that night. She had never in her life been out at night alone in a city, she had never been in Brooklyn, and she had never made any kind of speech in public. But she found the church after several hours' wandering and entered, completely worn out from the storm, only to find that the meeting was about to close.

But couldn't she speak, she begged, just for a few minutes? Couldn't she tell them what she wanted? Fifty dollars was all she was asking, fifty dollars to keep one boy in school so he could have his chance for a year; that was all it cost in the log cabin by the Possum Trot road. And before she realized it, she had made her speech, and a few women in the audience were in tears, and someone had given her fifty dollars and some names of people she might go and see. And she was out in the snowstorm again. She had actually succeeded in begging some money!

In the little hall bedroom, then, she wrote hopefully to the list of names she had received. If only each one would give fifty dollars!

But very few answered, and none gave money. And only one man, down on Wall Street, replied that he would give her an interview if she cared to tell him the whole story. By the financier's desk, a few days later, she stammered her story, while the great man stared at her curiously.

"What salary do you get?" he inquired.

She did not get any salary, she told him.

"But what do you get out of it?" he inquired.

"I"—she stammered. "Why, I get—I see my boys getting their chance—I see their lives opening out into happiness and knowledge and character—"

"Oh, I see," he returned thoughtfully.

She rose then. Had she overstayed her time?

"If ever you feel you can help just one boy to have a year"—she began.

But he motioned her to sit down, while he drew a check. "I'll give that—and as much more as I can," he said. And he bowed her out of the door, the folded check in her hand. He seemed most polite.

She did not dare open it until she was out on the street. And then the very buildings seemed to whirl around her, her eyes filled with tears, and she hurriedly boarded a street car to get away from the people she suddenly felt were looking at her. The check was for five hundred dollars!

She was on the wrong car, she realized five blocks later.

Six weeks later when she went back to the schoolhouse in the woods, she had laid the financial foundation for the school of her dreams. What was more, her trip had taught her that her dream could come true at last, if she was willing to beg for it, if she was willing to give up her life to the thing—just as Judge Wright had said she would have to.

I wish I could give you here in detail all the events of those next ten years—all the endless work and achievement, heart-breaking discouragements, and little success of them—while Miss Berry gathered one by one a little group of men and women to work with her in the school; while the woods and broom sedge gave way gradually to tilled fields and roads, and one by one log buildings sprang up, and the graduating classes grew year by year from one to five to twelve to twenty and thirty, and a real, "working" school came into being.

Gathering at first administration building

Just a catalogue of the disasters and discouragements would fill many pages—the burning of the first little whitewashed schoolhouse and the consequent necessity of holding school on porches, under the trees, in cellars; the ragged boy who came from thirty miles away, from the hills, and promptly fell sick of the measles and pneumonia, to be nursed week after week by Miss Berry, while the rest of the school promptly came down with the disease also, and the dormitory became a hospital without conveniences, without telephones or electric lights, without water, at times, when the well went dry. There were many hours during those first years, indeed, when it seemed as if the school could never survive.

And yet, it was not all gloom, of course; it was more an odd mixture of laughter and tears, like the night of the second graduation, when in the tent borrowed from the Baptist mission workers to keep off the rain, the canvas leaked, and one boy held an umbrella over the speaker of the occasion, while another protected the pianist, and the speaker forgot his surroundings and spoke eloquently of the boys going out from the massive walls of their alma mater—and then one after another the boys who were leaving arose and told simply what the school had done for them and what Miss Berry would always mean in their lives—and the people felt for their handkerchiefs! Or the summer she tried to raise peanuts, and the crop and seed all disappeared down the boys' throats. Or the lawsuit she had where the opposing lawyer called her a slave driver and tried to prove it by the hours of the school.

Through it all, indeed, went that curious thread of laughter and tears, while the boys were learning that farming did not mean just scraping the ground for a crop of something or other, while the two cows were becoming a small dairy where all modern sanitary and scientific methods were followed. And besides education, the boys were getting that shadowy thing, that priceless gift, called culture. Above all, they were learning the gospel of work. They were building the roads, washing the dishes, cooking the meals, studying the Bible, erecting the buildings, keeping the books. No place for a shirker, that school in the woods.

Early farm scene

Even for the teachers a regime of such work was one that called for devoted, self-sacrificing people. A rising bell at five o'clock, breakfast at six, school at seven, and then until sunset scrubbing and washing and ironing, teaching and milking and farming, making every minute count. A group of determined crusaders, those teachers and leaders. The school should not fail if they could help it.

And yet I doubt if [to] any of them did those years mean as hard work as they did to Miss Berry herself. Month after month, and year after year, then, she was devoting herself to the task of pushing on the school in the woods—learning, studying, building, working, planning, writing, speaking; now in Boston talking before some cultured women's club, now in a mountain cabin reassuring some fading old woman about her son's place in the school; traveling from city to city; getting a building in Philadelphia, a dormitory in New York—always and forever alone, her only faithful companion the little pad of daily expenses of the school she kept so that by her bedside she would know each dawn how much she must raise that day—her days spent interviewing Fifth Avenue, with her heart back in woods and wildflowers and mountains of Georgia—and her boys! A figure of pathos and infinite courage and endless, everlasting character. A figure of self-sacrifice rarely met with once in a lifetime!

Even to the White House her inspired energy carried her finally, armed with her photographic history of the school. Roosevelt was President then, and he took in the picture story with that extraordinary eagerness of his, pinning himself to the book as if it were the only thing of value in Washington, asking about this boy and that man. At the end, he brought down his fist with a crash on the table.

"This is the real thing," he said. "I can't give you money for your school, Miss Berry, but I can introduce you to some people who can."

A few days later, she found herself at dinner in the White House at the President's right, with a group of men as dinner companions who were famous for their support of worthwhile educational undertakings.

When dinner was partially over, Roosevelt rapped for silence. "I want Miss Berry to tell you about her school," he said.

And she did. When she got through she had secured some of her most steadfast supporters—men who have never left her.

But what about the girls? The question hit Miss Berry with abrupt force one night around her log fire in the old cabin, while she stared into the flames. Why, she had done nothing for the girls thus far, she realized abruptly. And year after year it had been so pathetically plain at commencement time and when the families came visiting from the mountains, that the boys were forging ahead of their sisters, of the girls whom they would naturally choose as wives. She must do something for the girls now, before she was a day, an hour older!

The boys could be enlisted to dig the foundations, and construct the very houses and dormitories themselves! The industrial shop turned out real carpenters now, who could make everything there was about a building or a house or a barn, except the plumbing.

Why could not it be started that way, with just a few thousand dollars? A month later, she had secured the trustees' consent, and out on the hills a mile from the boys' school, she watched the enthusiastic boys building the first of the new buildings of her girls' school. Sunshine Shanty, they were calling it! Her school was a real thing at last.

That was twelve years ago.

Sunshine Shanty

When you go out the new, hard-surfaced road from Rome today, just twenty years from the day Miss Berry began, and turn in at the tree-shadowed avenue that leads to the school, you are conscious at first only of the curious mixture of buildings and landscape, of Georgia woods and beautifully kept fields. Through the trees of the campus you can glimpse first a white-pillared building, and then a log house; in the distance a fine brick hall, and on your right a beautiful brick Colonial church such as Washington worshipped in at Alexandria, and beyond it all a sweep of fine farms and huge barns, and in the distance blue hills rising toward the wooded horizon into the mountains. That is your first impression.

The next moment, you are struck by the conviction that here for the first and perhaps the only time in your life, you are gazing on what you have always heard described as pure, unadulterated, plain, common sense—common sense in the form of a school.

You can feel it talking to the teachers, sitting at breakfast with them at six-thirty in the big, high-ceilinged mess hall, while the boys rush in from their rooms or the barns, and the clatter of dishes begins as soon as the morning prayer is said—you can feel it there, or you can feel it at night in Miss Berry's cabin, sitting around the fire with sixteen or eighteen of the boys, talking over the day's achievements.

The same thing is true of the girls' school, with a very decided difference. Practical home-making is the aim of the girls' school, of course, and yet through all the buildings, the log cottages and recitation rooms, the shrubbery-lined walks and beautiful flower gardens, through them all there lies the inescapable impression that here, somehow, although each single thing is practical, visible by itself, the net result nevertheless is that shadowy thing called culture.

The flower garden and its greenhouse, with its lesson of the value of beauty around your house and color on your table; the immaculate kitchens with the appetizing butter rolls cooking on the ranges and the girls singing while they work; the little tables for tea around the fireplace in Sunshine house, and around you all the products the girls make on the old-fashioned looms—porch rugs, huckaback towels, table runners of curious and beautiful design, neckties, sport skirts, counterpanes of ancient design and weave—the effect is one of indescribable beauty of vision.

Three hundred boys in the High School, two hundred and fifty girls, and a Foundation School of one hundred and fifty boys preparing to enter the main school—this is Miss Berry's family, today. She is giving them a chance for an education that could hardly be bettered in any way, one that is unique not only for being a working school, but for its magnificent inspiration.

An ever-widening circle of influence for America's finest ideals her efforts have set in motion. There is plenty of glory, reputation and success in that circle. Five hundred stars in a service flag; agricultural colleges modeled after Berry and run by old Berry School men; lawyers, senators, farmers among its list of graduates; beautiful, well-kept homes where happiness dwells and character guides; words of praise from statesmen, presidents, educators, editors, from Roosevelt to McAdoo, both of whom visited the place and were moved beyond adequate words!

"I would rather have built the Berry Schools than to have dug the Hudson Tunnel," said McAdoo simply, as he stood in the Chapel.

"I believe Miss Berry and those associated with her have been doing one of the greatest practical works for American citizenship that has been done within this decade," said Theodore Roosevelt, as he faced a crowd of enthusiastic boys.

Yes, plenty of glory for the school that was once a log house in the woods.

It was during his administration as President of the United States that Mr. Roosevelt summoned Miss Berry to the White House as his guest to speak to a group of his friends whom he had assembled to hear her tell the story of her work in the mountains of Georgia.

It was still the spirit of Theodore Roosevelt that called Martha Berry again to the White House May the fifteenth, 1925, to receive the medal for distinguished service. In designating Miss Berry as one of the three recipients of the medal this year, the Roosevelt Memorial Association was carrying out a wish of his, well known to his family and friends, to encourage a work in which he very thoroughly believed.

In presenting Miss Berry to President Coolidge, Mr. Garfield, president of the Association said: "For the medal for Distinguished Service in behalf of women and children, I have the honor to present the name of one, who, seeing a great need, turned from the pleasant places in which her lines were cast, to bring light and opportunity to children, who, but for her, would have walked all their lives in the darkness of ignorance."

Turning to Miss Berry Mr. Coolidge said, "Greatly as Theodore Roosevelt would have been gratified if he could see a distinction bearing his name bestowed on these old friends," indicating Governor Pinchot and George Bird Grinnell, "he would yet be most stirred to see this Roosevelt medal bestowed upon you. He believed in you and your work; and it was characteristic of him, that, believing in you, he should have upheld your hands and done what he could to win you friends.

In building out of nothing a great educational institution for the children of the mountains, you have contributed to your time one of its most creative achievements. Because of you thousands have been released from the bonds of ignorance, and countless other thousands in the generations to come will walk not in darkness but in light. You have built your school by faith—faith in your vision, faith in God, who alone can make visions substantial."

How Miss Berry received the medal, how she bowed and smiled and stepped back and addressed the President with that grace of hers that "can walk with kings nor lose the common touch," was told to the student body at Berry by one of her old pupils whom Miss Berry took with her to the White House. "Mr. President," she said in her clear, pleasant voice, "I accept this medal very humbly for myself, but very proudly for the girls and boys whom I represent. With apologies to Governor Pinchot, the Berry Schools are in the work of conservation—the conservation of one of our country's greatest natural resources—the children of the mountain forests. My ambition has been to free them and to give them to America strong of heart and mind and soul. May they take up their life-work fired with the zeal of conservative Americanism and intense loyalty to the Constitution and to the flag."

And yet to Miss Berry the amount she could still do seems so much greater than anything she has been able to do so far, that she is still trying hard to catch up with that dream! Yes, there are a thousand more boys and girls, writing in, writing in—and she cannot take them because she has not the money.

At the present writing, indeed, the value of the property, measured in sordid [sic] dollars, is well toward a million! And the amount of money she has to raise is still seventy-five thousand dollars a year, just to keep what she has going. For every new boy she has to raise more.

"One hundred and fifty dollars to send a child to school for a year! Who will give that?" Few people who have ever heard Martha Berry utter that cry will ever forget it.

No one who meets her ever asks the question, "What would happen if you gave up the work?" They only ask, "But what will happen to the work when you die?"

I wonder how many of us achieve that for an epitaph?

Martha Berry and the Pilgrims' silver roll

CHARTER AND BYLAWS

Berry was incorporated on April 6, 1903, as the "Boy's Industrial School." The petition for that first charter and indication of its approval follow:

PETITION FOR CHARTER
OF
BOY'S INDUSTRIAL SCHOOL

GEORGIA, FLOYD COUNTY:

TO THE SUPERIOR COURT OF SAID COUNTY:

The petition of Martha Berry, John H. Reynolds, Moses R. Wright, Paul J. Cooper and Thomas Berry, all of said County and John J. Eagan of Fulton County, Georgia and their associates shows:

First: Your petitioner, Martha Berry, has had erected certain school and other buildings upon her lands, north of Rome in said County, and is now carrying on, conducting and operating therein and thereon a boy's industrial School. These lands comprise about eighty-three acres, it being her intention to donate the same to the Corporation hereinafter named, with certain reservation to be expressed in said deed.

Second: Petitioners desire to be incorporated under the name, "BOY'S INDUSTRIAL SCHOOL", for the term of twenty years with the right of renewal and as such to have and use a common seal, to sue and to be sued, to buy and to sell and to otherwise dispose of real estate and rights therein, to receive gifts, donations and bequests of realty and personalty, to enforce good order for the management of said School, to erect buildings, to employ teachers, to grant scholarships and to carry on a School to meet the needs of poor boys from the rural districts.

Third: The place of business of said Corporation shall be Floyd County, Georgia.

Fourth: Said School shall forever remain undenominational, except that the Bible shall be taught; the teachers shall be members of some protestant Church, and the training of scholars shall be with the view to aid in their moral, industrial, and educational uplifting.

Fifth: Said incorporators shall, during the existence of said Corporation, be a perpetual Board of Trustees for the management of the affairs of the same; and upon the death or resignation of any of their members, shall have the right to fill vacancies by election; but in filling vacancies the wishes of petitioner, Martha Berry, shall be consulted as far as practicable; it being the wishes, desire and intention of petitioners to give to said Martha Berry the active management of said school, with the right in her to name her successor as manager by last will and testament.

Sixth: Said Board of Trustees shall have the right to enact by-laws for the government of said School, its Teachers, the Scholars in attendance and the members of said Board not in conflict with the settled policy of the State or the law of the land.

WHEREFORE, petitioners pray for themselves and their legal successors to be made a body corporate and politic with all the rights, privileges and immunities fixed by law.

MOSES WRIGHT
Atty. for Petitioners
Filed in Office January 10, 1903------D. W. SIMMONS, Clerk

CHARTER OF BOY'S INDUSTRIAL SCHOOL

GEORGIA, FLOYD COUNTY:

IN THE SUPERIOR COURT OF SAID COUNTY: JANUARY TERM, 1903

Martha Berry, John H. Reynolds, Moses R. Wright, Paul J. Cooper and Thomas Berry, all of said County and John J. Eagan of Fulton County, all of said State, having filed in the office of the Clerk of the Superior Court of said County their petition seeking the formation of a Corporation to be known as the "Boy's Industrial School", for the purpose of carrying on, conducting and operating a boy's industrial School, and having complied with all the requirements of the law for such cases made and provided, and the Court being satisfied that said application is legitimately within the purview and intention of the code, the same is hereby granted, and the above named persons, their associates and successors are hereby incorporated under the same name and style of the "BOY'S INDUSTRIAL SCHOOL" for and during the period of twenty years, with the privileges of renewal at the expiration of that time, and said Corporation is hereby clothed with all the rights, powers and privileges asked for in the petition and all the rights, privileges, and immunities, and made subject to all the restrictions and liabilities fixed by law.

This, the Sixth day of April, 1903.

W. M. HENRY, Judge of
SUPERIOR COURT, Floyd County, Georgia

Filed in Office, April 17th, 1903------Recorded, April 30, 1903

D. W. SIMMONS
Clerk

The name of the institution was changed to "The Berry School" by amendment to the charter on January 31, 1908. The charter was further amended on August 21, 1909, and on May 20, 1913. The name of the institution was revised to "The Berry Schools" by amendment of the charter on June 11, 1917. The initial charter of incorporation was for 20 years. The charter was amended again and renewed for another 20 years on April 6, 1923, the day the initial charter was to expire.

The next amendment of the charter was on April 14, 1932, when it was renewed for 100 years; and the institution was authorized to operate a college and grant degrees. A resolution was unanimously adopted by the Board of Trustees of The Berry Schools, on October 30, 1931, to petition to have its charter amended to include the following:

(1) This company shall have the power, in addition to its other powers, to conduct, maintain, and carry on a College in Floyd County, Georgia; the College to have such curriculum or curricula as may be from time to time provided or authorized by your petitioner's Board of Trustees or its authority.

Said College shall have the right to issue diplomas and to grant degrees in the several courses taught or to be taught by it upon completion of the studies prescribed from time to time by your petitioner in the respective courses; but no degree shall be granted until after the completion of a course of study leading to such degree at least equal to that prescribed by the State of Georgia or its authority, if the State of Georgia or its authority shall have then prescribed such course of study; nor until the applicant for said degree shall have shown such proficiency in the studies so prescribed as is at least equal to that required by the State of Georgia or its authority.

Your petitioner desires to have the right to prescribe such courses of study and the degree of proficiency therein to be required of the applicant for degrees, as its Board of Trustees or the authority of the Board of Trustees shall deem proper; provided, that at no time shall it prescribe a course of study and the proficiency therein on a basis less than that prescribed or required by the State of Georgia or its authority.

Your petitioner desires the right from time to time to grant such honorary degrees as it may deem wise; provided, however, that no such degree shall be granted in circumstances of qualification on the part of the recipient of said degree less exacting than is prescribed or required by the State of Georgia or its authority, if such qualifications shall then be so prescribed.

The charter was subsequently amended on May 14, 1962, and on March 29, 1982. On the latter date the corporate name was changed to "Berry College, Inc." A copy of part of that document appears on the following page.

The charter was further amended on February 20, 1988, and March 26, 2001. The most recent amendment increased the number of trustees from 19 to 23.

The current Charter of Berry College, Inc., and the Bylaws of the Board of Trustees follow the page from the 1982 charter.

I, David B. Poythress, Secretary of State of the State of Georgia, do hereby certify that

The articles of incorporation of "THE BERRY SCHOOLS" have been duly amended under the laws of the State of Georgia changing its name to "BERRY COLLEGE, INC." on the 29th day of March, 1982, by the filing of articles of amendment in the office of the Secretary of State and the fees therefor paid, as provided by law, and that attached hereto is a true copy of said articles of amendment.

IN TESTIMONY WHEREOF, I have hereunto set my hand and affixed the seal of my office, at the Capitol, in the City of Atlanta, this 29th day of March in the year of our Lord One Thousand Nine Hundred and Eighty Two and of the Independence of the United States of America the Two Hundred and Six.

SECRETARY OF STATE, EX-OFFICIO CORPORATION COMMISSIONER OF THE STATE OF GEORGIA

CHARTER OF BERRY COLLEGE, INC.

Article I: NAME, LOCATION AND DURATION

Section 1. The name of the corporation shall be "Berry College, Inc."

Section 2. The principal office of the corporation shall be located in Floyd County, with the privilege of establishing and maintaining branch offices, colleges, centers, and subordinate agencies elsewhere.

Section 3. The time for which the corporation shall have existence shall extend to April 14, 2032, when its present charter expires, with the privilege of extending such time and renewing said charter as provided by law.

Article II: PURPOSE AND OBJECTIVES

Section 1. The purpose of the corporation is to promote education directly and indirectly through maintaining and conducting a college and other educational agency or agencies of less than college grade.

Section 2. The more specific objectives of the corporation are to offer educational programs that meet the needs of young men and women who desire to increase their effectiveness as persons, citizens, and practitioners of the arts, sciences, and professions, and to afford the opportunity to worthy and qualified young people to obtain an education through necessary work.

Section 3. The college and other educational agency or agencies maintained by the corporation shall forever be Christian in spirit and democratic in procedure.

Section 4. The corporation is organized and shall be operated exclusively for charitable, educational and scientific purposes. The corporation is not organized and shall not be operated for the purpose of trade or pecuniary gain or profit, but for promoting the general design of the institution and looking after the general interest of such establishment. The corporation shall have no capital stock or shares of stock and no part of its net earnings shall inure to the benefit of any of the incorporators or of any individual. No part of the activities of the corporation shall consist of carrying on propaganda or otherwise attempting to influence legislation.

Article III: GENERAL POWERS

Section 1. The corporation shall have the power to have succession by its corporate name for the period limited in its charter and throughout the period of any renewal or renewals thereof; to sue and be sued in any court of law or equity; to make contracts and adopt and use a corporate seal and to alter the same; to hold, to purchase, to acquire by gift, bequest or exchange, and to dispose of and convey real and personal property of every kind, wherever located, consistent with the purposes of its existence, and to deal with, mortgage, pledge, encumber, lease, invest and reinvest funds in any such real and personal property with its franchise; to receive, hold, invest, reinvest, and use endowment and trust funds, and the income therefrom; to borrow money and contract debts when necessary or proper for the transaction of its business or for the exercise of its corporate rights, privileges or franchises or for any other lawful purpose of its incorporation; to issue promissory notes and other obligations of indebtedness, whether secured by mortgage, pledge or otherwise, or unsecured; to borrow money for payment of property purchased or acquired or for other lawful objects; to purchase, hold, sell, assign, transfer, mortgage, pledge or otherwise dispose of the shares of the capital stock of or any bonds, securities or evidences of indebtedness created by any other corporation or by the United States, any state of the United States or political subdivision thereof, or any government; to operate a college and other educational agency or agencies of less than college grade; to confer degrees, including honorary degrees, and issue diplomas, subject to the provisions of law; to operate timberland, agricultural business, industrial and other lawful undertakings for the full utilization of its present properties and that are hereafter acquired for the benefit and furtherance of the objectives of the corporation; to appoint such officers and agents as the affairs of the corporation shall require and to allow them suitable compensation; to make bylaws not inconsistent with the Constitution or laws of the United States or of the State of Georgia or the corporation's charter for the exercise of its corporate powers, the management, regulation and government of its affairs and property, and the calling and holding of meetings of its trustees; to wind up and dissolve itself or be wound up and dissolved as provided by law; to amend, renew or revive its charter as provided by law; to enforce good order; to do all and everything necessary and proper for the accomplishment of the objects enumerated in the charter or any amendments thereof or necessary or incidental to the protection and benefit of the corporation and in general to carry on any lawful activity necessary or incidental to the attainment of the objects of the corporation; and to have such other and further powers as are now granted or may hereafter be conferred upon similar corporations.

Article IV: TRUSTEES

Section 1. The business and all affairs of the corporation shall be governed and managed by a Board of Trustees, which shall be the ultimate and exclusive source of authority of the corporation under the law, charter and bylaws.

Section 2. The Board of Trustees shall consist of twenty-three (23) persons, of whom twenty-one (21) shall be elected by a majority of the board in such manner and for such terms as may be provided by the bylaws, one (1) of whom shall, by virtue of and for the term of his office as such, be the president of the Berry Alumni Association or its successor organization, and one (1) of whom shall, by virtue of and for the term of his office as such, be the chairman of the Berry College Board of Visitors. The twenty-one (21) elected members of the board shall have co-opted succession. In the event of any vacancy or vacancies upon the board, the remaining trustees shall be empowered to act for the corporation until the vacancy or vacancies are filled.

Section 3. The Board of Trustees shall be empowered to enact, by favorable vote of two-thirds of the board, bylaws for the government, administration and operation of the corporation.

Section 4. Twelve (12) members shall constitute a quorum of the Board of Trustees for the transaction of its business.

Article V. LIMITATION OF LIABILITY OF TRUSTEES

A Trustee of the Corporation shall not be personally liable to the Corporation for monetary damages for breach of duty of care or other duty as a Trustee, except for liability (i) for any appropriation, in violation of his duties, of any business opportunity of the Corporation, (ii) for acts or omissions not in good faith or which involve intentional misconduct or a knowing violation of law, or (iii) for any transaction from which the Trustee derived an improper personal benefit. If the Georgia Nonprofit Corporation Code is amended after approval of this Article to authorize corporate action further eliminating or limiting the personal liability of Trustees or Directors, then the liability of a Trustee of the Corporation shall be eliminated or limited to the fullest extent permitted by the Georgia Nonprofit Corporation Code, as so amended. Any repeal or modification of this Article shall be prospective only and shall not adversely affect any limitation on the personal liability of a Trustee of the Corporation existing at the time of such repeal or modification.

BYLAWS OF THE BOARD OF TRUSTEES

PREAMBLE

Berry College, Inc., was conceived and nurtured on faith in God, a belief in the dignity of worthwhile work, well done, and a conviction of the value of learning. In adopting these bylaws, the Board of Trustees reaffirms the above basic concepts as guides in developing policies for the corporation and its college and agencies.

Article I: THE BOARD OF TRUSTEES

Section 1. The charter fixes the number of voting members of the Board of Trustees at twenty-three (23). The charter also specifies that ex officio the president of the Berry Alumni Association and the chairman of the Berry College Board of Visitors shall be two (2) of the twenty-three (23) voting members of the board.

Section 2. a. All trustees (other than the trustees ex officio) who attain the age of seventy (70) years on or before the first day of January preceding the first meeting of the Board of Trustees held during each calendar year shall be retired as trustees at such meeting, notwithstanding the terms for which elected a trustee.

b. Upon nomination of the chairman of the Board of Trustees, any trustee who retired under Section 2a of this Article I or who resigns from the board prior to reaching the age of 70 years may be elected a trustee emeritus for life by the affirmative vote of a majority of the trustees then in office. Trustees emeriti shall be invited to and shall be entitled to attend all meetings of the Board of Trustees and may participate in the discussions thereat, but shall not have the power to vote, and shall not be counted for the purpose of ascertaining the presence of a quorum. Such trustees emeriti shall be available for consultation with and advice to the Board of Trustees, but shall not be members of the Board of Trustees for any purpose.

Section 3. The Board of Trustees, in recognition of meritorious service or benefaction, may elect honorary trustees. The number of honorary trustees shall not exceed twenty-five (25) at any one time, and they need not be elected for stated terms.

Section 4. Twenty-one (21) members of the board shall be elected by the board for three (3) year terms. There shall be three (3) groups of seven (7) trustees each, so arranged that the terms of seven (7) trustees begin on July first each year. A vacancy shall be filled only for the remainder of the term of the trustee replaced.

The election or re-election of trustees for full term shall be at the first regular meeting after January first each year. The election of trustees to fill vacancies for unexpired terms may be held at any meeting.

An affirmative vote of a majority of the trustees then in office shall be required for any election.

Section 5. Before any election of trustees, either at a regular or special meeting, the chairman shall appoint a nominating committee of five (5) members which, through the secretary of the corporation, shall send to the members of the board, thirty (30) days in advance of the meeting for election, a list of nominees selected by said committee and a resume of their qualifications. Any trustee desiring to nominate other persons shall do so by sending to the secretary for distribution to the members of the board, fifteen (15) days in advance of the meeting for election, a list of nominees and a resume of their qualifications.

Section 6. Members of the board shall not receive compensation for their services as trustees, but may be reimbursed for expenses of attending board or committee meetings or conducting official business for the corporation.

Section 7. No employee of the corporation shall be eligible for election to such board.

Section 8. By majority vote of the board, a trustee may be removed from membership on the board for failure to perform duties as prescribed in the bylaws. A trustee may not be so removed, however, unless (a) a notice of the meeting states that the purpose, or one of the purposes, of the meeting is removal of a trustee, and (b) the Executive Committee shall have first recommended to the board that the trustee be removed from office.

Article II. MEETINGS OF BOARD OF TRUSTEES

Section 1. Three (3) meetings of the board shall be held in each calendar year at times and places designated by the chairman, within or without the State of Georgia, provided, however, at least two (2) of the meetings each calendar year will be held at Mount Berry, Georgia. Special meetings of the board shall be held on call of the chairman, or on call of the secretary on written request of at least seven (7) members, at such times and places within or without the State of Georgia as stated in the call.

Section 2. At least ten (10) days before the date of any regular or special board meeting the secretary shall notify the members in writing, stating the time and place of the meeting and enclosing tentative agenda and supporting documents to indicate the nature of the business to be transacted, provided, however, that action of the board shall not be limited to matters on the agenda.

Section 3. The order of business shown by agenda may vary from time to time but will usually include roll call; correction and adoption of minutes of previous meetings; consideration and action or reports of standing and special board committees; reports of the president and other officers of the college and agencies; further consideration of unfinished business, and consideration of new business.

Section 4. The board may adopt such procedural rules as it desires for conducting its business, but in the absence of stated rules, the parliamentary procedure described in Roberts Rules of Order shall be followed. As required by the charter, no business may be transacted at a board meeting without twelve (12) members of the board being present and voting. Board members may not vote by proxy on committees or at board meetings.

Article III: OFFICERS OF THE BOARD AND THEIR DUTIES

Section 1. The trustees shall elect from among members of the board a chairman and a vice chairman of the corporation. The trustees shall also elect a president, a secretary and a treasurer of the corporation, none of whom need be members of the board.

Section 2. The board may also elect from time to time such other officers of the corporation as it may deem appropriate and assign their duties. In addition to the above provisions for the election of other officers of the corporation, the president shall have the power to appoint certain officers. Such appointments shall be limited to the office of acting secretary and acting treasurer. No such appointments shall be made without the concurrence of either the chairman of the Board of Trustees or the chairman of the executive committee. Such appointment shall only be made when there occurs an absence or incapacity for any reason to serve or act by the secretary or the treasurer, as the case may be, and there exists a need for the execution of some corporate document by or on a certain date and the appropriate signature of some officer cannot be secured. The president shall prescribe the term of any such appointment.

Section 3. The election of officers of the corporation shall be held at the first regular meeting of the board after July first of each year, and the term of each such officer shall continue until the successor is elected and qualifies. Vacancies in any such office shall be filled for the remainder of the unexpired term by election at any meeting of the board.

Section 4. The chairman of the Board of Trustees shall preside at meetings of the board.

Section 5. The vice chairman, in the absence or disability of the chairman of the board, shall perform all of his or her duties. In the absence of the chairman and vice chairman from a board meeting, the members shall elect one of their members as chairman *pro tempore.*

Section 6. The president is the chief administrative officer of the corporation. As directed by the board, the president shall act for it in all matters requiring attention of the chief administrative officer and shall perform the duties required under Article VI. Unless directed by the board, the president and the secretary shall jointly sign all deeds, mortgages, deeds or bills of sale to secure debt, and promissory notes for, in behalf of and in the name of the corporation as authorized by the board.

Section 7. The secretary of the corporation shall attend meetings of the board and, when possible, meetings of its standing and special committees, and, as secretary, shall make and preserve true minutes of the proceedings. Committee chairmen may designate an acting secretary, if the secretary of the corporation cannot be present, who will record the minutes and provide these to the secretary of the corporation. Promptly after each meeting, the secretary of the corporation shall transmit to each trustee a copy of the minutes of such meeting. The secretary shall be the custodian of the official archives of the board and of its committees and shall have custody of the corporate seal with authority to affix it to all documents where its use is required by law or by direction of the board.

The secretary is empowered to sign, in behalf of and in the name of the corporation, all documents except for those which other persons are required by law or board action to sign and except for those documents mentioned in Section 6 of this article and which are to be signed jointly by the president and the secretary.

The secretary shall transmit promptly all notices required by law, bylaws, resolutions, and other board and committee action. The secretary shall give written notice of meetings, and shall perform for the corporation such other duties as may be assigned.

Section 8. The treasurer shall serve as fiscal officer to the executive, budget and finance, and investment committees of the board. The treasurer shall arrange for safe custody of all corporate funds and securities. The treasurer shall make such studies for and reports to the executive, budget and finance, and investment committees as they may require, and report annually to the board on the financial condition of the corporation, showing all his or her transactions as treasurer.

The treasurer shall make and deliver to the secretary, who is custodian of all board archives, a surety bond in an amount determined by the executive committee or by the board. This bond shall insure his faithful performance of duties as treasurer. More specifically, the bond shall indemnify the corporation for the loss of any funds, securities, books, papers, vouchers, or any other property of the corporation in his possession or under the treasurer's control.

Article IV: COMMITTEES OF THE BOARD

Section 1. Standing Committees.

a. The standing committees of the board shall be an executive committee, an academic affairs committee, an advancement committee, a budget and finance committee, an investment commitee, and an Oak Hill committee. These committees and their chairmen shall be appointed by the chairman of the board. In order to assure proper liaison, the chairmen of the advancement, budget and finance, and investment committees shall be among trustees appointed to the executive committee.

b. Each standing committee shall be composed of at least three (3) members, except for the executive committee, which shall be composed of seven (7) members. These committees may choose their own places and times of meeting. A majority of the committee members shall constitute a quorum, and a concurring vote of the majority of those present shall be required for committee action. The secretary of the corporation, or an acting secretary designated by the committee chairman, shall serve as secretary to these committees, and the minutes and other records of their actions shall become a part of the records of the corporation.

Section 2. Executive Committee.

a. When the board is not in session, the executive committee shall have all of its powers, except the following: to dissolve the corporation and surrender its charter, to amend the charter of the corporation, to amend the bylaws, to elect or dismiss officers of the corporation or trustees, to dispose of or encumber the principal of the endowment fund, and to dispose of or encumber real property of the corporation unless such powers have been specifically delegated by the board to its executive committee.

b. The executive committee, in consultation with the president of the corporation and in liaison with any other appropriate committee of the board, shall study the program of the college and agencies and recommend to the board programs that should be initiated, discontinued, modified or expanded.

c. Independent of the president and chief business officer of the college and agencies, the executive committee shall designate a licensed certified public accountant to make an annual audit of the financial affairs of the corporation. The contract for this audit shall cover the full scope of the business operations of the corporation. It shall be presented in person to the executive committee, and the formal audit report shall be presented and interpreted to the board by the chairman of the executive committee.

Section 3. Academic Affairs Committee. The academic affairs committee shall keep itself informed on key academic matters to fulfill the committee's responsibility to the board for long-range planning of the academic area and its relationship to the other two areas (i.e., work opportunity and religion-in-life) of Berry's threefold program.

Section 4. Advancement Committee.

a. The advancement committee shall be responsible to the board for formulating and giving effect to immediate and long-range plans for raising funds to support, improve and expand the college and agencies. The committee shall work with the president of the corporation in formulating and carrying out fund-raising programs.

b. The advancement committee shall negotiate and recommend to the board settlement of bequests, legacies, deferred gifts and other major contributions.

c. The advancement committee, with the president, shall have major responsibility for recommending to the board public relations policies calculated to sharpen and focus the image of the college and agencies as noted for educational excellence, Christian commitment and spirit of service.

Section 5. Budget and Finance Committee. The budget and finance committee shall have general oversight of, and through the president and treasurer, shall direct the preparation and administration of the operating budgets of the college, its departments and agencies. It shall be responsible to the executive committee for a thorough review of the annual budget proposed for its approval by the president and treasurer. The budget and finance committee, in consultation with the treasurer, shall periodically review the institution's systems for budgeting, accounting, financial reporting and internal auditing and shall initiate and/or authorize appropriate changes as it deems necessary.

Section 6. Investment Committee. The investment committee shall have discretionary power to invest and reinvest such monies and other property as may from time to time be committed to it for this purpose, and shall exercise such power either in meetings by resolution or in writing signed by a majority of the members of the committee. Such investments may be made in stocks, bonds, securities, mortgages, security deeds, notes, real estate, real estate improvements and any other property such committee may deem best. The Board of Trustees, by resolution, may authorize two (2) or more members of such committee to execute jointly, on behalf of and in the name of the corporation, such transfers, stock options and other instruments as may be necessary to facilitate the management and handling of such investments.

Section 7. Oak Hill Committee. The Oak Hill committee, with the president of the corporation, shall be responsible to the board for long-range planning and broad policy formulation for the development, promotion, operation and maintenance of Oak Hill to include the Martha Berry Museum and Art Gallery, the Berry home, gardens and grounds and all improvements thereon; operation and use of the guest cottages and House o' Dreams; operation of the handicrafts and gift shop; arrangements and hosting/guiding visiting groups and tours and preservation, use and enhancement of historical sites.

Section 8. Ad Hoc Committees. From time to time as the needs of the corporation require, the chairman of the board may appoint ad hoc committees of five (5) or fewer members. The secretary of the corporation, or a person designated by each ad hoc committee chairman, shall serve as secretary to these committees. Ad hoc committees shall be required to submit a report and be discharged at a specified date unless the time is extended. Minutes and other records of the ad hoc committee meetings shall become a part of the record of the corporation.

Section 9. Consultants. When authorized by the board, both standing and ad hoc committees may employ consultants, and when requested, the board's attorney shall provide needed legal counsel.

Article V. THE AGENCIES OF THE CORPORATION

Section 1. Berry College, a coeducational college, and other educational agency or agencies of less than college grade shall be the academic agencies of the corporation.

Section 2. Agricultural, forest and other enterprises of the college shall be considered as parts of these agencies.

Article VI: ADMINISTERING THE COLLEGE AND AGENCIES OF THE CORPORATION

Section 1. The Board of Trustees shall be responsible for the policies governing the conduct and administration of the college and its agencies. The president shall be responsible for carrying out and administering these policies. The president shall develop for approval of the board a set of statutes for the internal organization of the college and agencies, which shall include a position description for administrative officers, shall define their duties and shall show their administrative working relations to each other.

Section 2. In the president's absence or disability, the chairman may designate a suitable person to serve as acting president with all the duties, privileges and authorities of the president while so acting.

Section 3. All administrative officers, faculty and staff, and students of the college and agencies are ultimately responsible to the president who shall be the official medium of communication between them and the board. The president, reporting to the board and its standing committees, shall have from the board all authority necessary to direct the program of the college and agencies, including the authority to employ all members of the staff and faculty. The president shall be empowered to delegate this authority.

Section 4. The authority, responsibility and duties of educational administrators and of the faculty shall be those commonly delegated to these officers in astutely managed, accredited colleges and agencies and shall be outlined in the statutes for internal organization developed by the president and approved by the board.

Article VII. INDEMNIFICATION

Section 1. Any person who was or is a party or who is threatened to be made a party to any threatened, pending, or completed action, suit, or proceeding, whether civil, criminal, administrative, or investigative (other than action by or in the right of the corporation), by reason of the fact that he or she is or was a trustee and/or officer of Berry College, Inc., or is or was serving at the request of the corporation as a trustee, director, officer, employee or agent of another corporation, partnership, joint venture, trust, or other enterprise, shall be indemnified by the corporation against expenses (including reasonable attorneys' fees), judgments, fines, and amounts paid in settlement actually and reasonably incurred by him or her in connection with such action, suit, or proceeding, if he or she acted in a manner he or she reasonably believed to be in or not opposed to the best interests of the corporation and, with respect to any criminal action or proceeding, had no reasonable cause to believe the conduct was unlawful, to the maximum extent permitted by, and in the manner provided by, the Georgia Nonprofit Corporation Code.

Section 2. The Board of Trustees in its discretion may authorize indemnification by the corporation of its employees and agents to the maximum extent permitted by, and in the manner provided by, the Georgia Nonprofit Corporation Code.

Article VIII. HONORARY DEGREES

Honorary degrees shall be conferred by the board only after consultation with the Berry College faculty. An affirmative vote of the majority of the trustees then in office shall be required.

Article IX. CORPORATE SEAL

The seal of this corporation shall be two concentric circles with the words "Berry College, Inc." between the lines of the circles at the top, and the words "Martha Berry Founder 1902" between such lines at the bottom, and the shield which is the symbol of the institution in the center.

Article X. ADOPTION AND AMENDMENT OF BYLAWS

Section 1. These bylaws, adopted by the Board of Trustees in session this 17th day of February 2001, shall supersede all previous bylaws and repeal those in conflict herewith.

Section 2. These bylaws may be amended or repealed at any regular or special meeting of the board provided thirty (30) days' notice in writing of any proposed change has been given before the vote is taken thereon. A two-thirds (2/3) majority vote of all board members present and voting, or a majority of all board members, whichever is greater, shall be required to amend or repeal these bylaws.

A Letter from Our Principal

Dear friends:

The Anniversary Celebration is over and we are well under way toward another year of glorious history for Berry.

I hope you who came back received even a fraction of the encouragement and inspiration that your presence gave us. The Anniversary Chapel Service, the Barbecue, the great Pageant and the brilliant Alumni Banquet in the New Dining Hall were highlights that will always stand out in the lives of all Berry men and women.

<u>The launching of Berry College is our next great goal of achievement</u>.* You who have been through Berry know what a clean, wholesome, inspiring, uplifting place it is. You know how thorough and practical the training is and you know that men and women who are ambitious and willing to work can get an education here without money. Miss Berry is going to offer this opportunity for an education to all grades from the primary through college. What a heritage this will be to you, and to those who come after you and to thousands of other worthy men and women. We expect an enrollment of seventy-five college men and women next year. Perhaps some of you will want to return for more training or you may be able to send us some good material.

Please remember us in your prayers and drop us a line now and then so that we may know where you are and what you are doing. Our one great joy is hearing from our boys and girls.

Most sincerely your friend,
G. LELAND GREEN

<u>The Berry Alumni Quarterly</u>, June 1927, Volume 11, No. 1.
** Underlining by editors.*

Dr. Berry's Letter

Dear "Boys and Girls":

It is only about six weeks until Commencement, now, which will be May 3rd. I am hoping to see many of you here for the exercises. I want this Commencement to be a real "homecoming" at Berry.

We have had a wonderful year, in many ways. As you all know, Mr. and Mrs. Ford have given a new dormitory for our Girls' School. We greatly appreciate this gift, and we hope that we may soon have a dormitory on the Junior College campus, as we do so need another one for the college boys. We are also in great need of another dormitory at the Foundation School.

I am hoping to make our college course a four-year course,* and to enlist the aid of friends to develop it as I had originally planned it.

I have been hoping to visit many of you in the midst of your work and homes, but as that is impossible the next best thing would be to see you at Berry. After all, that would be the most natural place to see you. I trust that your training you received at Berry is proving most helpful to you in your work.

Hoping to see you here at Commencement, and with affectionate greetings,

Faithfully yours,

Martha Berry

The Berry Alumni Quarterly, March 1930, Vol. 13, No. 2.
* *Underlining by editors.*

Major Anniversary Celebrations

Significant in the life of Berry College and the earlier Berry schools are the special celebrations marking milestones in the institutions' progress. Included here are momentos of five: the twenty-fifth, at which the founder's day program focused on students and alumni with no outside speaker; the thirtieth, the fiftieth, the seventy-fifth, and the ninetieth, each of which featured a distinguished speaker as well as special participation by students and alumni. Among the memorabilia included are letters inviting alumni to some of the celebrations, programs, and, in following pages, articles from *The Berry Alumni Quarterly* summarizing the programs, as well as a poetic history of Berry's presidents written for the Diamond Jubilee and updated with an epilogue for this publication. Goals for Berry's centennial celebration and some planned activities for the year 2002 follow the poem "Diamond Jubilee."

A LETTER FROM OUR FOUNDER

Dear "Boys and Girls":

This is the last Quarterly that will be published before we meet at Berry in April to celebrate the twenty-fifth anniversary—my silver wedding with the Berry Schools. It seems just yesterday since I started with a few pupils in the little whitewashed schoolhouse and Brewster Hall. My thoughts always turn back to the early days, especially the days I lived on the campus in the little room of the log cabin, where I met every Sunday afternoon with the boys around the fireplace. It was there I dreamed my dreams for Berry.

The years have passed swiftly in one way, and yet, when I look over the struggles and the efforts to raise money, it seems that the road has been a long one. My most cherished dream, which I am sure will come true, is that I shall have the job of meeting each one of you around our festive board on April 30th. Come back and give me the joy of knowing that you love the Berry Schools enough to put your personal affairs aside to meet with us for one day! I feel that it will be a high spot in my life to meet with all my Berry family.

I cannot hope to celebrate the 50th anniversary with you, but I am looking forward to this silver anniversary with the keenest pleasure. I hope that not one will be missing and everyone who has been helped at Berry will answer to roll call.

We can give you a great welcome, and I, personally, will appreciate beyond words the joy of having you with us.

Faithfully yours,

MARTHA BERRY

The Berry Alumni Quarterly, *Silver Anniversary Number, March 1927, Vol. 10, No. 4.*

A LETTER FROM OUR PRINCIPAL

Mount Berry, Ga.,
March 15, 1927.

Dear Friends:

Commencement is almost here once more. The graduating class this year numbers ninety-four, the largest senior class in the history of Berry. It is indeed a happy coincidence that the largest class should get their diplomas at the Twenty-Fifth Anniversary Celebration.

The tentative commencement program appears elsewhere in this issue of the Quarterly. Please note that Anniversary Day is Saturday, April thirtieth. Resolve right now that you will be at Berry on that date and you will never regret your decision.

Attend the inspiring service of Thanksgiving and Consecration in beautiful Mount Berry chapel, where in years gone by, you have felt the presence of the Holy Spirit urging you upward to a richer and fuller life and where you have made your noblest resolutions.

Come to the Anniversary Barbecue at the Foundation School, where you will have the privilege of renewing old and sacred friendships. It will be a time of feast and fellowship never to be forgotten.

Do not miss the Pageant and Musical Entertainment on the Girls' School Campus. By song and drama you will be carried back to the early days of the Schools and then a series of heart-gripping scenes will reveal to you the marvelous growth and development of Berry during the past twenty-five years. Before your eyes will be re-enacted Miss Berry's heroic struggles as she rears the structures and molds the ideals of the great institution that has become world famous and that has enriched and ennobled the lives of six thousand men and women of the Southland.

After you have witnessed the Pageant, the greatest Alumni Banquet ever served at Berry will greet you at the new Girls' School Dining Hall. You will want to see this building, undoubtedly one of the finest in America. The banquet will mark the end of a perfect day, that is, it will if you are here to help make it so.

In closing, I want to leave this last and greatest thought with you. Even though you may live across the Continent, you owe it to Miss Berry to attend this Twenty-fifth Anniversary Celebration. It will be the greatest day of her life. For twenty-five years, with devotion unparalleled in history, she has placed herself upon the altar of service for you. Can you afford not to be here the thirtieth of April, just to clasp her hand and tell her how much you care?

Trusting that we shall see you here 100% strong on Anniversary Day, I remain,

Most cordially and sincerely yours,

G. LELAND GREEN

The Berry Alumni Quarterly, Silver Anniversary Number, March 1927, Vol. 10, No. 4.

COMMENCEMENT PROGRAM 1927

SATURDAY, APRIL 30, ANNIVERSARY DAY

10:30 A.M. SERVICE OF THANKSGIVING AND CONSECRATION
Mount Berry Chapel

1:30 P.M. ANNIVERSARY BARBECUE
Foundation School

4:00 P.M. HISTORIC PAGEANT AND ENTERTAINMENT
Girls' School Campus

7:30 P.M. ALUMNI BANQUET
New Girls' School Dining Hall

SUNDAY, MAY 1, BACCALAUREATE DAY

9:45 A.M. SUNDAY SCHOOL
Recitation Hall

11:00 A.M. COMMENCEMENT SERMON
Mount Berry Chapel

4:00 P.M. MUSICALE

MONDAY, MAY 2, CLASS DAY

9:00 A.M. MUSICALE

10:00 A.M. FOUNDATION COMMENCEMENT EXERCISES

2:30 P.M. CLASS DAY EXERCISES

7:30 P.M. ANNUAL LITERARY SOCIETY PRIZE DEBATE

TUESDAY, MAY 3, COMMENCEMENT DAY

10:30 A.M. COMMENCEMENT EXERCISES
Mount Berry Chapel

Dr. Edwin Mims of Vanderbilt University, author of "The Advancing South," will be the Commencement Speaker.

The Berry Alumni Quarterly, March 1927, Vol. 10, No. 4.

THE SILVER ANNIVERSARY
1927

The Silver Anniversary Celebration during the past Commencement covered four days that will stand out in the memory of all at Berry, especially every old teacher, former student and graduate, of our beloved Berry. The first day was "Alumni Day," coming on Saturday, April 30. No more touching scenes or words have ever been seen or heard in our beautiful Church than was witnessed on "Alumni Day." It was their day! Everything was turned over to the "Old Grads" and "Old Teachers." At the morning thanksgiving service, the different Berry Clubs over the South, sections and states, were ably represented by their chosen spokesman who spoke with pent-up emotion and feeling for his Alma Mater. It was a great service! Miss Berry was touched and in turn touched the hearts of her boys and girls by her heart-felt response. Her face was wreathed with motherly smiles of joy and satisfaction when her boys and girls spoke of Berry, and when they gave their contributions toward the Alumni Endowment fund, amounting to $9,000.00. In all, the Alumni and old students have raised $17,000.00 for various funds at Berry. Out of the twenty-one classes, the first nine were small, ranging from one to sixteen. We are just now getting old and settled enough and growing enough to show our love and appreciation for Berry in many ways.

The day was a full one for the "Old Grads." After the morning service, lasting from 10:30 to about 1:00 P.M., the students marched out, each placing a silver dollar on a table at Miss Berry's feet. They lined up in two lines leading down toward the library and chapel. Miss Berry drove old Roany down this "lane of loving hearts," followed by the Alumni.

From the Church we went to a barbecue near Lake Victory, back of the Girls' School. After a happy meal there we returned to the lake to witness an historic pageant, showing the early history, development, and present growth of Berry.

It was not long after the end of this program until we were in the New Girls' Dining Hall where sumptuous banquet tables greeted our eyes. It was our love-feast. As boys and girls gather back home for a family reunion, we had gathered back—many of Berry's children—around our Founder. Representatives of classes, in multiples of five, beginning with the outgoing Class, expressed the feeling of their brother and sister classmates. All were happy; it was the "Silver Anniversary" of Our Founder's life wedded to Berry.

The Berry Alumni Quarterly, June 1927, Vol. 11, No 1.

FOUNDER'S DAY
1932

Founder's Day on January 13th was most fittingly observed. It was the school's thirtieth anniversary and from such notables as President Hoover, Nicholas Murray Butler, Bruce Barton, Rev. S. Parkes Cadman, Albert Shaw, Mrs. Theodore Roosevelt, Mary Woolley and many others came telegrams, congratulating Miss Berry on her thirty years of noble endeavor.

Among the guests on this occasion were Honorable Josephus Daniels, Secretary of War under Woodrow Wilson and Governor Richard B. Russell Jr., of Georgia. Mr. Robert G. Alston, of Atlanta, president of Berry's Board of Trustees, presided at the exercises. These took place in the chapel and were attended by the faculty, workers and students of the three schools as well as by many visiting Alumni.

Following the rendering of songs by the schools and quartets and the reading of telegrams by Mr. Alston, Miss Berry in her own inimitable way recounted the school's history, showing how step by step her dreams had been realized and how happy she was that the coming years would see their entire fulfillment.

After Miss Berry's address she was presented with thirty American Beauty roses by Mrs. Inez Wooten Henry, representing the Alumni Association. Next she was presented a purse by Mr. H. G. Hamrick in behalf of the Alumni working at Berry. Both Mrs. Henry and Mr. Hamrick made a profound impression by the spontaneous eloquence of their remarks. So did Governor Russell who, on next being presented, stated that it would be futile to attempt to translate into words the feeling of Georgia's people for Miss Berry, whom he pronounced the state's foremost citizen.

Last came the ringing happy speech of Mr. Daniels, who classed Miss Berry with George Washington and Julius Caesar when he said that today in referring to her we no longer have to apply titles of distinction like "Miss" or "Doctor" as we do ordinary people. Turning to Governor Russell, Mr. Daniels humorously exclaimed,

"I hope that in time your excellency will grow into such a distinguished class." Relating several interesting stories of President Wilson and touching on the depression and its remedy, Mr. Daniels paid Miss Berry and the schools this beautiful tribute: "My faith in dreams was increased a thousandfold when I came within the 'Gate of Opportunity' and beheld this marvelous school. The story of her growth contains more romance, thrill, and inspiration than all the best sellers of fiction. Like a twentieth century Joan of Arc, Miss Berry has heard voices and seen Heavenly visions and obeyed them while she was young. She obeyed her dreams by telling Bible stories to children on Sunday and now after thirty years we see the Berry Schools standing in all their uniqueness and fame, one of the most noted schools in America."

The Berry Alumni Quarterly, March 1932, Vol. 14, No. 3.

The Berry Schools

Twenty-Eighth Commencement

Mount Berry Chapel

Tuesday, May 3, 1932, 10:30 A. M.

Program

Prelude — Marcia Maestoso — *Calkin*

Processional Hymn No. 12—Holy, Holy, Holy — *Heber*

Invocation. . . . . DR. WILBUR M. JONES

Address. . . . . .PRESIDENT HENRY NELSON SNYDER
Wofford College, Spartanburg, South Carolina

Reading of General High Standing List. . . . . DR. S.H. COOK

Awarding of High School Diplomas . . . . HON. ROBERT C. ALSTON
Chairman Board of Trustees

Awarding of College Diplomas. . . . . DR. MARTHA BERRY

Song. . . . . QUARTET

Recessional Hymn No. 187—Onward Christian Soldiers — *Gould*

Postlude — Allegro Con Brio — *Kohlmann*

College Graduates

BACHELORS OF SCIENCE IN AGRICULTURE:
Clarence Harwell Mallory
Hillias Worth Martin
George Albert Nesbit, Jr.
Linton Ormond Ward

BACHELORS OF ARTS:
Wallace Edward Moody
Horace Radford Sims
Maude Tallent

BACHELORS OF SCIENCE IN HOME ECONOMICS:
Lurlie Ham
Clyde Reynolds
Elizabeth Jane Smith
Gracie Lee Smith
Myrtle Elizabeth Wright

BACHELORS OF SCIENCE
Frances Ellen Bell
Conie Brooks
Mossie Lee Hackett
Arthur Milton Smith
William LeRoy Wallin

General High Standing List

Frances Ellen Bell
Clarence Harwell Mallory
George Albert Nesbit, Jr.
Arthur Milton Smith
Elizabeth Jane Smith
Gracie Lee Smith

The 50th Anniversary 1902 - 1952

Celebration of the 50th Anniversary of the founding of The Berry Schools was begun on Saturday, January 12, at Joint Chapel, when Dr. James G. McClure, president of the Farmers' Federation, Asheville, N. C., told the faculty, students, and visitors that the people of the world do not need our money nor our guns but the magic Christian formulae for action. John A. Sibley, Chairman of the Board of Trustees, introduced Dr. McClure, and Dr. S. H. Cook, president, introduced other guests. Dr. McClure discussed his plan of "God's Acre," whereby each farmer gives the income from one acre to the church.

Joan Underwood, representing the student body, pledged support by every student at the Schools in raising funds for the Martha Berry Memorial Endowment. "Each student at Berry wishes to have a part in the golden anniversary, and we consider it our golden opportunity to contribute to the Martha Berry Endowment Fund." Miss Underwood said.

Following Joint Chapel, Mrs. Emily V. Hammond and Mr. John A. Sibley got in the old buggy which Miss Berry used at the beginning of the Schools, and several of the smaller children of the campus were in their laps, sitting at their feet, and standing in the back, while some of the senior boys pulled the buggy through the lines of students and Alumni.

After this ceremony was concluded, Mr. Sibley planted a magnolia tree in the Martha Berry Memorial Forest, facing the archway at the Girls' School.

Dr. Wallace Alston, president of Agnes Scott College, Decatur, preached the Founder's Day and Baccalaureate sermon in the Mount Berry Chapel at 11:00 A.M. Sunday, January 13. On Sunday afternoon all the visitors and staff members were invited to a tea at Oak Hill.

The largest attended part of the celebration was the graduation exercises on Monday at 11:00 A.M., when Mrs. Emily V. Hammond of New York, a long-time personal friend of the founder, spoke to the graduating classes and students, faculty, alumni, and friends. At this meeting, H. Grady Hamrick of the Masonic Home in Macon, and President of the Berry Alumni Association, brought greetings from the Alumni, and pledged wholehearted support of the organization and urged a campaign for $2,000,000 endowment for the Schools. The graduates, 65 seniors from high school and college, received their diplomas and degrees from President Cook.

Mrs. Hammond, who marked her 32nd visit to Berry, and who has brought more than 600 people to visit the School, was enthusiastic in her talk to the graduates. She received the first honorary degree from Berry College in 1923, and she is an author and poet. Tracing her friendship with Miss Berry, and her interest in The Berry Schools for the past thirty years, Mrs. Hammond called Miss Berry "a great humanitarian, a great educator, and a great leader, who proved that all things are possible for those who have faith in God. Human nature can be changed," Mrs. Hammond told her audience. "We must change ourselves, then national economies can be changed, world history can be changed, and nations can be changed."

The Berry Alumni Quarter, January 1952, Vol. 41, No. 1.

A Celebration of Founder's Day on the 75th Anniversary of The Berry Schools

Berry College and Berry Academy Mount Berry, Georgia

FOUNDER'S DAY CHAPEL
Berry College and Berry Academy
Mount Berry, Georgia
January 13, 1977

John R. Lipscomb, *vice president for resources*

Some people celebrate anniversaries. Some of us just observe them. Today, we all celebrate something that happened 75 years ago today—the founding of The Berry Schools.

Faith Gay, *president of Berry Academy Student Government Association*

The Schools Psalm (121st)

I will lift up mine eyes unto the hills, from whence cometh my help. My help cometh from the Lord, which made heaven and earth. He will not suffer thy foot to be moved: he that keepeth thee will not slumber. Behold, he that keepeth Israel shall neither slumber nor sleep. The Lord is thy keeper; the Lord is thy shade upon thy right hand. The sun shall not smite thee by day, nor the moon by night. The Lord shall preserve thee from all evil: he shall preserve thy soul. The Lord shall preserve thy going out, and thy coming in, from this time forth, and even for evermore.

David McAlpin, *Berry College senior*

Let us pray. Lord God, we come before you this morning and we adore you. We come before you praising you for your greatness. And, Father, I thank you this morning that you are God who is powerful, who is almighty and all-knowing, and who has chosen to involve himself in the affairs of everyday man, of ordinary man. We thank you, Lord, that you are very much alive and very active in the world today and in our own lives. But, God, we also come and, Lord, we confess our sins to you and our utter need for you.

Father, I thank you that you provided a way that we all might know your goodness and your love and your eternal life through Jesus Christ, through his atoning blood. Father, we thank you this morning that through faith in him we can know you and we can have a relationship with you. God, we thank you this morning that you love us and that you sent your Son to die for us. Father, we thank you for the vision and the faith that have put these schools here, for the vision and the faith of those in the past—for their faith in the living, loving God.

And, Father, we would ask this morning that as we look at ourselves and as we look to our leaders today that you would give them that same vision and that same faith of those in the past. Oh, God, we pray that they would humble themselves in prayer before you and seek your faith for leading and guidance, and we thank you for them and we promise to pray for them. And I pray, Father, that if everyone of us could come back in 75 years, we would be able to pray the same kind of prayer that we pray today—looking back in thanksgiving and looking forward in hope and faith. Thank you, God, for loving us and for being with us today. Bless us in this convocation, and we promise to give you all the praise and glory. In Christ Jesus' name we pray. Amen.

Terri Hinton, *Miss Berry College*

Good morning and welcome to the 75th anniversary of the founding of The Berry Schools. We at Berry are very proud of what our schools have become in the past three-quarters of a century. The traditions that Martha Berry held dear, such as worship, hard work, study and service, are still very important to us today. And it is my prayer as we celebrate this happy day, remembering those good things that have made these schools what they are, that we will continue to live in such a way that we will truly be a light that shines for right.

The Schools Hymn: "O God, Our Help in Ages Past"

Berry Academy Chorus: "Climb Every Mountain"

Berry College Concert Choir: "Alleluia"

Berry College Student Government Association Officers: "Why Are You Here?"

Patty Etchison, *vice president, college SGA*

What does Founder's Day mean to you, anyway? It seems to me that if Berry is to survive, each of you needs to answer that question. Does our heritage make any difference to you? Is this just a ritual or is there useful knowledge to be gained by looking at the past? Ten, 50 or even another 75 years, those who come after you will be faced with many of the same questions and will have no answers to what is the importance of Berry's heritage unless you begin to understand the meaning—the true meaning for each of you now—of Berry's past with regard to our present and to our future.

Bud Hall, *treasurer, college SGA*

You go to class and play the game, but are you really learning anything? Are you here because you had nowhere else to go and nothing else to do? Or is Berry a stepping stone just to get ahead, or are you here just for the sake of learning? Isn't part of why you're here to learn something about life? You need to know the kinds of things books and classes and professors can teach you. But if you can't understand the person behind the book or appreciate those students around you or comprehend the humanness of the professor, have you really learned?

Francy Jessup, *secretary, college SGA*

In the beginning everybody worked at Berry. But how many of you do now? I don't mean how many get a paycheck every two weeks—not just how many put in time—but how many actually work? If you aren't putting any of your sweat and tears into it, how can you get out of it what Miss Berry intended? And if your work doesn't improve, perhaps Berry would be better off without it. But then, those who follow you will miss a great deal of the meaning of education. The world out there doesn't stop for four years when you enter the Gate of Opportunity—it just begins.

Bill Roseen, *vice president, college SGA*

[Why are you here?] In the chapel of all places. Or doesn't that take on any of those traditional religious connotations these days? There are still services here, true, but are you ever here for that or for anything to do with God? There was a lot of prayer to go along with all the hard work that has made this place, and it will take as much or more on the part of each of you to keep Berry a strong Christian school. Or do you care? Does it matter if Berry remains Christian? Because if it doesn't, then this place shall surely die. And, after all, if we don't care enough to entrust and leave Berry in the hands of Almighty God, to use as only he knows best, then Berry should choose to die rather than to merely exist as a "common place."

Evelyn Wheeler, *president, college SGA*

Okay, so why are you here? Is it out of a sense of pride in our heritage, or to work to make things better, or to learn something or to sing praises to God? It should be these things and more. You should be here to be you, to give what only you can give, to work and sing and pray as only you can—to be yourself, your best self—always!

Today, I am to introduce someone who really needs no introduction. For the past 20 years he has worked to make The Berry Schools what they are today—the president of The Berry Schools, Dr. John R. Bertrand.

John R. Bertrand

Thank you, Evelyn, Bill, Patty, Francy and Bud, trustees, other honored guests, alumni, students, faculty and staff. It is my privilege now to present the chairman of Berry's Board of Trustees.

William R. Bowdoin became a Berry trustee in 1960. He serves as chairman of the Trust Company of Georgia Associates, headquartered in Atlanta. Mr. Bowdoin also is widely known for his interests and activities in civic, service and educational affairs. He is a member of the Emory University Board of Trustees and chairman of Emory's Woodruff Medical Center. Emory awarded him an honorary doctor of laws degree in 1969 in recognition of his service to the university and to higher education. The Association of Private Colleges and Universities in Georgia has also honored Mr. Bowdoin for his outstanding contributions to higher education in Georgia.

A Georgia native and an alumnus of the University of Georgia, he was an officer in the United States Infantry in World War II and in 1970 was inducted into the Hall of Fame at Fort Benning. Mr. Bowdoin took leaves of absence from his financial post to serve as chairman of Georgia's Ports Authority under Governor Herman Talmadge, as state supervisor of purchasing under Governor Ernest Vandiver and as chairman of the Governor's Commission on Efficiency and Economy in Government under Governor Carl Sanders.

It is now my distinct honor to present the chairman of Berry's Board of Trustees for comments on this 75th founder's day celebration and the founder herself. Mr. William R. Bowdoin.

William R. Bowdoin

Thank you very much, Dr. Bertrand, persons being honored here today, Mr. Sibley, trustees, members of the Board of Visitors, staff, faculty, students, parents and friends of The Berry Schools. If I have omitted anybody, I hope you'll forgive me. Mrs. Bowdoin and I are honored to be here today on this great occasion. In all probability I'll not be able to be with you for the next 75th celebration, so we're making full use of the one here today.

I want to join in extending you a very warm welcome today and tell you how delighted we are to have you with us on this occasion. I am particularly glad, and we are particularly honored, that Mr. and Mrs. John Sibley can be with us today. As most of you recognize, he is not only one of Georgia's all-time great citizens, he was a very close friend and confidant of Miss Martha Berry and for many years chairman of the Board of Trustees of this institution. So we have many reasons to be honored by your presence here today, Mr. Sibley.

I also want to express my gratitude for this very delightful program that has been arranged for this occasion, and I don't think I ever saw a more unique presentation of what Berry really stands for than was given by members of the Student Government Association along with the beautiful music and other presentations that you have had. I think it was a great job, and I want to thank everyone responsible for it.

My first real knowledge of The Berry Schools came some 48 years ago when I was honored to participate in a program at the University of Georgia honoring Miss Martha Berry for her great contribution toward the betterment of agriculture in Georgia, and it was then that I fully realized the uniqueness of this institution of learning which has contributed so much through the years to a better life for so many. And there certainly was no way on that day in Athens, even in my most vivid imagination, could I picture myself as a part of this fine institution that in reality has become the dream and vision that Miss Berry had.

The dedication, loyalty and contribution made by so many people under Miss Berry's leadership and guidance for these 75 years are too numerous to mention for fear that I might omit someone. I think, though, that we must recognize all of those who have had such a tremendous part through the years in building what Berry is today.

But one cannot talk about 75 years at Berry without really talking about Miss Martha Berry. The dynamic presence for 40 years of the schools' formal existence and the lingering spirit of Miss Berry through remaining years is accountable for so much of this success, along, I think, with the fine and outstanding leadership of Dr. Bertrand, who has been here 20 years, which makes a rather unusual situation when in 75 years you've had really two directors—one for 40 years in the beginning and one today for the last 20 years. So I congratulate you, John, too. Annabel, I congratulate you, too, because you have been tremendously helpful to Berry and have had John to look after.

Berry is no ordinary school, and I pray that it never becomes so, because the great lady who was its founder and nurturer through the years and whose name it bears today was no ordinary person. I didn't have the privilege of knowing her as so many of you did, but I did have the opportunity to meet her on the occasion that I referred to a moment ago, and I remember that very distinctly. I was president at that time of the Georgia association of the Future Farmers of America and in that capacity presented her with an honorary membership in that organization. It was an occasion I shall never forget. I can still see in the mind's eye this lovely, white-haired lady, small in stature, with sparkling eyes and ready smile, rosy cheeks, simply but impeccably groomed, who accepted this honor from me, representing the Future Farmers of America, just as graciously as if it had been presented by the President of the United States.

From reading the fascinating books *Miracle in the Mountains* by Harnett Kane and our own Dr. Inez Henry, *A Lady I Loved* by Mrs. Evelyn Hoge Pendley, whose father for so many years was a great stalwart here on the Berry campus, *The Sunday Lady of Possum Trot* by Tracy Byers, and many others, together with Miss Berry's own writings and by talking at length with those who did know her well through the years, it is not difficult to form an enduring and affectionate opinion of this strong-willed, dedicated and courageous lady.

Just recently I was asked the question if I didn't think Miss Berry would be greatly surprised if she could return to our midst and see the growth and expansion of the schools that she started and nurtured for so many difficult years. Since Miss Berry departed our midst to her celestial home, there has been much conjecture of what Miss Berry would or would not do, or would or would not say, under given circumstances and conditions. No one knows for sure what her reaction would be to the schools as they stand today, but it's my guess that she would not be surprised as she looks down upon us on this occasion.

There would be no surprise on Miss Berry's part because she built the institution on the strongest possible foundation—faith in God, the dignity of worthwhile work well done, the importance of education and the proper discharge of good citizenship responsibilities. Hopefully, she would be pleased with those who have followed her and have been able to fulfill in some measure her further hopes and ambitions for The Berry Schools. Her only possibility of surprise, or maybe I should say dismay, might be the resistant attitude that a few show from time to time toward the importance of maintaining the fundamentals of The Berry Schools in our present-day society. Miss Berry was not averse to change, provided that change was for the betterment of the schools, but she was not very tolerant of change just to satisfy individual whims. Her tendency at times to be idealistic was always well balanced with a liberal portion of practicality.

We who are privileged to gather here today should rededicate ourselves to the proposition that the next 75 years of this institution's history will be to protect and strengthen its foundation and expand even further its usefulness. Here are embodied the principles that for generations have been the rallying point to build courage when courage seemed to fail, to regain faith when there seemed little cause for faith and to create hope when hope became forlorn.

I think often of the recorded comment by Miss Berry as she stood one day with a member of the senior class at Berry College beneath one of the giant oaks on the campus. As she gazed admiringly through its branches, she remarked partly to the student and I expect partly to herself. She said, "All the buffeting it has had, all of the knocks. But it is the knocks that have made it grow." And to the student she said, "The troubles you have had are what make you." That's a great philosophy. I have quoted many times the statement of Miss Berry, "The pursuit of easy things makes us weak. It is the pursuit of the difficult that makes us strong." I feel sure that statement had its origin in her thoughts of the difficult years experienced in building The Berry Schools—thoughts that went back to a spring Sunday afternoon before the turn of the century in the little log cabin where she started reading scripture and telling Bible stories to those children who had not had the good fortune of an education. She must have also been thinking of those, including some members of her own family, who attempted to discourage her in the deep-rooted desire to bring opportunity to those whose thirst for knowledge and a better life would not otherwise be quenched.

Although born into wealth where she could have lived a life of luxury, her vision, courage and Biblical inspiration led her in another direction. Miss Berry possessed those qualities that uplift mankind and make tolerance a virtue and not just an excuse. Her patience and understanding of those who tried and possessed a deep and abiding ambition to better themselves and other people was wonderful to behold. But her wrath could be felt by others given to mockery, subterfuge and downright disloyalty. She sought advice and counsel from those whose knowledge and experience she respected, whether they be trustees, staff, faculty or students. But when the final decision was made, she expected everyone in the schools to adhere to it. Freedom of speech to Miss Berry didn't include making your own rules or defying those made by others in authority, because she considered discipline, respect for authority and the proper discharge of responsibilities placed upon you an integral part of our educational processes. That's the way it should be, in my opinion. And that's why the uniqueness of The Berry Schools must always be retained and maintained.

In her work and in her writings, it was evident she recognized the fact that this nation was not built by common people as often suggested. It was built by uncommon folk. Uncommon in the sense of possessing a desire to work. A willingness to sacrifice if need be. To study. To build a better world with loyalty and understanding among all of our people. Adherence to this philosophy is what Berry is all about. That's why Berry's mark of excellence for 75 years has contributed so much toward a better life for so many, not just in the field of academics, but in the broad scope of a well-lived life that contributes so much to the well-being of others.

Therefore, it is not sufficient that we just preserve this heritage, but we should so nurture and improve upon it that we leave it to future generations richer in advantages and opportunities in freedom than have been ours to receive. Miss Berry was strong in her beliefs that those who did not subscribe to the fundamentals upon which Berry was founded do not belong at Berry. I also subscribe to that feeling and attitude.

As we move into the next 75 years in the life of this great institution, let us do so with a firm conviction to keep strong the foundation upon which the school was built—faith in God, the dignity of worthwhile work well done and the importance of education.

By doing this we can continue to send forth our graduates to the communities of their choice, both here and abroad, "not to be ministered unto, but to minister."

This goal can be achieved and in doing so the generations yet to come can point to our stewardship and say as Paul said in his last moments on this earth, "I've fought a good fight; I've finished the course; I have kept the faith." Many happy returns of the day, and may God bless you.

Dr. Bertrand

In Georgia, throughout the South and over much of our nation you can with ease and without further ado say simply, "May I present Mr. John A. Sibley."

Today, however, I would add that while this man has meant much to Georgia, to this region and to our nation, he has meant that much and more to The Berry Schools. Martha Berry invited him to serve on the Board of Trustees. To achieve Martha Berry's goal of excellence she sought trustees of strong Christian belief and great personal achievement and character.

Outstanding among a great line of trustees at Berry is John A. Sibley. He joined the board in 1935, which was then under the long-time chairmanship of Robert Alston. Later, John Bulow Campbell became chairman and served for about two years until his untimely death.

Then, at the urging of Martha Berry herself, John Sibley accepted the chairmanship and served from 1940 to 1955 when he prevailed on William McChesney Martin, Jr., to succeed him as chairman. Mr. Sibley continued to serve as a trustee until he requested retirement from the board nine years ago.

Less than two years ago John A. Sibley received the 1975 Shining Light Award presented by WSB radio/television and the Atlanta Gas Light Company. William R. Bowdoin presented Mr. Sibley at that time. I should now like to share with you an excerpt from Mr. Bowdoin's presentation:

His unusual qualities of human understanding and compassion for all with whom he comes in contact have touched the lives of people in all walks of life—rich and poor, black and white. He has achieved a most unusual place in the esteem and affections of all who know him. His vision for progress and dedication to that cause are equaled by few and exceeded by none. These great attributes are already recorded in the annals of law, banking and other business enterprises, education, agriculture and areas of renewable wealth in our state.

As we look at the gift of his many talents to the people of Georgia, none exceeds the contribution he made in 1960 to public education. As the result of the ruling by the United States Supreme Court with which we are all familiar, the day of reckoning finally came to Georgia and with it bitterness, divisiveness and heartaches not experienced since the days of Reconstruction.

Governor Ernest Vandiver appointed a very representative commission to study the situation and make recommendations to him that would hopefully solve the agonizing problem. For chairman of the commission, he immediately turned to the most logical choice—Mr. John A. Sibley. The hearing had scarcely gotten underway when the vast majority of people recognized the chairman as a warm, compassionate, impartial individual of judicial calmness who sought the truth and who had the courage to fight for the right as he saw the right. You all know the final outcome. We took the high road instead of the low. By virtue of his strong leadership in one of Georgia's darkest hours, we emerged to the sunshine of opportunity that has given us nearly two decades of unprecedented growth and development.

The Berry Schools would not have been complete without John A. Sibley. And this day, this 75th anniversary Founder's Day, would not have been complete had he not been here.

Mr. Sibley, I am aware of the fact that nine years ago on your 80th birthday you vowed to make no more speeches. However, because of the special occasion honoring the memory, vision and achievements of the remarkable Martha Berry, with whom you were so closely associated, all of us hope you will consent to make some remarks, not a speech, but some remarks of whatever length you may wish. Ladies and gentlemen, here is John A. Sibley.

John A. Sibley

Dr. Bertrand, I'm very grateful to you for that introduction. And Mr. Bowdoin, I'm very grateful to you for bringing my wife here today! She will wonder who in the world the doctor was talking about.

You know, this is an occasion that no one should miss. I don't know when I've felt so deeply and have seen so clearly reenacted the spirit of Miss Berry as I have here today.

I wish she could have been here as we saw the occasion open with that beautiful 121st Psalm, "I will lift up mine eyes unto the hills, from whence cometh my help. My help cometh from the Lord, which made heaven and earth." When she heard the young man open the occasion with that beautiful prayer, she would have recognized that her spirit was still alive. And she would have been grateful for the people who are carrying on this work—so unique, so different—as an educational institution.

We owe so much to the people with whom we associate, and I owe so much to her because, while generally speaking I've had a wide acquaintance, I've never come in contact with anyone so thoroughly dedicated to certain principles in which she believed.

She was dedicated to the spirit of excellence, and that excellence she wanted to see developed in the young people of this state and this nation. She did not believe that excellence could be obtained merely by the efforts of the persons themselves. She felt there was a potentiality in the life of ordinary people—and that if they gathered the strength from the spirit above, then they became extraordinary people. She thought a part of the development of ordinary people into extraordinary people was through the help of God: the recognition of God and the things taught by the Creator were an essential element in their development. So education to her was much more than intellectual development.

Education to her was to take those hidden potentialities which are in the breast of all of us, and then by gathering new strength, a strength that is renewable day by day, and planting it in the lives of young people, she was helping to educate them.

She realized that potentiality could only be reached through the attitude of usefulness on the part of the young people. And that, too, was education, not work apart from education or religion apart from education, but that was education itself, just as much as intellectual development was a part of education. Now the world is coming to that today.

There are two things on the horizon. One of them that we're beginning to see is that there's an exhaustion of natural resources. There's a big cliff that the world can step over. We're also beginning to see on the horizon a great cloud of danger growing out of the technological ability of man, of true technology, the ability of man to destroy the world.

People are beginning to see that those two conditions can only be met by the renewal of man's spirit and the attitude of man toward life. And that attitude toward life has to recognize, as the young man said today so beautifully in his prayer, that it's a living thing, not just an historical fact, but an historical fact that has day-to-day life. Everything that we're seeing here—everything that's happened here today among you, among the faculty, among the leaders, has been the recognition of that great fact.

The other great educational institutions have got to reform themselves because they have brought us to the position in which we can destroy the world, but they haven't given us the things that can save the world.

And the little lady of Possum Trot brought together those elements, each of which enters into the development of the potential spirit of man. That spirit takes into consideration that man himself is not all of it. There's something bigger and something larger, and in order to develop himself and ultimately for him to save himself, he must take that into consideration in meeting the issues of life.

I didn't like your telling my age—I wanted some of these girls to smile at me! And I never have seen a girl, if she knew it, who would smile at an 89-year-old man! Thank you.

Audience Sings Berry's "Alma Mater"

<u>The Rev. Larry Green, *chaplain, Berry College and Berry Academy*</u>

God's blessing is richly a part of this occasion, because God's blessing has been upon us through the history of this place, and with all of those who have brought us to this time. God's blessing is with us now because of the struggle in which all of us are engaged to make life meaningful and education an appropriate part of that within the context of the Christian commitment of this place. And for that we give thanks. May that blessing be with you in the name of God the Father, the Son and the Holy Spirit now and forever. Amen.

A DIAMOND JUBILEE REVIEW 1902-1977 and EPILOGUE: APPROACHING BERRY'S CENTENNIAL (2002 A.D.)

By Evelyn Hoge Pendley

I am Martha Berry, at least I speak for her.
Three quarters of a century it's been
Since I began my schools.
And it's been nearly half that time, as people say,
Since I passed away.
And yet, I have not passed away.
My dreams grow on; my spirit is alive.
As long as this is true, I too survive.

How often do I wish that those who said
My schools would wither when I left the earth
Could see them now,
Could count the souls who've functioned in my stead,
Could recognize the rocks on which I placed my faith:
My faith in God,
And then my loyal girls and boys—
The ones I knew and others in their train—
Old friends and new ones to support, sustain.
The Board of Trustees, serving without fees;
Self-perpetuating, dedicated; in proportionate degrees
Unselfish, wise, and true,
Never swerving from the tasks I left for them to do.
They have made decisions, have provided
Chief administrators, who in turn have guided
The continuous flow of tri-fold education here
Through struggles and successes,
All the changes year by year.
But let these leaders speak.
As I told my story, they can tell

Their own experiences.
First Gardner Leland Green, our first president,
A man of foresight, whom I knew so very well.

Dr. Green
I, Leland Green, am a soft-spoken man.
I hope you all can hear.
Toward Martha Berry I felt awe and respect,
But never fear.
She sought me in Vermont, my native state,
Told me of her schools, persuaded me how great
The needs were, that somehow she knew
My future was with hers, deep in the South.
And this proved true. Ah, yes, this was so very true.
My tasks were to hire teachers and to see
That the academic work possessed real quality.
Scholarly standards were a challenge of my day.
High school accreditation came, this without much delay.
Then we began the college, and, I must confess,
I was the one to argue, and with firm foresight to press
For higher learning. It was plain to see
We needed at that time to widen
Our Gate of Opportunity.
Miss Berry sought the funds; we laid the plans,
Confronted many foes, met new standards and demands.
We also gained new friends, a growing faculty.
The dream of Berry College became reality.

We struggled and we sacrificed through the depression
days.
We were one big family then in, oh, so many ways.
Then came the war and then the time
That our dear Founder died.
Hers was the open honor; mine the secret pride
For all that we accomplished.

Some of myself I set in poetry.
My *Upward Quest* and then *These Will Remain*
Reflect my family life of love and harmony,
My inner self. Thus, all who wish may see
My life of sweet tranquility as well as stress and strain,
And what a joy it was to live on such a lofty plain.

Miss Berry
Dear Dr. Green, a man of gentle ways,
Who disciplined with calm control and reassuring praise.
A man of quiet courage, clear of purpose, undismayed.
Berry College certainly has grown on foundations that he laid.

It was Marcus Gordon Keown I chose to take my place,
An alumnus and a lover of the land,
Of trees, of animals, and space.
His shrewd and unsophisticated skills
In meeting folks, his bargaining,
His foresight helped to accumulate
Much of our land. We'd ride around and contemplate
Our growing holdings. Together we rejoiced
In the richness of the earth.
Often, like Will Rogers, he would spread
A background of droll mirth.
But hear him speak, for in his special way
He was a man of purpose, unpretentious, and articulate.

Mr. Keown
Well, here I am—Marcus Gordon Keown,
Just a country fellow from a tiny little town
Where the biggest job was postmaster,
So that's what I came to be.
But "Prime Minister" was another name
That some folks had for me.
Yes. I loved the land, and I loved opportunity

For young folks, and for a future
That would be full and free.
Almost for two years after Miss Berry died, I did the best
I could
To carry out her wishes through the trials of war years.
In far too many ways, mine was the vale of tears.
Still, the military came, kept our buildings in repair.
The girls took over the boys' work; we all did our share.
The trustees asked professionals
To evaluate our ways.
And criticism seemed to mount
Instead of words of praise.
I listened; I sat steady, trying to uphold each goal
Until a well-trained college man
Could come and take control.

<u>Miss Berry</u>
Ah, Gordon Keown. He was so dear to me.
His love and loyalty were strong and deep.
I'm sure he wept, for he could weep!
But the moment after, he could lead us back to laughter.
His was a rare and winsome personality.

William Jesse Baird was the man the trustees found
To be the next administrator. He came down
From Kentucky with a history of success.
But his two years at Berry were unsettled times of stress.
Folks had said the Angel Gabriel couldn't fill my place.
And, while I know this wasn't so, this was a unique case.
Let's hear from Dr. Baird and thereby we can find
The plans and new procedures that he promptly set forth
and designed.

<u>Dr. Baird</u>
I, William Jesse Baird, had a background in
education

In a school quite like Berry, so without orientation
I set about the task of reorganization.
I made changes that were recommended, adjustments
that were needed.
And, being quick and candid, in some things I succeeded.
I replaced some old employees, some for better, some for
worse.

I irritated others who, too often, thought me terse.
I didn't bother to be frugal; so much needed to be done.
I adjusted academic offerings. I could not please every-
one.
The townspeople seemed to like me, and after I resigned
The editorials in the paper were affirmative and kind.
I went back to Kentucky, to a college presidency;
Following my careful judgment, that seemed the place to be.

Miss Berry
It could have been that Dr. Baird
Was impatient to begin.
Perhaps a man who knew the schools
Better from within
Could have struggled for solutions in a more subtle way.
Or perhaps it was that Dr. Baird simply did not care to
stay.

At any rate, the next president,
One unanimously selected,
Had been at Berry several years,
Knew more what was expected.
James Armour Lindsay, tall and pleasant and polite,
Was serious about his challenge, always anxious to do
right.
His background included high school administration
And also good experience as a professor of education.

He had taught at Berry College, then had headed the
Boys' High,
And he was full of theories that Berry ought to try.
But let him straightway tell you what he did and why.

Dr. Lindsay
I, James Armour Lindsay, was president for
five years.
My wife was my great asset, always by my side.
Well-trained and poised, she was a good helpmate and
guide.
We analyzed and theorized,
Evaluated, tabulated,
Went through studies and suggestions,
Copious planning and proposals.
We experimented and advised,
Had new methods instigated.
We laid logical foundations
For a student government association.
A faculty council kept abreast
Of the workings of the rest.
Weekly news was disseminated.
Much of our land was designated
As a wild life sanctuary.
Higher pay came too at Berry,
But it lacked much to compare
With what teachers made elsewhere.
I was always working, trying
To advise in ways I should.
But so many called it prying,
Claimed they fully understood
What their jobs required of them
Better than I ever could.
Yes, there were loopholes in my training.
I'll not waste much time explaining
That I was no business man.

When the Korean conflict came,
With it came increased inflation.
Real finances were a game
Leaving me in consternation.
Thus, the trustees formed an office
To handle business and finance.
It also covered lands and forest,
Almost anything by chance
That had to do with monies. So it came to be
Berry almost had two presidents—this other man and me.
We worked together as we could,
But many things were not too good.
Enrollment lowered; tuition rose.
Maintenance told a tale of woes.
Nevertheless,
As we seemed sliding down the slopes
Morton Hall refreshed our hopes.
A gift like that was most inspiring.
But even then, I still was tiring.
A year away seemed wise for me,
A year to think, develop skill.
I didn't know that I was ill.
And so we left, not knowing then
We would not be back again.

Miss Berry
Good Dr. Lindsay did his best.
Sometimes our best is not enough—
Times for him were tense and tough.
Many of his contributions
Became developmental frames
For growth within our institution.
I hope before he died he understood
How much he did was needed and was good.

Sam Henry Cook was human—true—and yet
He was the most Christ-like man I ever met.
Coming to Berry back in 1910,
He was a young red-headed teacher then.
As he grew with Berry, so his duties grew.
He was our bachelor dean who knew
Every single student by his name.
It was he who dutifully came
To serve, as well as dean, as president until
Hopefully a proper person could be found to fill
The vacancy, now once again created.
For over two full years he worked and waited.
Tell us, Dr. Cook, how you endured.
In those hard days, what kept you calm, assured?

<u>Dr. Cook</u>
Lan' sakes alive, Miss Berry, don't you know
I'se best at tellin' Uncle Remus tales?
Brudder Bar and me, we likes to fetch our pails
And tease Brer Rabbit at de fishin' hole.
But den, I know dere is a weightier tale dat must be told.

Seriously, my experiences through the years prepared me well
For all the problems and the pressures of this place.
I could look back at earlier days,
Recall when perseverance had prevailed.
The role of president was not my choice,
But I was willing to assume the task
Until the proper person could be found.
Indeed these were some tense and testy times.
An added year of high school in the state
Cut college applications everywhere.
The men's enrollment almost disappeared.

Morale among the women was quite low;
We had too many stuffy, worn-out rules.
Again, evaluators came and warned
Of standards we must raise so we could keep
On offering the baccalaureate degree.
Some fine employees reached retirement age.
It broke our hearts and theirs as they grew old.
With pay so low it was hard to attract
Replacements who were young and qualified.
And yet among us was a solid core
Who kept the faith—who kept on keeping on.
Builders with Miss Berry we had been.
Our challenge was to keep her work alive.
These times would pass; there would come better days;
And so we worked and waited, analyzed and prayed.

Miss Berry
Yes, dear Dr. Cook, you kept on keeping on—
Not merely for two years, but on and on and on.
For over two decades more, how much you gave and served.
Myriad memories that honor you are well deserved.

Robert Stanley Lambert, a minister, was next.
In education, he said he was a neophyte.
And he was right.
That does not mean
He did not try to serve with vigor and foresight.
All he had heard and seen of Berry
Had won his admiration.
If he had had experience in education
Perhaps he would have had more than his twenty-two months' stay.
But let us pause and listen, hear what he has to say.

<u>Dr. Lambert</u>

I, Robert Stanley Lambert, came to Berry
 with great plans.
Each time I think of them, my memory expands.
My goals were timely, touching many a need.
And, with the proper help, I knew I would succeed.
I hired a second dean, tried to eliminate
Some deadwood, I felt I could create
A happier, more social atmosphere.
My critics said I brought about factions, grief, and fear.
I had an elaborate, formal inauguration.
I felt this would be prestigious
To my role in education.
During my stay the trustees closed the school for girls
And also Possum Trot.
They had a thorough study done
Of what was needed and what was not.
They had a special inventory of education
And a new committee on accreditation.
Well qualified were their consultants.
They knew what we should do.
But when the board did not support me,
I would not see things through.
Perhaps I used poor judgement when I hastily resigned,
For they failed to reconsider when I was so inclined.

<u>Miss Berry</u>

Dr. Lambert was a handsome and an ambitious man.
He had good intentions; this I know.
But first comes service; then comes recognition.
To work for joy, not title and position—
This is what gives to life its inner glow.
Still, this man gave to Berry in his special way.

He had a secret, selfless side that was not on display.
Unknown to most, he returned the salary he was paid.
Fine furniture and paintings were other gifts he made.
He had a love of beauty; his heart was full of caring.
He left his footprints on our paths, footprints of quiet sharing.

Again there was an interim.
William McChesney Martin, new chairman of the board,
Found many duties quickly laid on him.
Again dear Dr. Cook assumed the role
Of leadership on campus and kept calm control.

<u>William McChesney Martin</u>
Miss Berry, you know that we were friends.
You used to call me Bill.
Won't you do that still?
When I became chairman of the board,
I felt that I had heard a special call
To serve the schools in this capacity.
Thus, when the president's office was vacated,
For a year until a full-time man was designated,
I was known as acting president
And worked with Dr. Cook untiringly.

<u>Miss Berry</u>
John Raney Bertrand was the man Bill Martin found.
He is my kind of man, I'm sure.
Practical, close to earth, well-trained and disciplined,
Courageous, kind, a gentleman, honest, fair and pure.
He was "the Moses of Mount Berry." Thus said Dr. Green.
And gracious Annabel is like a gentle, helpful queen.

Dr. Bertrand
I am John Raney Bertrand, a Texan,
As most of you know well.
In 1956 I came to Berry
With my good wife Annabel.
We brought our four young children.
Berry became our home.
Soon we made friends throughout the South,
On campus, and in Rome.

I tried at once to watch and learn
From men who'd served before,
To build on their foundations,
To keep on adding more.
I could not walk on water,
But Dr. Green and Dr. Cook
Showed me how to find the rocks,
Where to step and where to look.
So I followed in their footsteps.
I advised from day to day
With them and many others
Before I went my separate way.
We achieved accreditation and updated many rules.
We opened new avenues into The Berry Schools.
We honored old workers, helped them realize their worth,
Tried to bless and undergird them through their last lapse on this earth.

We kept old friends, found new ones
To help us build and grow.
We conducted special studies to help us think, to know
Our weaknesses, our needs, our strengths,
Which directions we should go.
We've built a stronger Berry with more buildings, faculty,

More staff, more students, and more plans for good things
yet to be.
We've fostered academic freedom and rights of privacy,
Augmented benefits and salaries despite the economy.
We've added student scholarships and offered study
grants.
Special consideration has been given to many a
circumstance.
Education is our business; we must never cease to be
An optimistic oasis of opportunity.
I've had some thorns prick in my flesh—and deep in my
heart, too,
But I have tried to do my best—all that I knew to do.
A leader never works alone. Colleagues, guides, and
friends
Have constantly supported me in work that never ends.
Alumni giving answers now Miss Berry's ardent prayer.
The Boards of Trustees and Visitors have given their full
share.
Through turbulence and changing times, we have worked
and grown.
We're building for the future still, a future quite unknown.

Miss Berry
He is a kindred spirit, this solid John Bertrand.
For more than twenty years at Berry, as he has worked
and planned,
He, too, has known the loneliness and burdens of
command.
I'm sure, in time of doubt, he's stopped and looked up to
the hills,
And found new guidance to go on and sense the joys and
thrills
That bless the inner lives of those who minister unto
The world about, who keep the faith, who bravely see
things through.

Yes—all of these men who followed me have been links in a chain.
More than they know, the works they did will wondrously remain.
Berry now is larger than ever in the past.
And Berry still is beautiful. Oh, may that beauty last!
And may this ever be a place where youth may come and find
Good ways to learn, to live, to serve our Lord and all mankind.

Epilogue: Approaching Berry's Centennial (2002 A.D.)

Dr. Gloria Shatto
Dr. Shatto looked at Berry with
The eyes of an economist.
It was as though her task was to polish
The silver platter on which the Schools
Were handed her.
There must be change for progress,
But not all change is necessarily good.
Thus, there were times of trial and success,
And there were times of error.

Gloria liked statistics, reports, ratings—
And Berry did not disappoint her.
Scholarship, athletics, beautification
All were ranked superior.
Seasoned faculty and alumni in key places saw to that.

Truett Cathy took
What was left from the Academy
And fashioned it into new
Opportunities for education.
O.W. Rollins tried to salvage the sinking lake,

And supported new ventures in agriculture and
renovations.

Courses were updated to fit the modern world.
Another library addition was built.
Romans continued to be better neighbors
As old animosities died away
And new friendships flourished.

Estates of people of the past, such as Macy and Campbell,
were settled.
Business and alumni prospered,
With Berry receiving admirable shares.

So sad it was that Dr. Shatto's health slipped away,
And, after eighteen years,
Another president needed to be found.

As always in the past, Martha Berry turned to prayer.
"Prayer changes things," she often said.
She liked strong men. There should be one
Ready to guide the students she so loved.

Dr. Scott Colley
As if waiting in the wings, this scholar, gentleman,
This strong Scott Colley came upon the stage,
A lover of the land and learning, he stepped forth
graciously,
A friend to all.

With respect for the past, with future plans,
With quiet understanding, he renewed,
Revived, revised the dreams of Martha Berry.
Sinkholes in the land
Did not lead to sinking spirits, rather to
A sensible assessment of the tasks at hand.

With appreciation, admirable attitude, he sets his goals;
He speaks his thoughts.

So, as the curtain of 2002 rises higher,
So do the dedicated plans of Berry rise
With new support and leadership—
A place where all can study, pray, and work
To build a better Berry,
To bring about a better world.

— EHP

Evelyn Hoge Pendley, associate professor of English emerita, Berry College, is a 1938 graduate. She was married to Dr. Walter Pendley (deceased), also a Berry graduate.

Berry College Centennial—2002

Goals of the Centennial Planning Committee:

Reflection on the college's past and articulation of our vision for its future.

World awareness of our unique mission of education of the head, the heart, and the hands of our students, and of our commitment to service.

World awareness of our distinctive academic program.

Participation by all college constituencies in this celebration.

Collaboration with Berry's capital campaign committee, which is tying its efforts to the Centennial.

Some events planned for the Centennial:

Centennial banners flown on our campus and in city of Rome throughout the year.

Founder's Day, January 13.

Alumni Weekend, May 31–June 2.

Mountain Day Weekend, October 4–6.

Performance of "Voices of the Past" by alumni.

Recognition of 100 Hours of Community Service performed by alumni and members of the college community.

Centennial Lecture Series.

Centennial Concert Series; performance of anthem composed by Dr. Stanley Pethel.

Several performances of "Martha!" (musical drama) written by alumnus James Way.

Student essay contest and tee-shirt slogan competition.

Regilding of Memorial Library dome.

Publication of *Martha Berry, Sketches of Her Schools and College.*

Publication of *Berry Alumni Centennial Directory.*

Publication of *Berry Trails, Centennial/Third Edition.*

Faculty Academic Tenure

Berry College

Introduction

Academic tenure denotes a relationship between certain members of an academic staff and the institution itself. Simply stated, it is the assumption on the part of each that the contract of employment will be continuous from year to year. Certain advantages accrue to each party from the tenure relationship. The advantages to the staff member are (a) economic security and (b) the recognition of professional status. The advantages to the institution are (a) to improve staff procurement through a more attractive employment contract and (b) to encourage the permanency of desirable staff members. Of advantage to both the staff member and the institution are the benefits derived from long-range planning and research made possible and encouraged by the tenure status.

The Tenure Plan

I. Establishment. A systematic and permanent tenure program is hereby established for Berry College, effective July 1, 1957.

II. Participation. The tenure program shall apply to full-time ranked academic and library personnel. Tenure shall not apply to the administrative assignment of ranked academic and library personnel. Tenure shall not be applicable to persons who have reached "normal" retirement age.

III. Probationary Period. The probationary period of employment is established as follows:

A. Three academic years at Berry College for the ranks of Assistant Professor, Associate Professor, and Professor.
B. Five academic years for rank of Instructor.

IV. Initial Application of Plan. In making appointments for the initial year of this tenure program, the Board of Trustees will pass in each individual case upon whether or not tenure is to be granted to presently employed faculty members who are eligible for tenure consideration under the provisions of this plan. Faculty members eligible to be considered for tenure, initially or in the future, may be employed "without tenure" by action of the Board of Trustees for additional probationary years.

V. Notice of Intent Not to Renew Contract of Faculty Members on Probationary Appointments. Berry College shall give at least three months' written notice of its intent not to renew the contract of faculty members on probationary appointments. However, in no case shall notice be given later than April 1. The same procedure stated in Paragraph VI to be used for terminating the contracts of persons on tenure shall be used for terminating before the expiration of the contract of a faculty member on a probationary appointment.

VI. Procedure for Termination of Contracts of Personnel on Tenure.

A. Termination shall be only for one or more of the following causes:

1. Incompetence.
2. Moral turpitude.

3. Financial exigence of Berry College, demonstrably bona fide.

B. The process of terminating contracts of personnel on tenure shall be:

1. A statement of charges, in writing, shall be presented to the accused by Berry College.
2. If the accused desires a hearing, he must request it within ten days. The date for the hearing shall be set not sooner than thirty days nor later than ninety days from the date of the request for the hearing.
3. Any hearing shall first be conducted by a committee composed of nine members of the faculty of Berry College as defined in Section II. Six members of this committee shall be elected by the college faculty and three members shall be appointed by the President.
4. The recommendation of the faculty committee shall be reviewed by the President, and by the Board of Trustees as it sees fit.
5. The accused shall have the privilege of counsel at the hearing and at the reviews.
6. If he so desires, the accused shall be heard in his own defense by all bodies that take action in the case.

Approved by the Board of Trustees on May 25, 1957.

The Berry Schools

Proposed for Tenure, July 1, 1957

Name	Rank	Years of Service
Ruth Clendenin	Instructor	20
Garland Dickey	Associate Professor of Physical Edu. & Soc. Sci.	10
Ralph E. Farmer	Associate Professor	12
Elizabeth Mayes	Professor	6
L. E. McAllister	Professor	25
Willis N. Pirkle	Associate Professor	12
Ollie M. Scoggins	Assistant Professor	5
Alta Sproull	Associate Professor	31
Joe Stone	Associate Professor	12
G. D. Wilson	Associate Professor	4

Samuel Henry Cook

Dean Emeritus of Berry College
(1887-1975)

Dr. Samuel Henry Cook, dean emeritus and advisor to the president of Berry, died of cancer at 3:55 p.m. August 7, at McCall Hospital in Rome. He was 88. Born on February 9, 1887, in Brunswick, Georgia, he was the son of the late Samuel Henry and Virginia Ralston Cook. He was awarded the Bachelor of Arts degree with honors, the Master of Arts degree, and the Doctor of Pedagogy degree by Davidson College, Davidson, North Carolina.

Dr. Cook was teaching gymnastics at Davidson in 1910 when the late Miss Martha Berry asked him to come to Mount Berry. For many years thereafter, Miss Berry introduced Dr. Cook to her guests by saying: "I wrote to the president of Davidson to send me a young man to teach math, history, English, athletics, stay in the dormitories to teach good behavior, preside in the dining hall to teach courtesy; a man who didn't have any bad habits—did not smoke, chew, drink or curse. I received this reply: 'Miss Berry, you will have to write to St. Peter for your man. There are no angels in this world, but I am sending you the nearest I have—red-haired Sam Henry Cook.'" Though Sam Henry Cook intended to be at Berry for only one year before going to divinity school, he remained for the rest of his life.

Miss Berry later called Dr. Cook "the most Christ-like man I have ever known."

No one can recall ever having heard him speak harshly of anyone. Indeed he was laconic, tender, and to the end rather stoic, never complaining of the pain during the last weeks of his illness.

At Berry, Dr. Cook taught English, mathematics, history, geography, reading, science "and just about everything except home economics." He also served as athletic director; coached basketball; played the organ; taught Sunday School and a mission-study class; helped found the Mount Berry Church, which he served as a deacon, usher, and treasurer; and once even led a window-washing crew which prepared the campus for a visit from ex-President Teddy Roosevelt.

Dr. Cook was a bachelor and contented himself with being wedded to Berry and the thousands of students he helped to educate. Perhaps his closest friend was Harvey Roberts, a former director of public information at Berry (and Berry alumnus) who shared everyone's astonishment at Dr. Cook's phenomenal memory. "If anybody came back to the campus 30 years later and 200 pounds heavier, he would know him," Roberts explained.

Dr. Garland Dickey, alumnus, professor and chairman of the physical education department and director of intercollegiate athletics at Berry, recalled: "Dr. Cook could sit in the balcony at church, look at the back of everybody's head, and tell who was absent."

Berry president Dr. John R. Bertrand remembers Dr. Cook as a "source of strength and inspiration." Shortly before his colleague's death, Dr. Bertrand recalled, "Annabel (Mrs. Bertrand), Dr. Cook, and I were having lunch together in Blackstone Dining Hall, where he had taken his meals for more than 50 years. As he counseled with me about some matters of concern to the three of us, Dr. Cook quoted from an author who was unknown to him. Almost prophetically, he said: 'In the last days when the Good Lord looks you over, it'll be for scars and not for honors and medals.'"

In accordance with his request, only simple grave-side services were held with interment alongside Berry College Chapel on August 9. He also had requested contributions to the S. H. Cook Chair of Mathematics at Berry College in lieu of flowers. His many friends, with the aid of Berry Chaplain Larry Green, decided to hold a memorial service of triumph for Dr. Cook in the Berry College Chapel on August 17.

The Berry Alumni Quarterly, Summer 1975, Vol. 62, No. 2.

TO: Faculty

FROM: Doyle Mathis
Dean of the College

DATE: September 26, 1991

SUBJECT: Administrative Reorganization of Academic Areas of the College

Over the years and from a variety of sources have come suggestions for improvement of the academic organization of the college. Included among these ideas have been references to the numbers of administrators and departments in relation to the numbers of faculty and students, departments with few faculty other than the department head, the inclusion of all department heads on Academic Council creating a large body with insufficient representation of "teaching faculty," and the lack of coordination among similar departments in planning programs and courses.

These observations, along with budget matters, have been considered as a part of the institutional-planning process; and the decision has been made to reorganize the academic administration in order to operate more effectively and efficiently.

The current 16 academic departments will be placed in four new academic units: School of Business, School of Education, School of Humanities and Social Sciences, and School of Sciences and Mathematics. Each of these four units will be headed by a dean reporting to the Vice President and Dean of the College. A new academic-organization chart is attached, although it may be further revised. The position of Dean of Academic Services is currently titled Associate Dean of the College, and the position is not expected to be extensively changed. Dean Ouida Dickey will continue in this position.

All 1991-92 contracts will be honored, but the positions of Associate Dean for Arts and Sciences and Associate Dean for Professional Studies will be abolished after this year. The title of department head probably will not be used after this year. There will be a need for some administrative assistance for the four deans, such as area or program coordinators to help with scheduling, budgets, etc. However, there will be fewer of these positions and more time allotted to teaching. The details will be determined during the next year.

The four schools initially will have a similar number of student majors, although the number of faculty will vary considerably. The schools with the smallest numbers of faculty have graduate programs and other special operations. Each school could handle advising for its declared majors. Each dean and one or more faculty members from each school could serve on the Academic Council.

Including similar programs within the same school should result in better coordination and less duplication of curricula. This grouping might also result in more interdisciplinary courses and programs and better utilization of faculty. Emphasis and recognition could be placed on each of the four schools rather than attempting to select a few programs from the many currently offered by the departments. Business, education, and the sciences could be emphasized for their own programs, and the humanities and social sciences could receive recognition for their major programs and also for providing most of the general-education courses for each of the other schools. Perhaps one or more of the schools might attract a donor who would endow the unit and have it named for him or her.

The new organization will begin to function October 1, 1991. The Associate Dean for Arts and Sciences will serve as dean for the School of Humanities and Social Sciences and the School of Sciences and Mathematics. The Associate Dean for Professional Studies will serve as dean for the School of Business and the School of Education. The relationships of the department heads reporting to Dean Ben Hawkins or Dean Barbara Mixon will not change this year from the present situations, except for the head of the Department of Agriculture, who will now report to Dean Mixon. Searches for deans of the School of Education and the School of Humanities and Social Sciences will begin now, and the new deans are expected to begin work next summer. Dean Hawkins and Dean Mixon are expected to continue to work as deans of the other two schools for next year.

These plans will continue to be reviewed and perhaps revised somewhat. Your ideas and questions are welcomed and your support during this time of change is requested.

Presiding Officers of The Board of Trustees

John J. Eagan	1903-1924
Robert C. Alston	1924-1938
J. Bulow Campbell	1938-1940
John A. Sibley	1940-1955
William McChesney Martin, Jr.	1955-1973
William R. Bowdoin	1973-1983
James M. Sibley	1983-1989
H. Inman Allen	1989-1995
H. G. Pattillo	1995-2000
William B. Johnson	2000-Present

Presiding Officers of The Board of Visitors

Ben Gilmer	1969-1972
Roy Richards, Sr.	1972-1975
William E. Reid	1975-1977
MacDonell Tyre	1977-1979
Edwin Dodd	1979-1981
William Stokely III	1981-1983
David C. Garrett, Jr.	1983-1985
R. Earl Roberson	1985-1987
John Lie-Nielsen	1987-1989
J. T. Parker, Jr.	1989-1991
E. L. Baker	1991-1993
W. Joseph Biggers	1993-1995
Roy Richards, Jr.	1995-1997
Colleen Nunn	1997-1999
Leila E. Trisman	1999-2001
Ted Owens	2001-2003

Chief Administrative Officers

Martha Berry, Director	1902-1942
G. Leland Green, President	1926-1944
M. Gordon Keown, Acting Director	1942-1944
William Jesse Baird, President	1944-1946
James Armour Lindsay, President	1946-1951
S. H. Cook, Acting President	1951-1953
Robert S. Lambert, President	1953-1955
William McChesney Martin, Acting President	1955-1956
John R. Bertrand, President	1956-1979
Gloria M. Shatto, President	1980-1998
Scott Colley, President	1998-Present

Chief Academic Officers Of The College

G. Leland Green	1926-1944
S. H. Cook	1944-1957
O. N. Darby	1957-1959
Robert C. Whitford	1959-1960
John R. Timmerman	1960-1969
Thomas W. Gandy	1969-1971
William C. Moran	1971-1975
Doyle Mathis	1975-2000
Thomas E. Dasher	2000-Present

Part III

Selected Writings and Speeches

Uplifting Backwoods Boys in Georgia

Early History of the Berry School

Wash Day

Speech of Theodore Roosevelt

Miss Berry's Comments to Students, Founder's Day 1925

Lifters Not Leaners

Education and Opportunity in the South

Tributes by Notable Persons

Uplifting Backwoods Boys in Georgia

How the Poor Whites in the Pines Were Awakened to the Need of Progress—Children Taught to Scrub, to Cook, to Farm, to Build Houses, to Save Money—Boys Who Built an Industrial School and Who Learned in it How to Live—a Record of Experience

By Martha Berry

I have always lived on a plantation in the northwestern part of Georgia. The poor people of the neighboring hills and piney woods had often appealed to my sympathy, but I had never thought seriously of their condition, or really tried to do anything for them, until one Sunday afternoon in the spring, about six years ago. On this particular Sunday afternoon, I was in a little cabin which I had fitted up as my "den," enjoying, all alone, the freshness and delight of the spring beauty and blossoms by which I was surrounded. I suddenly became aware of three little faces peering in at me from the window. They were bright faces, and the unspoken longing that I saw in them caused me to throw aside my book, to go forward, and to speak to them. But they were very shy, these three little "poor white" children, and it was only by tempting them with apples that I could coax them to come into the cabin and talk to me. After I had gained their confidence, I remembered that it was Sunday, and I began to tell some Bible stories. They had never heard any of these stories before, and they listened with an almost pathetic eagerness. Their bright faces, their keen interest, and their need of knowledge so touched my heart that I told them to come back again the next Sunday, and to bring all their brothers and sisters, and I would tell them more stories out of the Bible.

My own interest was now keenly awakened. After this, the children came regularly to my little cabin from Sunday to Sunday, bringing not only their brothers and sisters, but their mothers and fathers as well—often with an accompaniment of dogs, and of babies in arms—all gathered together in the one room, shy, but eager to listen and to learn. The only music that we had at our meetings, besides our own voices, came from an antiquated little melodeon, which, while I played it, was held up by several of the small, bright-eyed, bare-footed children, whose interest was so great that there was usually a scramble to hold the broken pedal, or to support its feeble frame. These exercises were exceedingly simple. One song book was enough for us all. So few of them could read or write that it was necessary for me to "line out" every hymn until it became familiar. My congregation grew so rapidly that soap-boxes, skins, shuck-mats, and even the doorsill, were all used as seats. The average attendance was from thirty to forty every Sunday. The shuck-mats were made by the country people, and brought as gifts to the cabin.

I took long walks with these children in the piney woods, told them about the different varieties of plants, mosses, ferns, and wildflowers, and the names and habits of many of the birds, insects, and butterflies. Their interest in everything that I told them, and their quick intelligence, encouraged me to continue the work. Very soon they began to bring all sorts of things to decorate our cabin, such as grasses, leaves, ferns, and even wasp nests and colored stones, which they would arrange according to their fancy.

It was not long before I began to visit these people in their homes. I would ride my pony for miles through a zig-zag path in the resinous woods, leading up to some isolated little cabin. The whole family would come out to welcome me. And these words grew quite familiar: "Yonder comes the Sunday Lady! Hitch yo' nag and 'light—'light and come in. We-uns be pow'ful proud to see you!"

It was not always easy to "light and come in," because the doorway was usually blocked with dogs, cats, chickens, and a tow-headed baby, lying serenely happy in the sunshine, in a crude wooden box which did duty for a cradle. My appearance among the children was always the signal for a rush, pell-mell, to the dilapidated old well. This pleased me very much, and it showed that my admonitions to wash and be clean were literally carried out. There was always a scramble among them to get possession of the family tin basin. Then, after a hasty dip, they would come forward, one after another, to give a loving greeting to the "Sunday Lady," their bright little faces and caressing hands shining and dripping with water.

These cabin homes are built of rough logs and the interiors of most of them are smoked and dark, and, some of them, none too clean. They are usually lighted by one or two small window-openings, but with cracks and crevices large enough for a dog of fair size to leap through. An old musket, strings of red and green peppers, and a miscellaneous collection of herbs decorate the rafters, and pots and pans are usually scattered about the floor of the one living-room. The only other room is a small "lean-to," adjacent to the cabin proper, used as a bedroom. As the cabin door always stands open, there is, fortunately, plenty of ventilation, and the children live in the open air all the year. But the people are poor—some very poor; and they have no money to educate their children, or to have them trained to useful work or remunerative labor, even when both parents and child are willing and know the value of training.

During one of these visits, my simple desire to do something for their betterment became a determined resolution to devote my entire time and means to teach them the way to help themselves. I saw that they needed only opportunities and a guiding hand to make them useful and successful men and women. They needed to know how to scrub, to cook, to care for their rooms, to dress neatly, to farm, to build houses, to save money—in short, to do the practical things of life in the best possible way.

From the little cabin school on the plantation, which had had its beginning in my "den" on a sunny Sunday afternoon, we moved to a place half a mile away, which my father had given to me when I was a child. Here we built a house of one large room, the rough lumber from the mill costing me $100, the men and boys doing most of the work. When this was finished, the county gave me a teacher for five months, and I paid the teacher to stay another month. I paid the teacher something extra to visit the pupils, to investigate needs and condition of each family, and their ability to pay for books and old clothing; and, also, to lend books from house to house, and to see that they were returned in proper condition. I even supplied the school with umbrellas and wraps, so that the children could come in bad weather. The school soon so increased in numbers that the one-room frame building had to be enlarged. As the work increased in a corresponding measure, my sister, Miss Frances Berry, helped me in the sewing-school for the girls, in a debating club for the boys, and in training the pupils to sing. It took all of the teacher's time and a great part of the time of my sister and myself to manage this school, to visit the sick, the tardy or the offended pupils, and to stimulate and to keep alive their interest and attendance.

Some of our pupils living eight miles away from the schoolhouse begged us to come and start a Sunday school at a place called "'Possum Trot." Encouraged at this show of interest, we found an abandoned schoolhouse at "'Possum Trot," and we immediately took possession, and opened a school. The first Sunday that I taught there, the roof leaked so badly that my muslin dress was wet. I told the people that we must have a new roof by next Sunday. Some of them answered that, "it mought not rain for a month." I said "yes—but it 'mought!'" I then told the men that, if they would get the boards, I would bring the nails, and that everybody who worked on the house would be treated to lemonade. The house was covered and ready for use by the next Sunday.

In the same way, we opened a day school supplementing the five months' term by an extra month, and supplying the school with an organ and a library of fifty books, requiring the teacher to hold a meeting on Saturday afternoons to introduce the people to the books. As our efforts were now meeting with so much success, we decided to open another school at a place called Mt.

Alto, where we repaired an old house, whitewashed it, and made it attractive with photographs, an organ, and books. My friend, Miss Elizabeth Brewster, a graduate of Leland Stanford University, now offered to give me her services in the furtherance of my work; and, shortly after the school was in progress at Mt. Alto, we opened still another twenty miles away, at Foster's Bend. This was a very isolated spot; but, as the needs of the people who lived there were so much greater than in our other fields of effort, we soon built up a fine school, which reached many more people in the surrounding country than we had anticipated. After four years of work and effort among these poor white people in the schools and in their homes, the results, while gratifying and hopeful, were still not what I desired. Their home influences were not always in sympathy with our school work; and the vacation was so long that they lost much of what we had given them.

Turn-of-Century class (ca 1900)

With the schools that I have described all organized and in good working order, there was still a need which I wished to meet—the need of helping the condition and the restricted advantages of the poor white country boys. To do this, in January, 1902 [This land was deeded to Boy's Industrial School in April 1903.], I deeded a plot of eighty-three acres of ground near Rome, Georgia, and erected a two-story building at the cost of $1,000, and, with the assistance of Miss Brewster, opened an industrial school for the boys of the surrounding rural districts. We built a modern dormitory, a kitchen, a dining hall, and a library. These were soon followed by a workshop, a laundry, a dairy, and an additional dormitory, built by myself and a few friends. Every boy was required to pay $5 a month for his board and tuition, or its equivalent in work or farm produce. He was required also to work two hours a day, doing any kind of work that he was called upon to do. They scrubbed, cleaned, cooked, washed, farmed, and did carpenter's work, much of which was new to them, and it took much patience to teach them to do all this with thoroughness and promptness. A neighboring carpenter was engaged a few days in every week to come and to direct the boys in putting up a workshop, a laundry, and a barn. We have no hired help, the boys doing willingly and cheerfully everything about the place, such as building fences, grading roads, and clearing land. As an example of sincere industry and real interest in their work, the following incident is an excellent illustration: Having an invitation to attend a Sunday school several miles from the school, one of the boys asked me to take dinner with his mother, who lived near. On Saturday, Ben came to me with a request to go home on that day. When I asked why he wanted to go then, he said, "Well, you know, I wrote and asked Ma to have the house all cleaned up when you got there, but I'm afraid she don't know how, so I want to go and get it all scrubbed up before you come." When I arrived the next day, Ben had scrubbed with so much vigor that the floors were quite damp, and his mother told me that since Ben had been going to the industrial school "he'd rather scrub than eat!"

As a result of what they have learned, several of our pupils are now working at the carpenter's trade and receiving $1.50 a day, while others are doing more intelligent farm work. The fence corners are cleaned out, the fences are repaired, and their farms are still in better cultivation than heretofore. My brother, Mr. Thomas Berry, is the director of the school farm.

Three of our young men have a first-grade license to teach in the county schools, and one of them is doing good work in a most neglected spot. The first thing he did was to scrub the floor of the schoolhouse, to wash the windows, to put strips around the house so that the pigs could not get under it, and to mend the broken chairs and benches. He got every child of school age in the neighborhood into his school, and he is a competent and very enthusiastic teacher.

Another instance of the practical results of the training of our school came to me last spring in a letter from the postmaster at Rome, requesting me to select a young man out of my school to fill a vacancy in the post-office. He pleased me by saying that a young man who had had the discipline of our industrial school for boys would make an efficient assistant. The young man is now receiving a salary of $50 a month in a little country town.

Our boys and pupils understand that, as we have very little outside help in our work, it is of the utmost importance to work with economy, frugality, neatness, promptness, and thoroughness. As an example of how such discipline is heeded and carried out, we had a boy who complained of his assistant in the kitchen as being wasteful. He declared that he would "peel his potatoes too thick"—a thing which to his mind and teaching means a loss to him personally and to every boy in the school.

The home life of the school is also a discipline in social intercourse and in the training of gentlemen. At the beginning, I left my own home and went to live at the school. The teacher and the pupil are brought into daily contact in various ways. They eat at the same table, and they share the same fare, always of the simplest. In this way, an error or lapse of speech in conversation or in manners may at once be corrected without offense to the pupil, who almost invariably appreciates our efforts in this direction. They rise when I enter the room, they ask the blessing at table, they conduct the evening prayers and the singing, and they have been taught to be uniformly courteous and polite. One of the chief principles that we inculcate from the very first entrance of a pupil into the school is that whatever is worth having is worth working for.

Old clothes given to the school are sold to the boys, who pay for them by working on their holidays, at the rate of five cents an hour; a suit of clothing being sold to them for twenty-five or fifty cents. An amusing incident occurred, which illustrates, in rather a comical way, the good-natured, earnest willingness of the boys to work for what they get. Last spring a large box of clothing was donated to the school. In it was a sober bishop's suit of black

Martha Berry and students at Roosevelt Cabin

broadcloth. This was bought for the sum of fifty cents by a young man of twenty years of age, who was not quite stout enough to fill it. On his appearance in the schoolroom the next day, a hurried note came to me from the teacher, requesting me to implore the wearer of the big bishop's suit not to appear in it again in the schoolroom, because his rather imposing and decidedly misfit ministerial appearance awed the other pupils, and made it impossible for her to conduct her duties with her usual firmness and dignity. This was, indeed, a comical situation, and called for all my powers of diplomacy. I called the unsuspecting young man aside, and, after warmly praising his industry, I told him that the suit he wore with so much pride was too nice for school wear, and ought to be kept for Sundays and state occasions. He agreed good-naturedly and the bishop's suit did not appear in the schoolroom again.

At the close of our school in May of last year, the Governor of Georgia was invited to make an address and to hear the boys speak. The schoolhouse was crowded to overflowing, the people having come for thirty miles. One poor woman, who had parted with her only milk cow to keep her boy at the school, was among those present. Picture to yourself this poor white southern woman, this dear mother, who had sacrificed all she owned, to see her boy become an educated and useful man—sitting there, weeping, but glad and proud—as she saw her boy modestly receive the prize for the best speaking!

I have frequently been asked why I gave up my home of ease and comfort to work and live among these people. The answer is simple. The more I studied them, their poverty-stricken environment, their restrictions and disadvantages, their lack of opportunities and of education—the bareness of their home lives and the absence of pleasure—the nearer I got to all this, and observed their intelligence, their aptitude and their eagerness to learn and to acquire the arts of usefulness and knowledge, the greater the contrast appeared between their lives of toil and ignorance and my own life of ease and plenty, of opportunities and knowledge undreamed of by them. Finally, the resolve was born to give my time and means to educating and uplifting these poor white people of my own State, and to trying through simple, industrial and educational methods to make them useful and respected citizens.

The aim of my institution is, as I have tried to show, to meet the educational and industrial needs of the poor white country-boys of Georgia; to reach the children of the farmers and the toilers, and teach them useful and remunerative trades and ways of making a living, to make them independent, thrifty, and self-respecting. But, while we have met with great success and encouragement, our needs are still very great. Last year we had seventy [new] pupils—boys ranging in age from twelve to twenty-three years—with 100 of the same class enrolled for another term, and daily applications of many more. We need more room, more teachers, and money to pay the teachers. We have only four teachers, including myself. We wish to enlarge the scope of our work, and to make it possible to accommodate and give the advantages of the school to all the earnest, bright, ambitious boys and young men of the section and State who apply to us for tuition and the privilege of working their way into useful citizenship.

Having lived for more than two years in the school, and coming into daily contact with all the pupils, I feel sure of the practical results of the undertaking; and I believe the boys trained in this school will make some of the most valuable citizens in all of our great country. I have lived and worked for and among these people for six years, and I feel that an industrial school, on their own ground and in their own State, is of untold value. I have entered into their joys and sorrows, and I have studied the problem on all its sides, and I believe that the work I have been engaged in for the past seven years of my life is a plain and practical solution of that problem.

The World's Work, July 1904, VIII, pp. 4986-4992.

Early History of the Berry School

The question is invariably asked "How did you happen to start a school with character?" The answer is that it grew out of a Sunday school. Though the beginning of the school dates from January 13, 1902, its real beginning is somewhat further back. For a number of years previous to the founding of an industrial school, I established and kept up several other Sunday and day schools in destitute places. In these little schools, I would often have to sweep the house and make the fires in addition to teaching and superintending the work. Such a picture as this would generally present itself—a crowd of men and boys spitting tobacco juice, huddled around a broken-down stove, littered with ashes. I would request someone to sweep up the rubbish and replenish the wood pile from the outside, but I would generally have to do it myself.

Feeling that the real need of the country and mountain people was a home school with refining influences, where we could teach them the dignity of labor and economy of time, this industrial school was started.

With five boys, we opened school. The first schoolhouse was rather unique in architecture. The middle part was put up of rough lumber, the labor being given by the men who attended the original Sunday school in the log cabin on my home place. Wings were added to the little white-washed schoolhouse until it was cruciform in shape.

From the very first, the students were required to do two hours of work each day in addition to their school work. Our industrial equipment was small. We had one horse, "Roany," known as the Sunday school horse, because he had done such good service in carrying me over the mountain roads to the various Sunday schools. We had one plow, a couple of hoes, a rake, two dull axes, and a mattock with which to dig stumps. Our cooking stove was too small for even our small family, so we had to supplement it by boiling a pot of beans or potatoes on the fireplace. After school in the afternoon, I would go out and direct the work hour, working with the boys to keep up their courage by example. We would offer a cake to the one who picked the most cotton.

As the school grew, we had boys of all sizes and conditions. One of the first things on arrival of a new student was to have him take a bath. I remember that one arrived and we thought it best for him to burn the dirty and ragged clothes he had. We had a time searching for suitable articles of clothing for him. A pair of my pants and a shirtwaist were pressed into service, and a near neighbor contributed the pants coat. After his scrubbing, Willie was initiated into our school, and the next day developed a case of measles which spread all over the school. It was a difficult problem to care for the sick, as we had not taken into consideration that sickness would befall us so early in the history of the school.

—Martha Berry

Wash Day

I told the boys that there was to be no hired labor on the place and we would have to do all of the cooking, scrubbing, washing clothes, etc. To wash clothes without any conveniences was a great task. Our tubs consisted of barrels sawed in two. These, with an old-fashioned scrub board and an iron pot out in the yard to heat the water and boil the clothes in, composed our equipment. One boy flatly refused to wash his clothes, saying that "he never had seen no man of any kind a-washin' clothes." I explained to him that if he did not wash his clothes that I would have to do it for him, thinking that if he was the kind of boy I thought he was that he would not allow me to continue long. He sat for awhile and cried out, "I'll wash them clothes, Miss Berry!"

A lady visitor came to see the school and took notice of the way we had to get the laundry work done, and she was so impressed with the earnestness of the boys that she gave the money for a steam laundry. There has never been a strike in the laundry work since.

—Martha Berry

Speech of Theodore Roosevelt

At The Berry Schools,
Mount Berry, Georgia.
Oct. 8, 1910.

I have been intending ever since I first saw Miss Berry to come down and see this school, not only for the sake of the school itself, not only for what is being done with you boys and girls here, but because I think that this school is an example that must be widely followed—I will put it a little stronger than that—in its essentials, be <u>universally</u> followed in the South, and in the North also.

It is harder to live for your country than to die for it: it is harder to do the little things that have to be done if you are going to be a good citizen. That is not only true as to good citizenship, but the curious thing is it is true in soldiery just as much, for a good soldier is usually a man who spends months of work perfecting himself in qualities that he shows for one day. I remember in my own regiment, during the Spanish-American War, having a young man of nineteen, quite a wealthy young gentleman who singularly lacked the training which you get here at this school. After three days, he came to me and complained. He said: "Colonel, I came and joined this regiment to fight the Spaniards, and here I am put to digging a kitchen sink!" I said: "All right, my friend, you go ahead and dig it well. We shall see about fighting the Spaniards later on."

I did not want anyone in the regiment who would not do a job at hand because he felt that he would like to do some bigger one later on. **Good citizenship consists in continually doing the duty there is at hand.** Every time a boy turns in and works so hard and intelligently that he helps his father improve the farm, or helps lift a mortgage off it, he is being a good citizen. He is adding his contribution to good citizenship. Every time a girl makes it a little easier for her mother or father, by herself doing something that otherwise the mother would have to do, she is being a good citizen. **Words are not of any value at all except as they are translated into deeds.**

My friends, I am going to do for you what I don't think I have ever done for any other audience; that is, to speak a little about myself, personally. Insofar as I have been a success, it has been absolutely and solely through doing the ordinary things that any man could do—but that nobody does, or that so many people do not do to the point they ought to. It is often stated, among my very intellectual opponents, as a matter of complaint, that I preach what is commonplace and humdrum. I do, and so I intend to do. **Honesty, courage, decency, tenderness and force, combined, they are all commonplace virtues, but they are essential virtues.** They are the main things that I want to see developed in the American man and the American woman, and, therefore, in the American boy and the American girl. I never got anything in my life by an unusual display of genius, or even by an unusual display of talent. Whatever I got has always come through doing a number of things just as hard as I know how; each of them perfectly ordinary things, but ordinary things that ordinary people do not do, or, at least, did not do to the extent that was necessary in order to make a great success through the doing of them. Now, the longer I live the less difference it makes in my mind what position a man holds so long as he does his duty in that position in the highest possible way. Take the soldiers of the Civil War. It is mighty hard for me to discriminate in the honor in which I hold the veterans who wore the blue and the veterans who wore the gray. There were, as a matter of fact, two of my mother's brothers who wore the gray in the Confederate service, and they were Georgians.

Now, here is what I think when I meet a veteran, when I meet a man who fought in the Civil War, just as I met three or four ex-Confederate soldiers this morning and, as yesterday at Knoxville, I met both Union and Confederate veterans. I have no real interest as to whether the man was a private soldier or a major-general. That does not affect the regard in which I hold him. What does affect it tremendously is how he did his duty as a private soldier or a major-general. **The important thing is doing one's work well.** When I think of my own children and wish success for them, the kind of success that I want is to feel that each of them will "be a lifter and not a leaner," that each will pull his own weight in the world and then have a little strength to spare to help in pulling the general weight of the world. Now, I say this to you, I speak thus intimately of myself and the hope that I have for my children, just because I want to impress you, to whom I am talking here, with an understanding of what I am about to say to you.

Miss Berry has always laughed a little because the first time that we met, when she told me about some of the books in the library, when she came to speak of some of the masterpieces of literature, I said, "Oh, don't get the boys to reading these. Eloquence does not amount to a row of pins unless it expresses earnest convictions that can be turned into deeds."

I remember when I first went to the legislature, a man gave me excellent advice on which I tried to act. He said, "Now don't get up and try to be eloquent. Any number of people can try to be eloquent but it doesn't amount to that. Think. Don't speak until you have something that you feel ought to be said, something that must be said. When you have made up your mind you have something that must be said, think carefully how to say it as clearly as possible. Then get up, say it and sit down." **Words are not of any value at all except as they are translated into deeds.**

Now that is why I believed at once so implicitly in the work that Miss Berry was doing, and the reception which Miss Berry told you I gave her illustrates just exactly what I have meant in some of the things I have stated to you already. Miss Berry turned up at the White House. There were quite a good many statesmen in the room. I looked at the letter of introduction and then glanced at the pamphlet about the school. Then, I saw Miss Berry at once, and, as Miss Berry told you today, when they tried to interrupt us I said, "Let them wait." I thought Miss Berry's work was a great deal more important than the work of the statesmen who were waiting to see me at that moment. Now, I don't mean to say but that some of the work of the statesmen is very important indeed, but it cannot be more important than this, and it is **very rarely as important.** As soon as I had seen her and heard what Miss Berry had done, I saw in the first place that she was trying to do the right thing, and in the next place that she knew how to do it. Now, bear that in mind. I am a busy man and I haven't time to talk of vague good intentions, but instead of the practical power to do the work. I haven't a doubt but that very many other excellent women have vainly thought that they would like to be as beneficent as Miss Berry has shown herself. They are good women and I respect them, but I cannot waste my time with them because they cannot turn the trick. There is another thing that I was much struck by at once. Miss Berry said that this school was being made a Christian Industrial School. They are going to raise a mighty poor crop of Christians, if you can't have decent houses and have the men and women lead decent lives in them. So you have got to have the school industrial. And, on the other hand, I think that the greatest industrial efficiency is a curse to a nation if those able to practice it fail to have and live up to the ordinary Christian morality. This school does both.

What this school aims to do is to train mind and body and what is more than mind and body—character. It takes you boys and turns you out to go back to the farm with the mind and hand so trained that you can do infinitely better on the farm; in addition, with the character that makes you resolute to do better, resolute to do better for yourselves, and at the same time to do your part in benefiting others.

If the effort of this school was to train you away from the farm and merely to give you higher tastes without the additional ability to gratify them by your own efforts and to lead more useful lives, if that was the purpose and the effect of the teaching in this school, I should not have come here. I would have nothing to do with it. This school trains the boy to go back to the farm and to do his part in making farming a skilled profession; making it a profession like the law, like any other profession. It trains the girl so that she can go back to the farm, and, as wife and mother, do her part, and it is a part even greater than the man's in elevating the home.

One of the least desirable features of our present-day civilization is that, while there are a great many big men, men of note, who were born on the farm, most of them do not die on the farm. Now, that was not so in the early days of this country. Then our greatest men were men like Washington, who lived and died a farmer; a man out in the open country; and the great majority of our most eminent leaders were men who followed the career of a man who makes his living from the land. I am very glad to see, as all of us are glad to see, a city grown up. If the growth of the city supplements the growth of the country, it is a good thing; but if it is a substitute for the growth of the country, it is a very bad thing. That is something I want you to think of. I want you to go away from this school feeling the pride—those of you who go back to live on the farm—feeling the pride that you ought to feel in following the profession which stands at the base of our whole land. We can get along in this country more or less well without almost every other type of man, but the one man whom we cannot get along without is the farmer. I regard this school as one of the influences which is going to place the career of the farmer on a higher standard of dignity, of usefulness and of reward. If a farmer is an ignoramus, if the average farmer is utterly ignorant, of course, the profession will be looked down upon; but you boys who come here and go away have nothing to fear in comparison with the men in other professions. But more than that, you are trained, not merely in the ordinary literary exercises, but you are trained in the handicrafts, so that when you go back you will have the ability to put the farm on a better paying basis and to make the farm house an attractive place in which men and women can live and bring up their children.

Now, those are two of the things that this school is specially designed to teach—to give you a training that will enable you to help yourselves. Remember—and I am sure, looking at your faces, that I do not have to say to you to remember—that each man has got to lift himself. I misread you, my young friends, if you are not straight Americans. You have got that spirit in you. **Now until a man can lift himself, he cannot lift anyone else.** If there is a being more utterly contemptible than another, it is the shiftless creature who has a taste for corn whiskey and tobacco and who spends his time at the cross-road store saying how he is going to pass some governmental scheme for helping everybody, while he himself can live his miserable life only because his wife takes in washing.

Your first duty is to handle yourselves so that you can afford to marry, and that you can keep your wife and children decently, and as they ought to be kept. A woman's first duty is to be able to do her part, to take care of the household, see that it shall be a fairly attractive home, a home that will keep the husband there instead of tending to drive him somewhere else, and that will give decent surroundings in which the children can be brought up. That is the first, but that is not all. That is the industrial side of the school. You must have the Christian side in addition. **In addition to helping yourselves you must steadily try to help others.**

The great growth, the real growth in modern Christian civilization has been the growth of the type of man who is both the strong man and the good man. Whenever you go among savage tribes, as I did last year, you find that the strong man treats goodness as a sign of weakness. That is one of the great difficulties we always have in first dealing with the savage. The moment you are kind to them they will think they can impose upon you and it is your business to make them understand that they can't. Now, as civilization grows, I mean true civilization, the only civilization worth having, more and more people understand that strength can go and ought to go with decency, with honesty, and with respect for the rights of others. I want to see you all here turn out to be able to hold your own. If you submit to an imposition, I do not admire you, I despise you. I want to see you able to hold your own, and I want at the same time to see you scorn to do wrong to anyone else. Pay heed to your rights. Do not allow people to impose upon you. Do not submit to bullying, but pay even greater heed to your duties. Not only be as scrupulous of the rights of others as to the rights of your own, but be a little more scrupulous of the rights of others, because you will find it necessary to be a little more scrupulous to the rights of others or else you will find that you do not pay any heed to them at all. It is a good deal easier to pay heed to your own rights than to the rights of others, being close at home. Begin by thinking of the rights of your mother, your sister or your wife. That is the most important place to begin, right in your own home. No man is a good citizen, if when he is away from home, there is a general breath of relief from the rest of the family. Handle yourselves so that when you come back to your home there will be joy and not anxiety. Then handle yourselves so that you do your full duty by your neighbor, the next man. Show yourselves the kind of men whom your neighbor likes to deal with, likes to work for, or to have work for him, or work alongside of. Be that kind of a man that the other man will not have to be forever wondering whether you are keeping up your end or not. Show yourselves good citizens in all those ways and then finally, my friends, show your good citizenship in other ways still. You here have exceptional advantages. It is your duty when you go back to communities in which you live to set standards of others. Take it in politics. You make it felt, by your example and by your precept, that the man who takes a bribe to cast a vote in any given way, and the man who gives a bribe, are creatures to be so intolerably scorned that they should be hunted out of American social and political life. We can afford to differ politically among ourselves, to have different convictions, [but] we cannot afford to differ on the question of insisting upon honesty in public life and in private life alike.

Honesty by itself does not make a good public servant any more than it makes a good man in private life, but without honesty, the man who is a public man is a curse and a menace. No community can afford to tolerate him. And without honesty the man is as thoroughly a bad citizen in private life no matter how able he may be or what other qualities he may possess.

I believe in this school because it was initiated and is being carried on and extended in a spirit which combines in an extraordinary degree adherence to a very lofty ideal with the most practical common sense in realizing it. I believe in it because it recognizes what are the prime essentials necessary to good citizenship in our people, and takes the boy and the girl and trains them in practical efficiency so that when they go out they shall go back to the farm and to the shop able to do infinitely better work for themselves, able to lift the profession to which they belong and at the same time also resolute to do their duty by their neighbors and by their State. Those are the reasons why I so believe in this school. Those are the reasons why I believe that Miss Berry and those associated with her have been doing one of the greatest practical works for American citizenship that has been done within this decade.

Now you boys and you girls, I want you to show your appreciation and this is the way you can show it, and the only way. Go back to the farm, go back to the actual industrial work and live your lives outside so that all who are brought in contact with you shall feel and shall heartily recognize the debt of obligation they are under to Miss Berry and to the Berry School for the kind of citizenship it has produced.

Miss Berry's Comments to Students
Founder's Day, 1925

I want to ask all the new boys, those who entered in the January term, to hold up their hands.

I think that everyone is familiar with the origin of the Berry Schools. I think of how I was sitting alone one Sunday afternoon in the little log cabin just in front of where I live, thinking and dreaming—when I heard the voices and laughter of little children playing on the outside in the pine groves. I called them in and in talking with them, I found they were children from 'Possom Trot, some few miles away; they seemed so neglected and poor, and I asked them how many brothers and sisters they had, and I found they were rich with brothers and sisters, some of them had eight, some had ten, and some twelve, and I asked them what they did on Sunday afternoon, and they said "narthin'" so I told them to come back to Sunday school next Sunday and I would tell them some Bible stories. And so they came and brought the fathers and mothers, the boys and girls, the babies and the dogs, and we had all these in one little cabin Sunday school. I loved that little Sunday school. I went every Sunday on horseback or walked over the mountain trail. My youngest sister helped me to teach and we did the best we could. We always managed to be on time and I never heard a complaint about Sunday school being so far. The weather was very hot and my mother made me a big white and black slat sunbonnet; it had some paste-board stiffening in it, and it kept my head from getting so hot. I have always loved sunbonnets, and for that reason, I love to see the girls in sunbonnets.

I saw there was a great need for these boys and girls to have a chance in life, and that somebody had to give something—and I decided that I had something to give so I took the deeds to the seven thousand acres of land which my father had given me, and I quickly saddled the old Sunday school horse "Roany" and rode into town to Judge Wright's office and asked him to deed this property to a school for the boys and girls in the rural and mountainous districts throughout the South who needed help; only those who lived in these county and rural districts and could not afford to go to school elsewhere, and he looked at me and said, "What's the matter with you?" I said "Why, I'm all right. I feel all right—don't I look all right?" He said, "You know women have a way of changing their minds. You had better go home and think this over; you know when you deed this property over to a school, you can't get it back. Your heirs can't get it; its gone forever." And I said, "Well that is just what I want, I don't want it back; I don't want my heirs to have it. I want the boys and girls of the rural districts of the South to be my heirs." Then I said, "Very well, if you won't make out these papers, I'll have to find somebody that will do it." He said, "Well, it can be done and I can do it." And so I had the deed made out and the school incorporated, and a strong charter drawn up so the trustees would have to be members of some evangelical church and the teachers would have to be members of some Protestant church. I have always tried to protect the school in every way.

The next step was to secure the lumber to put up a suitable frame building; we had a small frame school building, but no place suitable to place the boys, and so I went to a sawmill and hired a man—a Mr. McKenzie. He came and worked by the day. I always went along and watched the things as they were brought to help the boys put up a building, the first dormitory, and I was so enthusiastic over this building. We had cedar posts which were brought from away down the country and I went into the sawmill where they were cutting these cedar posts to see that the men did not let a piece of bark fall off.

We began this building in October and it was ready by Christmas time. We called this building Brewster Hall. This was our first dormitory and I thought it was one of the most beautiful buildings in the world. I had heard something about some discarded war material (this was about the time of the Spanish-American War) and I went up to Chattanooga and bought some cots, but they were not all good lengths; one of the boys was over six feet tall and we had to put a chair at the end of the cot for him to rest his feet on. I suppose that I was thinking of life in a little cottage, because I bought a small stove suitable for a small family. We had a little bell to ring for the boys to come to meals and to class and it made me think of how Miss McCullough, who taught me, used to ring the little bell for me to come to school.

Students at Brewster Hall (Brewster burned in 1920.)

I found I would have to have somebody to help me and so I wrote Miss Elizabeth Brewster and begged her to come and help me teach and so she came and said she would stay awhile—she helped me so splendidly and I sometimes feel that I owe so much to those dear teachers who worked so faithfully in the early days. I had charge of the industrial work and Miss Brewster took charge of the school. I helped to cook breakfast in the mornings. I tied a towel around my head and put on a big cook apron and I knew how to make very nice muffins, and so I made some hot muffins, and when the boys came to breakfast, these muffins were gone before they sat down good [sic]. I sat at the table with the boys; I remember one boy particularly. I thought he could eat more biscuits than anybody I ever saw, and I said to him, "Some day you are going to be a great man" and he said, "Why, Miss Berry?" I said, "Because you can eat more biscuits than anybody I know and I don't think it's all for nothing," and so he did go to the University of Georgia and is now the baby Senator, and a short time ago, when I was in Atlanta, I had the privilege of sitting in his chair, and so I was the baby Senator for a few minutes.

We only had a little white-washed school house over back of where Mr. Hoge's house is now and this little school house had been added to and built around, but I thought it was a great school house. We opened a school; it happened to be on January 13th; there were five boys. Only one of them was paying his tuition. The others were coming for accommodation.

We had a very hard time getting water in the early days. We had to haul water from home and sometimes the boys would forget to cover the barrel and the bugs would get in it or it would slop out (about half of it) on the way over, so I've really been thirsty for the Berry Schools and I've been hungry for the Berry Schools. We finally got a well dug over by the shed where old Roany stays. Part of that shed was the boys' wash house; they took their baths over in the shed and we sawed the barrels in two for tubs. We were continually having trouble with our well; one of the boys accidentally dropped a cat in the well and we had trouble with that trying to get a drink.

Never a day passed at the Berry School without prayer. We had prayer meeting every Thursday night over at the little white-washed school house. I asked Miss Brewster if she would lead the prayers and she said, "No, Miss Berry, you will have to do it." So I went over every Thursday night with the boys. We had a little path from Brewster Hall over to the school building. We had to go all around the pines, walk around the trees. We just had the tops of them cut off and it was a very zigzagged little path from Brewster to the white-washed school house. Still the boys never complained. I had all the boys to learn the 23rd Psalm. I have always loved that Psalm. I never hear it that I don't think of the early days of the school. I went out to a little one-room school in the mountains, with no door steps, and I found here an old man teaching some boys, and I brought some of these boys to the school. Gordon Keown, who has been with me for twenty years and Allen Henson, the first graduate of the Berry Schools, came. I wondered what these boys would think of this school. I said to the teachers, "These boys are going to be very critical." This old man that has been teaching them knows Latin and all kinds of foreign language and I am going to be very careful. The first thing Gordon asked about was the curriculum. I told him that we could take him square through the top of the house and up to the stars if he could go that high; we could teach him everything.

I thought it was the most wonderful thing when the Berry Schools lived to be one year old. I had had a vision, just like you young men and women have dreams, but it was a hard thing to bring it down to earth. When we were just one year old, a boy came in and brought the measles and everybody in the school had the measles, except one boy and I had to be the nurse. At night I walked the floor and wondered whether that boy would get well; I felt his head to see if his fever would go down. I wondered if I should send for his mother. It was such a responsibility to have that boy away from home. I used to keep a big bottle of castor oil and every time one of the boys got sick, I would give him a dose of castor oil. It was difficult to get a doctor; the roads were so poor and rough and we had no quick way to get into town; no telephone, or anything, but when the doctor would come, he would always say, "You did the exact thing." I have been anxious about the Berry School—just as anxious as a mother has ever been about her delicate child; perhaps more so, because a school is a thing that is never grown up. I just sat up and wondered if it would live another year. The little white-washed school house burned about this time, but we still had school under the trees and commencement time came. This was the first commencement. The mothers and fathers of some of the boys came, and we borrowed a tent from some Baptist people in Rome who were having a tent meeting, and I thought it was the hardest thing to have this tent, but nobody grumbled. Everybody was trying to make the thing go. We had five boys to graduate, and all of them had grand speeches. I thought they were the most wonderful speeches that had ever been in America, and when Gordon Keown came out to deliver his speech, everybody told me he was the grandest orator, and the people all wept when he said his speech. I said to the lady next to me, "Will you loan [sic] me your handkerchief?" She said, "I can't, I am using it." There wasn't a dry eye in the house. Gordon had a long speech about the strong walls of the Alma Mater—there we were in an old tent. It was pouring rain; everybody was getting wet and we had to hold the umbrella over the speaker, so if any of us were Methodists that morning, we were Baptist by the time it stopped raining on us.

When the Boys' School was ten years old we started the Girls' School; they had a little log cabin called "Sunshine Shanty," but it is torn down now and they had very little to go on and it was a hard struggle to live through those pioneer days, but we had a wonderful spirit. Mr. Hamrick wanted a school started for small boys and so we started the Foundation School in a little log cabin with the cracks in the wall large enough to throw a dog and never know anything had gone through. All the schools were started in the simplest way, without anything. The Berry Schools have been started without money, without buildings, without equipment, without anything. We had boys and girls who had the spirit of doing something, and I can look back at the splendid workers who were with me in those days.

On the twenty-fifth anniversary, I am going to write them a letter giving them a most pressing invitation to come back and see how the schools have grown.

But now we come to the twenty-third anniversary and we want to keep growing. We never want to be static at the Berry Schools. We had a great loss in the passing away of the President of our Board, Mr. John J. Eagan, and I am hoping that some day something will start in the way of a living memorial for him at Berry. I wish that we might start an "Endowed Day" for John J.

Eagan and each one of us give something until we get it up to $2,500.00. It is not how much we do, it is the spirit.

This morning while sitting in my office, I heard the patter of little feet and I looked up and saw two bright little faces at the door—two little children living on the campus; they came tripping over to my desk. Little Martha Berry Johnson said, "Miss Berry, I have something to give you for the Berry Schools," and she handed me $10.00. Then little Eva Margaret came to me and said, "Miss Berry, I have something to give you." She gave me $5.00, and this morning I found on my desk from Inez Wooten, one of my girls who has helped me so splendidly in the office, and who was of so much help to me on my trip to New York, a nice little note enclosing a check for $50.00. One of the trustees, Mr. J. Bulow Campbell, sent a letter with $5,000.00 for the Berry Schools on this birthday. I have several letters and telegrams from different former students and graduates.

Now I want the Berry Schools to be always known for its Christian spirit and for its willingness to serve. This is what I hope and pray, on down through the years to come. Some of you, I hope, will be at the 50th Anniversary. I want you to remember that that is what we want to do—to have a living memorial going on at Berry. Each one of you can help to bring Berry into its own—to make it one of the greatest Christian schools in the world, so that people will say when they come into the Gate of Opportunity, that this is holy ground. I thank you.

Lifters Not Leaners

Martha Berry Has Dedicated Her Life to 'Larnin' Southern Mountain Youth

By James Hay, Jr.

Here is the dramatic and moving story of a triumphant adventure in the launching of human beings upon successful careers. It is the story of a young Southern girl, an aristocrat of aristocrats, who brought to realization her dream, cherished from her twelfth year, that she would bestow the blessings of education upon the poverty-stricken boys and girls of the mountains near Rome, Georgia. It is also, therefore, the story of the Berry Schools at Mount Berry a short distance outside of Rome.

Because Martha Berry was a pioneer, because she had unconquerable courage, because she transformed every difficulty and obstacle into a stepping stone to victory, the Berry Schools, which she founded in 1902, now own more than ten thousand acres of land in the Georgia foothills of the Blue Ridge, with more than ninety buildings which house and educate every year one thousand boys and girls.

Because Martha Berry has achieved all this, she wears many honors and is internationally famous. In 1927 she won *The Pictorial Review*'s award of $5,000 for the greatest contribution by a woman, through individual effort, to our national life in letters, arts, science, philanthropy or social welfare.

Before that, she was given the Roosevelt Memorial Association medal for "distinguished service," and it was presented to her by the then President Coolidge. And before that the legislature of Georgia adopted a concurrent resolution "that the State does now recognize the splendor of Miss Berry's work, the fineness of her character, the unselfishness of her ambitions; and, in appreciation of her life work, she is now declared to be a Distinguished Citizen."

A little more than twenty-seven years ago Martha Berry, graduate [Martha Berry attended only part of one year and did not graduate.] of the fashionable Edgeworth School for Young Ladies in Baltimore and "finished" by travel in Europe, found herself through the terms of her father's will the owner of six thousand acres of wooded land and a small amount of cash. And she knew what she wanted to do with both the land and the money.

She deeded every square foot of her 6,000 acres to the Berry Schools. [Martha Berry initially (1903) deeded only 83 acres to the Boy's Industrial School.] She used all her cash to build a ten-room dormitory for the boys she hoped to have as pupils. She went to an old and kindly judge who had been a friend of her father and with his help incorporated the schools, providing for their ownership and control to be vested in a self-perpetuating Board of Trustees.

Then she went into the mountains to round up a dozen pupils, and straightway difficulty beset her. No belted earl was ever more stiff-necked with pride than the Southern Mountaineers. They hate outside interference in their affairs, and they shudder at the thought of accepting "charity." And this offer of the young aristocrat to give their children education smacked of charity.

Martha, full of enthusiasm, buoyed by indomitable resolution, argued, begged and pleaded. She pointed out that each boy would have to pay her fifty dollars in cash and fifty dollars in work each year, and that, as no mountaineer family had fifty dollars, it would mean that each youth would do $100 worth of work on her buildings and land in return for the privilege of getting a good academic education, training in modern scientific agriculture, and acquaintance with all those things which would go to teach them to live fuller, happier and more useful lives.

When the boys started their classes, doing chores, thinning out timber and working the land, Miss Berry saw that she must have more money to keep even this small beginning from degenerating into failure. She announced to her friend, the judge, that she would go to New York to beg the money.

"Martha," he said in a kindly tone, "you gave your land to this undertaking, then you gave your money, and now you want to give your pride. Will you have anything more to give?"

"I'm afraid not, Judge," the fearless young crusader replied, "but I wish I had!"

She went to New York, found friends with whom she had been at school in Baltimore, was introduced to many people and wrote hundreds of letters asking financial help. A financier to whom she had written sent for her, and when she explained why she needed the money, he gave her a searching look and asked her how her own salary was paid.

"So far," she said, "I have not been paid. There has not been time for me to get the pay I want for this work. But if you and men like you will help me to carry on, I shall be paid some day by the sight of boys and girls standing on a platform waiting to receive their parchment symbols of their victory over ignorance. I shall be paid in full by the knowledge that young men and women have struggled out of the mountain darkness."

He gave her another long look, and reaching for his check book, wrote. She had asked him for fifty dollars, enough to carry one boy through one session. Out in the open street, where the snow fell fast and the wind blew, she unfolded the check and looked at it. It was for $500.

"Dear God," she breathed, tears of relief and gratitude on her cheeks, "it is the real beginning!"

She went to New York again and again, and each time she brought back to Mount Berry more money for the Berry Schools. The third year ended, and her first graduating class, consisting of one boy, was ready to go forth into the world. Miss Berry invited the Governor of Georgia to speak. Other distinguished guests were expected. The class of one was the valedictorian. All was in readiness when fire destroyed the one school building then standing.

But she who had created the Berry Schools was not beaten. She hired a big tent and had the Commencement exercises, her first, despite the fact that the day was rainy and water dripped down the Governor's back as he delivered his address.

Martha Berry kept on, kept going forward. More and more boys came to her. One day one showed up leading an emaciated swine by a rope halter. "This hyuh's to pay f'r my l'arnin'," he informed the proud girl who greeted him. At the end of the third year she had twenty-eight boys in school.

One day Andrew Carnegie arrived in Atlanta to dedicate a new library. Miss Berry was invited to the banquet in his honor that evening, but, because of the crowd, she could not get to him. The next morning, still in her evening gown, because she had had no time to change, she was shown into the steel magnate's private car for breakfast with him as he sped northward. When he heard her story—a story which she told surpassingly well—he said he would give her $50,000 if she would get together an equal amount to go with it.

A year later, having raised almost all of her $50,000, she was to address a federation of women's clubs in Boston to ask them to contribute the remainder. But she did not make her speech. She had worked so hard, the strain was so great, that she fainted on the stage before her name was called. And that evening the president of the federation came to her bedside and said, "Don't worry any more, Martha. We'll see that your $50,000 is made complete."

Then, soon recovering from that illness, Miss Berry invaded Washington to see President Theodore Roosevelt. Once more she told her oft-told story, and Roosevelt said, "Tell me more." His secretary came in and reminded him that Senators and Cabinet members were waiting to see him. "Let 'em wait!" he retorted. "This is the real thing."

To Miss Berry he said: "You must have a school for girls as well as boys. As President of the United States, I can't help you, but I can introduce you to wealthy and influential men who can and will help you." Thus, in a short time, the girls' school came into being, and Roosevelt went to Mount Berry to speak to the student body.

"When I think of my own children and wish success for them," he said, "the kind of success that I want is to feel that each of them will be a lifter and not a leaner."

"Be a lifter, not a leaner"

When he was gone, the Berry Schools, by vote of the student body, adopted as their motto: "Be a lifter and not a leaner."

By 1927 there were nearly 400 boys and girls at Mount Berry. Today there are a thousand. They come down from the foothills and the mountains, from the coves and the hollows. Their parents have long ago learned to think of the Berry Schools as the one place for them to go. Some bring animals to make their small payments, some drag in hay or garden truck.

Some declare that they have nothing and with tears in their eyes beg Miss Berry not to turn them away. She never does. They all get that "l'arnin'" for which they yearn. They yearn for it because they have seen older youths come away from the Berry Schools and soon win through to substantial success as farmers or workers in other lines of country life.

And every young man and woman who graduates from there carries the image of Martha Berry enshrined in his or her heart.

"The spirit of Martha Berry," said a middle-aged man recently, one of her "old" grads, "lives in the lives of her boys and girls."

Roosevelt once declared: "Martha Berry's work is one of the finest triumphs in the development of useful living I have ever heard of. It is unique. Nobody could have done it except Miss Berry, because she had the capacity to make her vision come true."

President Coolidge said: "In building out of nothing a great educational institution for the children of the mountains, you have contributed to your time one of the most creative achievements."

Presented by President Calvin Coolidge

Countless numbers of the great men and women of the world have paid like tributes to the founder of the Berry Schools.

"I've never labored for honors or praise or medals," Miss Berry said a few weeks ago. "If these schools don't go on after I am dead, if they are not far more enduring than my own life, then I have labored in vain."

So, as she did twenty-seven years ago on her first trip to New York, she still "goes a-begging" in the hope of building up an endowment fund that will insure the perpetuation of this dream that grew out of a patch of woodland and a log cabin to its present imposing dimensions of nearly 100 buildings and its numbers of 100-acre model farms, each one of which is managed for three years by a graduate student.

Occasionally Martha Berry, white haired now and in her sixties, journeys back to the foothills and is the guest for dinner of some man or woman who, having got a full and rounded "l'arnin'" under her management, has married and established a home with children playing in the yard. Then it is that she feels repaid a hundred times over for all the battles she has fought, all the obstacles she has overcome, to make richer and happier the lives of "the people of the mountains." Then it is that, with eyes a little dimmed, she realizes how true was her vision and how splendid are its fruits.

And many a tourist, going to Rome, Georgia, drives out to Mount Berry where, seeing young lives being lifted out of the Slough of Despond that is ignorance to the conquering heights that are education and appreciation of the finer things of life, he pauses to write a check for Martha's endowment fund.

Her most irresistible argument is the sight of the youth to whom, for so little cost in money, she gives the things that are beyond all price.

Prepared for American Motorist, a National Magazine for Automobile Owners (draft of article from F. H. Robison, acting managing editor, August 15, 1929).

Education and Opportunity in the South

Martha Berry, 1935

When thirty-five years ago I began teaching a few children in a childhood cabin used as a playhouse, I scarcely envisioned coming today before this body of educators. I only hoped to somehow glorify simple people and commonplace things through education. That God through the years would be so kind as to turn that first log cabin into a great campus fifteen miles long, adding a hundred buildings of stone, steel, concrete and brick to our plant, I had no idea.

If you could envision us thirty years ago, a rather frightened group of people floundering along muddy clay paths between two buildings lost in the woods that I gave to the Schools. If you could only see us as we were, and then come to see us now, as your splendid president, Dr. Few, has done, you would marvel with me. Today we have four large and separate educational developments: There is The College, where we have some 500 students working to earn their schooling. There are two high school and grammar school groups: one for boys, and one for girls. There is the newest community school project, the Possum Trot farms.

Education to me may not be what it is to everyone. People have always had their heads, but they didn't use them. They had their hands, but did not know how to synchronize them. At Berry we are trying to educate head and hands. We are seeking to reveal the Glory of the Commonplace. It was just a simple step across the road from my home to Berry. It was a commonplace move to begin teaching. Yet today, we have 10,000 visitors annually; presidents, statesmen, and educators from many lands have given us of their time and praise.

We have lifted a banner to which the common people could rally, making for our Southland a People's College in the truest sense. We are not competing in any way with any other institution. Our boys and girls do not come from the homes of alumni of your great and famous institutions. Their fathers and mothers are the fine-blooded Anglo-Saxons of the hills of the South; men and women of great potentialities, but not educated.

If I were asked my reasons for Berry College, I would say that it is essential for sociological, educational and patriotic reasons inherent in a Southerner. If our Southland is to take the rightful place it deserves in the Sun, our educational institutions must lead the way.

Advancement of the South can only come through progress of all its people. We have seen a great deal in the past few depression years of trying to lift a nation by working only the topsoil. We know now that lifting up must be carried to all strata of society and all classes. The South, peculiarly enough, has a great unlearned class of the highest type of man and womanhood—the Anglo-Saxons of its highlands. Berry College primarily is aimed at these, seeking to infuse new life and hope into a stratum of society which must be educated if the South is to reach its inheritance.

I believe deeply that God grants us many gifts which must be conserved. Conservation of our boys and girls is far more important than preservation of our forests, our animals, or anything else. When we started at Berry, it was enough to teach grammar school and high school subjects. This Association aided us greatly by recognizing the work we were doing and for many years our high school was a member. Later our Junior College was a member of the Association. We have been thankful for this privilege; somehow our Gate of Opportunity seemed officially sanctioned by the South, a Gate through which 10,000 boys and girls have passed in the thirty years of Berry.

Today our College is the crowning achievement of my life, the realization that we can carry the boys and girls from first grade through all their Schooling, and finally stamp them, "an approved Berry product," at the end of their toil in books and fields and shops.

We prepare our students for a useful and fruitful life, training them not only in head and heart and mind, but in the spirit, seeking to so accustom them to beautiful and good things that indelible habits will be stamped into them. We are offering them a priceless education to all boys and girls of strong character. The weak drop out at Berry, but the strong carry on through. I feel that our seasoned young people have the "right stuff" in them.

Education is not enough to me in teaching book lore alone. I feel that God gave us our hands to be helpful, instead of helpless. At Berry, we spend four days and seven nights a week with books, and two days at work—working in the fields, the orchards, the dairy, the shops, the kitchens, [the] laundry, the cannery, or [the] brick plant. They all learn to cook and to serve meals; to efficiently plan hours of study and play. Our Memorial Library is one of the busiest places at Berry, with an overturn of books that many larger libraries would envy.

Work cultivates a spirit of democracy and an understanding of life conditions sorely needed in America today. The Antioch plan, cooperative engineering courses and the recent New College experiment of Teachers' College, Columbia University, indicate that there is a definite trend towards requiring students to grapple with actual life situations before granting them a diploma. At Berry we are giving our students varied experiences on the campus, instead of sending them on hazardous travels to far sections.

We have critical inspections frequently in our dormitories, checking on conduct, on cleanliness and neatness. All students care for their own rooms. We have built up a faculty of strong Christian people, and I feel that by imitation and suggestion we will develop good character traits. Character-building must in the long run be the essence of education.

Helpful, hopeful Christians, patriotic, filled with a desire to serve their God and nation, of these America will be built. To this end Berry College is dedicated, that its boys and girls will go forth devoutly desiring to be of service to their country.

Culture may rest in the seeing and seeking of beauty in homespun.

Perhaps I have seemed to emphasize too much in speaking on education such things as patriotism, service, work, spirituality. I believe in all these things under those names, not disguised as something else. We are told by idealists that the end of education is culture. Then I feel that we achieve culture by teaching appreciation of homely things.

The poets surely have written their deathless sonnets of simple things, eternally cheap things; cheap like sunlight and fresh air, sunset and fragrant fruit blossoms in spring. The love and joy of primitive things, of native handicrafts thrills the connoisseur.

At Berry our faculty is drawn from many states, represents travelers in a score of lands and on every continent. The College boy and girl learn from them in the freest of academic discussions. We not only preach service, but seek to give it. All of our faculty members live on the campus, are of continual access to the student body, whose joys and woes are laid at their feet. The great medieval colleges and universities set this standard long ago.

This then to me is education, a vivid process of training minds and hands, of stirring imaginations, of creating character, of building souls and bodies fired with enthusiasm to serve God and country.

Henry Ford—a staunch supporter—with Martha Berry and student.

The Following Tributes to the Work Done By This School Are Selected from Many Which Have Been Received from All Parts of the Union

Dr. Thomas Jesse Jones, Educational Director of the Phelps-Stokes Fund:

"I am not interested primarily in Berry because of the splendid education it is giving the young men and women here. I am interested because there is being worked out here the kind of education which the whole world needs. While it is important to give an education to the young men and women of Northern Georgia and neighboring states, the great work that is being done here is that there is being worked out the type of education which can be used effectively throughout the world. In working out this type of education, Miss Berry and the officers of this institution have rendered a far greater service than just educating the young men and women of this locality.

"Education in other parts of the world is so ineffective. The comparison of what schools in different parts of the world might give with what they actually give, is disappointing; but coming to Berry and seeing this real interest in the realities of life is an inspiration."

Ex-President Woodrow Wilson:

"Will you not let me express my very deep interest in the school and all that concerns it. Mrs. Wilson had its welfare much at heart."

Ex-President Theodore Roosevelt, on a Visit to the School:

"I believe in this school because it was initiated and is being carried on and extended in a spirit which combines to an extraordinary degree of adherence to the very lofty ideal with the most practical common sense in realizing it. This is one of the greatest practical works for American citizenship that has been done within this decade."

William H. Taft, on Leaving the Presidency:

"One regret I have in leaving the office of President is that I was not permitted to visit the school of which I have heard such good reports. It is a hopeful sign when a cultured woman of the South surrenders her entire patrimony to endow a school for the mountain boys."

President Coolidge:

"In building out of nothing a great educational institution for the children of the mountains, you have contributed to your time one of its most creative achievements. You have built your school by faith—faith in your vision, faith in God who alone can make vision substantial.... Because of you thousands have been released from the bondage of ignorance and countless other thousands in the generations to come will walk, not in darkness, but in light."

William McAdoo, Former Secretary of the Treasury of the United States, on a Visit to Berry:

"I would rather have been the founder of this school than to have built the Hudson River Tunnel."

W. J. Harris, U.S. Senator from Georgia:

"Miss Berry, you have done more by founding this school for the State of Georgia than all the senators that the state has ever sent to Washington."

Hoke Smith, Former U.S. Senator from Georgia:

"I regard the entire spirit of this school as ideal. I am sure no better work can be done."

James R. Garfield, President Roosevelt Memorial Association:

"Seeing a great need, Miss Berry turned from the pleasant places in which her lines were cast to bring light and opportunity to children, who, but for her, would have walked all their lives in the shadow of ignorance. Her visions were born in human sympathy and given substance by the magical touch of faith. She is an educator who trains equally the head and the hand, the spirit and the heart. She is a builder who builds on rock, creating beauty where she goes, scarce knowing that she creates it, so natural an expression it is of the abundance within."

Chancellor Barrow, University of Georgia:

"The spirit and strength of the faculty and beauty of the location make it an ideal school for any boy."

Thomas A. Edison:

"I have heard much of the Berry Schools. I believe in a school where the students do the work, because in an especial sense it becomes their school—they belong to it and it belongs to them—and they put that priceless thing, their personality, into it."

Dr. Wickliffe Rose, Executive Secretary of the Southern Educational Board:

"I regard Miss Berry's as the best industrial school for country boys that I know. The school is also an object lesson to the public schools of the state."

M. L. Brittain, State School Superintendent of Georgia:

"I desire to commend in the strongest terms the work of the Berry School. As an example and inspiration this school is invaluable to the South."

Robert C. Ogden, Late President, Southern Education Board, New York:

"I have great confidence that Miss Berry is carrying on an educational enterprise that is inspired by a missionary spirit, and is also managed with consummate skill and ability. Her work cannot fail to confer lasting benefits on many worthy boys who otherwise would entirely lack opportunity for an education."

Dr. Albert Shaw, Editor of Review of Reviews:

"I do not know of anything in the whole South more interesting, more attractive or more worthy of hearty support."

Mrs. George Maynard Minor, Former President General National Society Daughters of the American Revolution:

"We are here in this world to be useful—to get things done—and I believe this school is doing some of the most worthwhile things for our country and our oncoming citizenship that can be done."

Clark Howell, Editor, Atlanta Constitution:

"I know of no educational institution in the state of Georgia, or elsewhere, that is doing better work than your school. I believe that a school of that kind established in every county in Georgia would do more toward the moral, educational, industrial and commercial development of the state than any other one thing that can be done by the state for the uplifting of her people and the promotion of her prosperity."

Mr. Fleming H. Revell, New York Publisher and Philanthropist:

"I was astonished, pleasantly astonished at what I found at the schools. I had heard much of them, but the half had not been told. I am interested in the work of two great schools of a similar nature, at Northfield and Mount Hermon, in Massachusetts. I must admit, though, that the Berry Schools have gone them one better. It is such schools as this that make for the regeneration of our country."

Excerpts from a booklet, "What They Say About Berry Schools," The Berry Schools, ca 1940s.

Part IV

Selected Letters

Letter	*Date*
My Dear Boys from Martha Berry	*June 25, 1907*
Dear Friend from Martha Berry	*No date*
My Dear George from Martha Berry	*October 22, 1908*
My Dear Miss Berry from Theodore Roosevelt	*July 13, 1910*
My Dear Miss Berry from Walter Johnson	*October 20, 1912*
Dear Miss Berry from Andrew Carnegie	*December 9, 1912*
My Dear Miss Berry from Ellen A. Wilson	*April 23, 1913*
My Dear Miss Berry from Woodrow Wilson	*November 21, 1914*
Dear Miss Berry from Booker T. Washington	*February 26, 1915*
Dear Miss Bostick from Martha Berry	*December 28, 1915*
My Dear Miss Berry from Bureau of Education (includes report)	*August 11, 1915*
Dear Miss Tarbell from Martha Berry	*February 26, 1916*
My Dear Miss Berry from Ida Tarbell	*March 29, 1917*
Dear Mrs. Hammond from Martha Berry	*April 11, 1917*
My Dear Miss McCollough from Martha Berry	*July 18, 1922*
My Dear Miss Berry from J. C. Penney	*July 3, 1924*
Dear Sirs from J. C. Penney	*November 11, 1924*
Dear Mr. Green from Mrs. J. O. Edwards	*January 27, 1925*
Mrs. J. O. Edwards from G. Leland Green	*January 30, 1925*
Dear Miss Berry from Juliette Low	*March 6, 1925*
Gentlemen from Asa Candler, Jr.	*July 3, 1925*
Gentlemen from Martha Berry	*November 4, 1925*
Dear Boys and Girls from Martha Berry	*December 1929*
Dear Friends from G. Leland Green	*December 1929*
Dear Miss Berry from William McAdoo	*December 23, 1930*
Dear Miss Berry from Franklin D. Roosevelt	*February 4, 1931*
Dear Miss Berry from Helen Keller	*May 9, 1931*

Letter	*Date*
My Dear Miss Berry from Mrs. W. K. Kellogg	*May 13, 1931*
Mr. W.K. Kellogg from Martha Berry	*June 17, 1931*
My Dear Miss Berry from Sara Delano Roosevelt	*November 10, 1931*
Dear Friends from G. Leland Green	*March 16, 1932*
Dear Miss Berry from Richard B. Russell, Sr.	*March 31, 1932*
My Dear Judge Russell from Martha Berry	*April 5, 1932*
Dear Dr. Berry from Corra Harris	*June 29, 1932*
Dear Miss Berry from Eugene Talmadge	*March 29, 1933*
Dear Miss Berry from Mrs. Thomas A. Edison	*May 9, 1933*
Dear Mrs. Ford from Martha Berry	*May 7, 1936*
My Dear Miss Berry from G. C. Sellery	*April 13, 1937*
Dear Dr. Sellery from Martha Berry	*April 19, 1937*
Dear Miss Berry from Walter F. George	*September 18, 1937*
Dear Miss Berry from Mrs. Laurence S. Rockefeller	*November 26, 1937*
Dear Miss Berry from E. D. Rivers	*August 15, 1938*
My Dear Miss Berry from Connie Mack	*September 26, 1938*
Dear Peter Marshall from Martha Berry	*January 24, 1939*
My Dear Miss Berry from Peter Marshall	*January 28, 1939*
My Dear Miss Berry from Mrs. Peter Marshall	*March 16, 1939*
Dear Dr. Green from Martha Berry	*September 14, 1939*
Dear Miss Berry from G. Leland Green	*September 15, 1939*
My Dear Miss Berry from Margaret Mitchell Marsh	*November 7, 1939*
Dear Miss Berry from R. W. Woodruff	*January 3, 1940*
Dear Miss Alston from Ralph Farmer	*April 18, 1940*
My Dear Dr. Green from Erwin A. Holt	*April 20, 1940*
Dear Mrs. Berry from Upton Sinclair	*February 13, 1941*
Dear Inez [Henry] from Clara Ford	*May 17, 1947*

MARTHA BERRY
FOUNDER AND DIRECTOR

THE BOYS INDUSTRIAL SCHOOL
(INCORPORATED)

ROME, GEORGIA,
25 June, 1907

My dear Boys,

I know you will be interested to hear from the BIS and to learn of the wonderful improvements we are making this summer. I am confident that next year will be the greatest in the history of the school and that we will have many new things and many good things to be thankful for.

I have been working very hard every day since school closed making talks in the interest of the work and writing many letters when I am at the school trying to make money to provide for the comforts and improvements I want to see made in our school. Then, too, I have been visiting various schools all over the country, but boys I find that ours is away ahead of most of the schools in every way. For instance, not a single one of the very rich schools I have visited has as complete and nice a bath-house as we have, and there are many other things that we have that they haven't.

We will have all of the old teachers, with the addition of one or two new men, who I think will prove a blessing to the school. They are men I have very carefully selected after visiting their school and seeing them at their work.

I hope it will be possible for every one of the old boys who love the school to return, as I feel those that have worked hard and have been faithful should have the benefit of the improvements we have made. I think of my boys all the time and earnestly pray that God will abundantly bless you in every way. I want you to have a nice, pleasant summer.

I shall expect an answer to my letter from each one of you telling me how you are spending the summer, and to state positively whether or not you will be on hand the 29th day of August to welcome the new boys to our home school. We have applications pouring in daily, but we cannot write and tell them to come until the old boys are given the preference. I cannot let them know then until a letter is received from you. I want to assure you of my sincere appreciation of your answer in advance. I may have to go off on another trip very soon, but Miss Neal will keep me posted how many of you think enough of my letter to answer it.

With your co-operation, we can all pull together and make this the grandest school in the South. I am counting on you, boys.

With every good wish, I am

Your friend,

Martha Berry

Miss Berry wrote her students and alumni frequently. This letter appears to be addressed to returning students

The Boys Industrial School

ROME, GA.

FOUNDED BY MARTHA BERRY

DEAR FRIEND:

Each succeeding year at The Boys Industrial School has witnessed continued growth and development. With this growth there have naturally been increased expenses. You are aware that our object is to furnish a Christian education to worthy boys whose means will not permit them to go to other schools. To this end our fee for board, tuition and all expenses is only $50 per year, which is but half the actual cost of each student. As we have no endowment to meet this deficit, we need the co-operation of friends who approve of the work.

We can accommodate one hundred and twenty-five boys next year, which means that I will have to raise about $7,000 to meet the current expenses of the year. To meet this sum I am seeking subscriptions of $100, $50, $25, $10, or any amount. No contribution is too small to be of use. We have also sought to meet our expenses by making a popular appeal to friends, who, owing to numerous local calls, are not able to give in large sums, but are willing to show their sympathy and interest in the work by smaller gifts. We wish to secure one thousand "sustaining members" who will contribute $5 a year toward the support of the work. May I ask your aid in our work to this amount?

We need a new dormitory, so as to be able to take the hundred boys we have had to turn away for lack of room, and many other improvements, and I am working very hard to try and raise money for this outside of Rome. In my efforts to raise money, it will be such a great help to state what friends in the city of Rome contribute towards the support of this institution.

When our school opens the third of September I earnestly hope we will have at least a part of this money in bank to meet the current expenses.

Yours sincerely,

Martha Berry

MISS MARTHA BERRY, Boys Industrial School:

I hereby give the sum of ....Dollars to be used for the maintenance of the Boys Industrial School.

Signed..........................

This letter inviting support was written to a friend from Rome.

THE BERRY SCHOOL
INCORPORATED
A CHRISTIAN INDUSTRIAL SCHOOL FOR COUNTRY BOYS
MARTHA BERRY, FOUNDER & DIRECTOR

ROME, GA., Oct. 22, 1908.

My dear George:

I am writing to all of my old boys to get them to send me a letter telling me just what they are doing. It will give me a great deal of pleasure to have a letter from you, and I want to preserve these letters in a book, so that when I am old and feeble I may refresh my soul by reading these letters from you boys and know that the world is better for your having attended the Berry School. It is not the big things we do but it is the little things we do that tell in life. If you are farming, tell me that you are trying to make a good crop. If you are teaching, tell me of your struggles and of what you are trying to do for the children entrusted to your care. If you are teaching Sunday School or using any effort to do Christian work, don't forget to put that in your letter. We have no endowment except our boys, and I feel that the old boys will be a living endowment far better than mere money.

I am looking to you to help hold up this school, and you know of the struggles I have made to keep this work going and to give the boys a vision of the best and highest things in life. I am sure that you will help me by answering this letter at once and telling me just what you are doing and what you hope to do, and also what it has meant to you to come to the Berry School.

I hope that you can come to us on Thanksgiving, for that is our home day for our old boys. This year we are making an especial effort to have all of our boys come to us on Thanksgiving, and we hope to make it a great day.

Thanking you in advance for your letter, I am,

Yours with all best wishes,

Martha Berry

A letter to an early graduate.

The Outlook

287 Fourth Avenue
New York

Office of
Theodore Roosevelt

July 13th 1910.

My dear Miss Berry:

I am having great difficulty about arranging to visit Rome. I need not tell you that it is imperative that I should use my time as economically as possible. It looks as if I would have to take the 5.10 p.m. train on October 8th from Atlanta, reaching Rome at 7.15, stay there an hour and forty minutes, and return by the train leaving at 8.53 p.m. Now can I see the school and make what speech you want me to make under these circumstances!

Faithfully yours,

Theodore Roosevelt

Theodore Roosevelt, 26th president of the United States (1901-1909), visited Berry in 1910.

Davidson, N.C.
Oct. 20, 1912

My Dear Miss Berry,

I have been thinking today of Berry and wondering how everyone is [there]. I know the faculty and students were very glad to have you back with them again after such a long absence. I hope that you were greatly benefited by your trip to Europe.

I thought I would get to see you as I came by Berry but I learned there that you had not returned. I was very sorry I did not get to see you. I certainly do miss Berry School and everybody there, but I am learning to like Davidson College and the fellows here.

Miss Berry, I haven't been able to see you since I finished at Berry and tell you what a great deal the school has meant to me, but will say now that I can not express in words what the Berry School has been to me. It was my home for nearly five years and it was indeed very hard for me to leave after I finished. I couldn't realize that I would not be back there this year until time came for the opening and I wasn't there.

I hope that this year will be one of the greatest in the history of the school and that great and lasting good will be accomplished. I remember you and the school in my prayers every day and trust that you will be able to carry out your plans for your great school.

Hoping you very great success in this year's work, I am

One of your boys,

Walter Johnson

Walter Johnson, 1912 Berry high-school alumnus, graduated from Davidson and served for many years as director of the Alumni Association Office.

Andrew Carnegie
2 East 91st Street
New York

Dec. 9, 1912

Dear Miss Berry:

What you are doing and have done in your school surprises me.

The boys should not have it alone and for the Girls' School foundation I will give you Fifty thousand Dollars if you succeed as you say you will, in getting friends to subscribe an equal amount.

I know of no better use to make of money. Success to you.

Ever yours,

Andrew Carnegie

An industrialist leader in the United States at the turn of the twentieth century, Andrew Carnegie contributed the earliest large gift to Berry.

THE WHITE HOUSE

April 23, 1913

My dear Miss Berry,

I am very sorry the pictures did not sell at Phila, but when I went to see them just after our lunching and saw for the first time what an out-of-the-way place they were in and how miserably lighted, I knew it would be so! They looked wretchedly in that dark room. "Better luck next time"! Some one out west wrote to ask for one of the small pictures and I am sending on the check received from him. With warm regards and all good wishes I am

Yours very cordially,

Ellen A. Wilson

Ellen Axson Wilson, first lady of the United States, 1913-1914, lived in Rome and is buried in Myrtle Hill Cemetery. She gave Martha Berry the income from some of her paintings.

THE WHITE HOUSE,
Washington, D.C.

November 21, 1914.

My dear Miss Berry:-

Thank you sincerely for your kindness in sending me the pictures of the young ladies who carried the beautiful flowers to Mrs. Wilson's grave.

Will you not let me express at the same time my deep interest in the school and in all that concerns it? Mrs. Wilson had its welfare very much at heart and, therefore, it touches me very deeply that the children of the school should think of her as of a true friend who has gone.

I am glad to find the name of the school spreading rapidly in this country and hope that as it is better known it will be more and more generously supported.

Cordially and sincerely yours,

Woodrow Wilson

Miss Martha Berry
Mount Berry, Ga.

Woodrow Wilson was 28th president of the United States (1913-1921).

BOOKER T. WASHINGTON
PRINCIPAL

EMMETT J. SCOTT
SECRETARY

WARREN LOGAN
TREASURER

THE TUSKEGEE
NORMAL AND INDUSTRIAL INSTITUTE
FOR THE TRAINING OF
COLORED YOUNG MEN AND WOMEN
TUSKEGEE INSTITUTE, ALABAMA

February 26, 1915

Miss Martha Berry,
Rome, Georgia.
Dear Miss Berry:-

As a partial recompense for not calling on you to speak before you left (and I fully meant to do so but did not know you were going to New York with Mr. Low's party), I am sending you the names of all the visitors with their addresses with the hope that you may interest them in your work. Perhaps some of them are already interested. Please do not use my name in any use you may make of the list.

I also hope you will consider this an invitation to come with any party that may be here next year.

We were so glad to have you and your secretary with us.

Yours very truly,

Booker T. Washington, African-American educator and author, founded the Tuskegee Institute in Alabama.

THE BERRY SCHOOL

FOUNDED BY MARTHA BERRY 1902

(INCORPORATED)

MOUNT BERRY

GEORGIA

December 28, 1915.

Dear Miss Bostick:-

I have just received your Christmas box and I am so rejoiced over its contents. How beautiful the oranges are and the red berries and moss. It looks too "Christmasy", and too Southern for anything.

My mother and I will enjoy them greatly and then I want some of the people at the school to see these beautiful berries and the lovely moss.

We miss you very much, but I hope and pray that you are better. I have been thinking about you constantly and have a nice plan in mind to get you well and strong.

We have had a quiet Christmas, but the boys and girls seem to have enjoyed it. I think many of them have for the first time sensed the real meaning of Christmas.

Hoping that your vacation will be a great benefit to you and deeply appreciating the splendid work you have done here, and with grateful thanks,

Sincerely yours,

Martha Berry

Miss Caroline Bostick,
Beaufort, South Carolina.

Caroline Bostwick established the department of home economics at Berry and later married Herman Hoge, Berry's first comptroller. They were the parents of Evelyn Hoge Pendley, author, two of whose works are included in this volume.

DEPARTMENT OF THE INTERIOR
BUREAU OF EDUCATION
WASHINGTON

JLM/NW.

August 11, 1915.

Miss Martha Berry, Principal,
The Berry School,
Mount Berry, Ga.

My dear Miss Berry:

I have been assigned the task by Commissioner Claxton of reviewing the progress in rural school extension for the school year of 1914-1915. This is to be a part of the chapter on Rural Education in the Commissioner's Report for 1915. I shall need this information from you at your earliest convenience, but it must reach me not later than September 15th to be of help in this review.

Please tell me what your school has done for rural life betterment that is worthwhile in such lines as (a) teacher-training, (b) better salaries, (c) a longer school term, (d) better school buildings and grounds, (e) consolidation, (f) more money for education, (g) the public health, (h) better conveniences for the farm woman, (i) correspondence courses of study, (j) extension centers, (k) lecture courses and entertainments, (l) community meetings, (m) rural life conferences, (n) night schools, (o) boys' and girls' clubs, (p) school fairs and educational rallies, (q) rural school libraries, (r) rural school supervision, (s) better agriculture, (t) land ownership, (u) cooperation in selling farm products and in buying for the farm homes, (v) rural games and sports, (w) the country church, (x) the rural Sunday school, (z) rural social life. [There was no *y* item in this listing.]

In the chapter on Rural Education, pages 110-115 of the Report of the Commissioner of Education for 1914, a copy of which has no doubt already reached you, you will find my review of what some of the State normal schools are doing in rural school extension. Have you such a department with a director in charge in your school?

Very Sincerely,

School Extension Agent.

Information requested by the school extension agent appears in the following report.

Report to Bureau of Education

1. The Berry School
2. Head of School, Miss Martha Berry, Director
3. School founded, Jan. 13, 1902 by Miss Martha Berry
4. Title to property vested in Board of Trustees (Incorp)
5. Self-perpetuating Board of Trustees--15--White
   Trustees present at meetings last year: 1st? 2d? 3d?
6. Teachers and Workers:
   41--White--19 male--22 female. 18 devote entire time to teaching. To other work 18. Teachers of non-industrial subjects 15. 3 agriculture 2 mechanical industries 3 domestic science
   Students do all work about buildings, campus, farm, shop, dairy, garden, etc. Student foremen in dairy, garden, and library under skilled supervision. 11 student officers responsible for discipline in dormitories at night. Teachers also reside in each dormitory.

7. Total enrolment -- 350 (at one time) no college work

	Grades	Boys	Girls	All Boarders
Grammar	1st	13		104 boys are getting
	2d	28		10 periods per week
School	3d	41		each of instruction
	4th	38		in either wood or
				iron work.
	Freshman	29		
High	Sophomores	23		
School	Juniors	17		
	Seniors	17		

	Grades	Boys	Girls	All Boarders
Primary	1st		6	All girls are taught agric., sewing, and basketry both in classes and by actually doing the work.
	2d		22	
	3d		23	
	Juniors		17	
	Middlers		14	
	Seniors		16	

8. Work and organization
   Industrial classes average 15 each. Academic about 20.
   All ordinary grammar and high school subjects (except Greek, modern languages and advanced Latin) also joinery carpentry, forging agriculture (4 yrs.)
   Practical work 2 periods per week in all agric classes; also 16 hours per week for at least 6 weeks of industrial productive work required to secure high school credit for mechanical or agric. classes.

It is the definite task of assigned employees to keep records of work of former students, to visit them and encourage them.

9. Three extension libraries are in circulation. Three Sunday Schools are assisted with teachers. Summer conferences are held as follows:

Teachers	1 day
Sunday School	2 "
Farmers and Families	3 days
Boys'	14 "

10. School plant:

Approximately 3000 acres. 250 cultivated by school. Most of it is woodland or is rented out in small farms. Campus proper is somewhat rolling, partially wooded, well cultivated and forms a beautiful park.

Buildings

Boys' Department	3 dormitories hold 67, 58, and 45 2 cottages of five rooms Hospital and Guest House 20 rooms Shop, laundry, cannery, dining hall seats 270, gymnasium, woodshed, store, dairy house and barns, recitation hall, science hall.
Girls' Department	4 dormitories hold 115 Hospital, laundry, dairy house and barn, practice cottage, chapel, science hall. Industrial cabin.

Teacher in charge of each dormitory with student officers as assistants on each floor. In boys' dept. students study in their rooms at night. Study hall is maintained for younger girls, smaller boys and a few who are behind in studies.

Recitation rooms fairly supplied with charts and maps. $500 worth of scientific equipment, wood-working benches for 18, iron forges for 18, and domestic science laboratory for cooking, sewing, weaving.

Special needs

Two pianos, Industrial bldg., and equipment
$400 scientific equipment Farm mechanics bldg and machinery.

New dormitory and new barns are imperative.

School community. Neighbors friendly and appreciative. Rome ladies now paying for model Practice Cottage at Girls School.

School Finances
Income

1.	Gov.	None
2.	State	"
3.	County	"
4.	City	"

THE BERRY SCHOOL

FOUNDED BY MARTHA BERRY 1902
(INCORPORATED)
Mount Berry
Georgia

February 26, 1916.

Dear Miss Tarbell:-

I am hoping that you will come South this spring and make us your promised visit. It will mean everything to us and we shall be only too glad to pay your expenses from whatever point you may be in this vicinity to have you come and help us by giving us a talk.

I am so anxious to meet Mr. Ford. I have never had a chance to do so, though I hear he is often in the South. I do want to get him interested in these boys and girls here, who are just the kind of Americans that would interest him. Would it be too much to ask of you to help me get him interested in some way to come to see us?

The work is growing and there is such a crying need of help. We are turning away so many for the lack of room; and just at this time it seems to me that we need to have as many boys as possible trained as efficient citizens to help our country. They are loyal to the heart's core, ignorant, but willing and anxious to be developed. I cannot help feeling that you will help us, and I would give anything to meet Mr. Ford and tell him about this work.

Mr. Earle Harrison has been here and has made a splendid set of pictures. I wish you would write us up and, perhaps, use some of his pictures.

Hoping that you will come to see us,

Sincerely yours,

Martha Berry

Miss Ida M. Tarbell,
1332 East 19th Street,
New York City.

Miss Tarbell was a journalist and author.

132 EAST NINETEENTH STREET

New York, March 29, 1917.

My dear Miss Berry:

Forgive me for being so slow in answering your letter of February 26th. I have been in the West on a lecture junket until a few days ago. I am afraid my visit South cannot come off this spring. The war situation has recently changed some of my plans, and then, too, I have a quantity of belated work on hand. I must go to Detroit at the time that I thought I might go to the Berry School. It is not impossible, however, that the visit to Detroit may in the long run be better for you, for I expect to be working for ten days or so in the Ford factory. I may not see Mr. Ford at all, but then again I may have a chance at him; and while to put a thing like your enterprise directly to him would be impossible, yet there might come a chance for me to interest him or Mrs. Ford. You may be sure that [I will] bear it all in mind, and if the time does come I shall take advantage of it.

With all good wishes, believe me,

Faithfully yours,

Ida M. Tarbell

Miss Martha Berry
Mount Berry, Georgia.

THE BERRY SCHOOL

FOUNDED BY MARTHA BERRY 1902
(INCORPORATED)
MOUNT BERRY
GEORGIA

April 11, 1917.

Dear Mrs. Hammond:-

I know that you will be glad to know that Dr. Pritchett was pleased with his visit to us and that he has informed us that the Carnegie Corporation has voted to give us the last $100,000 on the $250,000, after we have raised $150,000.

You remember at the meeting at your home Mrs. Ladd gave us $25,000 and we raised $5,000 then; and with our letters since then we have brought it up to something over $50,000, so we still have to raise $100,000.

I am so grateful for your interest and I feel that many good things have come to us from the meeting in your home. Would you please write or speak to Mrs. Carnegie and tell her how much you appreciate this gift. She wrote me such a lovely letter and told me that it gave her and Mr. Carnegie the keenest pleasure to have this amount given.

Dr. Pritchett was most enthusiastic about the school and I hope when you meet him you will talk to him about it. He told me he had a nice letter from you.

Won't you please pass this good news on to dear Mrs. Hope, and tell her I have been wanting to write her a letter, but we are having so many people visiting us from different schools, with so many things coming up that it is hard to find the time for the things I really want to do.

We are counting upon your visit to us next spring.

Cordially yours,

Martha Berry

Emily Vanderbilt Hammond, granddaughter of Cornelius Vanderbilt, brought numerous friends, called "pilgrims," to visit Berry between 1920 and 1962; the pilgrims became benefactors.

MARTHA BERRY
FOUNDER AND DIRECTOR

ROBERT F. MADDOX
(PRESIDENT ATLANTA NATIONAL BANK OF ATLANTA)
TREASURER

THE BERRY SCHOOLS
INCORPORATED
ESTABLISHED 1902

A CHRISTIAN INDUSTRIAL SCHOOL
FOR COUNTRY BOYS AND GIRLS

Mount Berry, Floyd County, Georgia
EXPRESS AND TELEGRAPH OFFICES: ROME, GA.

July 18, 1922.

My dear Miss McCollough:

I am counting on your aid and help next year. I have just returned from a trip to Mentone trying to make my mother satisfied and content with her sojourn there. I cannot begin to tell you how much you meant to the girls last year. The girls have told me so many times how much they love you and enjoy your teaching. We expect you to be with us next year without a doubt. We can make you comfortable and happy. Don't fail to be with us.

I cannot tell you how much it has meant to me personally to have you with us.

I am having a hard time this summer trying to make both ends meet. It is a struggle. I have been working hard in the office. I am leaving tomorrow for Western New York and shall try to make other engagements to speak. I shall have to put forth a great effort to interest the people.

Hoping that you will let nothing interfere with your being with us next year.

Affectionately yours,

Martha Berry

Miss Ida McCollough
Saluda, N.C.

Miss Ida McCollough served as governess for the Berry children and later assisted Martha Berry at the schools.

JAMES C. PENNEY
370 SEVENTH AVENUE
NEW YORK CITY

New York, July 3, 1924

Miss Martha Berry
Mount Berry
Georgia

My dear Miss Berry:

I feel heartily ashamed of myself, that I have allowed the multitudinous business cares and duties which crowd in upon me, to prevent my writing and thanking you for the jar of very fine jelly which you so kindly sent to me in care of my Florida home.

It was indeed very fine tasting and is evidence of the very fine work you are doing at the Berry Schools. This is a most wonderful undertaking, Miss Berry, and I am sure you are reaping the priceless compensation which can only come from such a harvest.

Wishing you a continued success, I am

Sincerely yours,

JCP:A

J. C. Penney founded the well-known department store that carried his name.

J.C. PENNEY
370 SEVENTH AVENUE
NEW YORK CITY

November 11, 1924

The Berry Schools,
Mount Berry, Georgia,

Dear Sirs:

I am enclosing my check for $150.00 in response to your request for aid addressed to the J.C. Penney Foundation, which at this time is not making any disbursements. Kindly send official receipt.

Very truly yours,

J.C. Penney

Acworth, Ga.,
Jan. 27. 25

Mr. L. Green
Mt. Berry Ga.

Dear Mr. Green:-

Am writing to you in regard to my little boy Harold Edwards. Upon visiting him this last week I was so surprised to find that he was not attending church and S.S.

Now please Mr. Green you know he is just at the tender age 15 when he needs this training more than anything.

He was also so shocked to know that the boys in his Dormitory used profanity. I'm sure you do not know this. Could you please change his work and put him in some other Dormitory with some boy that is religious and has some age on him? This I think would be of better influence to him. We can pay his way gladly but, this he does not want us to do. Could you give him some work to do that he could go to school and work his way while doing so?

Please write me concerning these matters.

I am very sincerely,

Mrs. J. D. Edwards.

Mrs. Edwards was the mother of a young, male Berry student.

MARTHA BERRY
FOUNDER AND DIRECTOR

ROBERT F. MADDOX,
CHAIRMAN BOARD OF DIRECTORS
ATLANTA & LOWRY NAT. BANK,
TREASURER

THE BERRY SCHOOLS

INCORPORATED
ESTABLISHED 1902
A CHRISTIAN INDUSTRIAL SCHOOL FOR
COUNTRY BOYS AND GIRLS

MOUNT BERRY, GEORGIA

EXPRESS AND TELEGRAPH OFFICES: ROME, GEORGIA

January 30, 1925

Mrs. J.O. Edwards,
Acworth, Georgia.

My dear Mrs. Edwards:

I was greatly surprised to receive your letter and to learn that Harold is not attending Church and Sunday School. This all of our boys are expected to do and and if he does not go he will be receiving demerits for each absencc. A boy gets two demerits if he stays away from required school exercises. When he receives twenty demerits we have to send him home. I will have a talk with Harold immediately and will see that from now on he does attend Church and Sunday School. Sometimes our new work boys do not understand the rules of the school or do not think that they mean what they say and on this account they get into trouble. I am also surprised to hear about the swearing and shall question Harold closely about this and will see who the offenders are.

I think it is very well for the boy to work his way along as far as possible and with your cooperation I feel sure that we can make a man of him.

Yours very truly,

G. Leland Green

G. Leland Green, Principal

G. Leland Green came from Vermont to serve as principal of The Berry Schools and later became president of the college.

Honorary President
Mrs. Warren G. Harding

Honorary Vice-President
Mrs. Woodrow Wilson

Founder
Mrs. Juliette Low

Officers
Mrs. Herbert Hoover, President
Mrs. Arthur O. Choate, Second Vice-President
Mrs. Julius Rosenwald, Third Vice-President
Mrs. William S. Sims, Fourth Vice-President
Mrs. E. M. Swift, Fifth Vice-President
Mrs. Nicholas F. Brady, Treasurer
Mrs. V. Everit Macy, Chairman Executive Board
Mr. Douglas Campbell, Counsel

Director
Mrs. Jane Deeter Rippin

Advisory Committee on Business and Finance
Mr. Frederic W. Allen, Chairman
Mr. Gordon Abbott, Boston
Mr. Robert Cassatt, Philadelphia
Mr. Herbert Lloyd, Philadelphia
Mr. Dunlevy Milbank, New York
Mr. Charles E. Mitchell, New York
Mr. John D. Ryan, New York
Mr. Frederick Strauss, New York
Mr. Felix Warburg, New York

GIRL SCOUTS

(Incorporated)

National Headquarters,
189 Lexington Avenue
New York City
Telephone Madison Square 4388

Executive Board
Miss Sarah Louise Arnold
Mrs. Leo Arnstein
Mrs. Selden Bacon
Mrs. Nicholas F. Brady
Mrs. Frederick H. Brooke
Mrs. Francis K. Carey
Mr. Francis P. Dodge
Mrs. Frederick Edey
Mrs. Arthur W. Hartt
Mrs. V. Everit Macy
Miss E. Gwen Martin
Miss Llewellyn Parsons
Mrs. Harold I. Pratt
Mrs. W. N. Rothschild
Mrs. W. H. Scudder
Mrs. A. Clifford Shinkle
Mrs. Edward A. Skae
Mrs. Percy H. Williams

329 Abercorn Street
Savannah, Ga
March 6th 1925

Dear Miss Berry:

The Lawtons tell me that you passed through Savannah lately & I am sorry not to have known that you were here.

My Girl Scouts are now established and I want to help the Berry School. I expect that if our town Players will give a little play & then if we could get a ballet danced by local talent, we might clear $100.00.

Especially if you could come & stay with me & address the audience.

Please let me have a reply stating the date etc if you like this idea?

Yours Sincerely,

Juliette Low

Juliette Low founded Girl Scouts.

Asa G. Candler, Jr.
1706 Candler Building
Atlanta, Georgia

July 3, 1925.

The Berry Schools,
Mount Berry, Georgia.

Gentlemen:

Enclosed please find my check for $12,500.00, which covers semi-annual installment of my $50,000.00 subscription to the Berry Schools.

Yours very truly,

Asa G. Candler Jr.

Asa Candler, Jr., was a member of the family instrumental in the early development of the Coca-Cola enterprises.

THE BERRY SCHOOLS
Martha Berry, Founder & Director
Mount Berry, Ga.

November 4, 1925

Messrs. Green, Hoge & Keown,
The Executive Committee of
The Berry Schools,
Mount Berry, Georgia.

Gentlemen:

Since we have decided for the good of the students and the good of the organization to discontinue Christmas vacations, especially on account of the students bringing back various diseases which cause a great loss of time in the school work, I think it best to have only Christmas Day as a holiday. Examinations should begin on Saturday, compelling the boys to stay. It is important not to give Saturday as a holiday because a number of students will want to go home over Sunday and it would not help us to do away with the trouble we have had in the past. There is always a let down right after Christmas Day, and the work should go right on after the holiday of one day.

I want to ask the Executive Committee to see that this is carried out.

Sincerely yours,

Martha Berry

G. Leland Green, principal; Herman Hoge, comptroller; and Gordon Keown, postmaster, resident trustee, and early Berry graduate, later acting director of the schools, were chief advisors to Martha Berry.

Miss Berry's Letter

Dear "Boys and Girls":

I have just returned from Europe where I spent three months. When I went to Battle Creek, Michigan, this summer, the doctors there told me that I had a very over-worked heart and that I just must go some place and rest. They thought my condition was so serious that I would have to be careful to live at all. I decided to go abroad and take a long rest.

I went to Nauheim, Germany and spent a month, under the care of one of the very best doctors I could find. Then I went to Carlsbad for a month. My stay in Germany was very interesting. They are rapidly recuperating from the war and the German people are orderly and thrifty. Being alone, I naturally felt very lonely at times but I did get a good rest. When I was in school I studied German, but had forgotten about all I ever knew about it, and the trip this summer gave me an opportunity to review the language.

I was so glad to return to the schools and find that everything had gone well during my absence. The splendid teachers and workers at Berry did their best. I often think of the early days of the school, and of all the struggles we have had through the years, and how faithfully the boys and girls have stood by the schools and helped me to "carry on".

On my way home a stockbroker asked me if I had lost much in stocks. I told him that I had never lost anything in stocks, and he was so interested to know what kind of wonderful stock I had invested in if I had never lost anything. I told him that I had invested in the splendid boys and girls of the Southern rural districts, and that they had paid a hundred percent in human dividends.

We who stay at the schools year after year always welcome letters from the Berry "boys and girls". It takes your splendid letters to cheer us on, and to help us to realize the worthwhileness of the work. Wherever you are, won't you please drop us a line telling us what you are doing, and if your Berry training is helping in your work? We are counting on you to make such splendid records that people everywhere will know, and love, Berry Schools.

May God bless each one of you and make your life a blessing.

Faithfully yours,

Martha Berry

The Berry Alumni Quarterly, December 1929, Vol. 13, No. 1.

This letter is addressed to former Berry students.

Dr. Green's Letter

Dear Friends:

As this number of the Quarterly reaches you, it will bring to your minds once more the sacred memories of school days at Berry. You will picture to yourselves the exciting contests of Field Day and Cross Country Run and you will again experience the fine fellowships of Mountain Day. This year, Lemley won Cross Country and Field Day, but Emery captured the Baseball series in the most exciting contest in Berry's history.

I know that many of you will also recall the special religious meetings held each fall term, where so many Berry men and women have made decisions which changed forever their habits and aims in life. We have had some wonderful services this fall and ask your prayers that 100% of our boys and girls may decide to become active, zealous workers in the Master's vineyard.

Our hearts are made glad that Miss Berry, who went to Europe for her health, is able to be with us once more and continue the great work for her boys and girls whom she loves so well and whom she has served so faithfully.

As usual, our Schools are filled to overflowing. Three times as many applied for entrance last fall as could be accommodated. You already know that Berry's high school has been on the accredited list for the past seven years, and now, the junior college has also been placed on the accredited list. Our junior college graduates may now enter the junior classes of standard senior colleges by certificate. The excellent records made by our junior college graduates in senior colleges have achieved this happy result.

Berry is winning victories right along. On December 6, she won her first intercollegiate debate with Bowdon College. This subject was: "Resolved that the present policy of co-education in American colleges is undesirable". The Berry team, consisting of Tom Wheelis and Tom Meacham, upheld the affirmative side of the above question. They put up a wonderful debate and won the decision of the judges.

As I close, I know you will be thinking of us during this sacred Christmas season. The Christmas carols in Mount Berry chapel and beautiful "Silent Night" are a part of your very lives. The carol service comes the night of December 21 this year. Some of you may be able to return for it. It is physically impossible to write you all a personal letter, but the hearts of all of us at Berry go out to our boys and girls this holiday season. Please write and let us know about your work and your problems.

May the love and peace of the Christ child abide with you all throughout the coming year.

Most sincerely yours,

G. LELAND GREEN

The Berry Alumni Quarterly, December 1929, Vol. 13, No. 1.

As Berry president, Dr. Green wrote regularly to the alumni a letter published in The Berry Alumni Quarterly.

LAW OFFICES
McADOO, NEBLETT & CLAGETT
LOS ANGELES, CALIFORNIA
WASHINGTON, D.C.

WILLIAM G. McADOO
WILLIAM H. NEBLETT
BRICE CLAGETT
EDW. H. MITCHELL
FRANK G. SWAIN
BEN H. NEBLETT
ROBT. B. POWELL
JOHN G. SOBIESKI

TRANSAMERICA BUILDING
LOS ANGELES, CALIFORNIA

December 23, 1930

Dear Miss Berry:-

Thank you warmly for the package of cotton bolls, which bring back some very vivid memories of my boyhood when I used to try to pick cotton. The price, in those days, was "fifty cents per hundred." After working with all my might and main and thinking I had picked about a thousand pounds, I used to find that I had gotten about twenty, but for a small boy of ten I suppose this wasn't so bad. I presume the cotton you sent me was raised by the students of your school.

Mrs. McAdoo and I often think of you and always with genuine pleasure. We hope that everything goes well with the Berry School and that you particularly may have the happiest kind of Christmas and New Year.

Cordially yours,

WG McAdoo

Miss Martha Berry,
Mount Berry, Ga.

WGM:W

William McAdoo, a native of Georgia, served as secretary of the treasury during Woodrow Wilson's presidency and was later U.S. Senator from California.

STATE OF NEW YORK
EXECUTIVE CHAMBER
ALBANY

FRANKLIN D. ROOSEVELT
GOVERNOR

February 4, 1931.

Dear Miss Berry:-

Thank you for your very nice letter. I do wish that I could definitely accept to go to Berry on May fifth. I have always been deeply interested in the work you are doing there. However, I do not go to Warm Springs until the Legislature adjourns, and after that I must sign or veto the thirty-day bills. As the date of the departure of the Legislature is determined entirely by the amount of work which they have to do, I cannot make any definite plans whatever. However, I should say, from previous experience, that I will undoubtedly be in Warm Springs by April twenty-fifth and, in that event, it would be impossible for me to go to Berry, as I do not leave Warm Springs at all during my short visits there.

I am sure you will understand and I do hope you will invite me after I have served this term as Governor.

Very sincerely yours,

Franklin D. Roosevelt

Miss Martha Berry,
Mount Berry,
Georgia.

RT

Franklin D. Roosevelt was governor of New York, and later thirty-second president of the United States (1933-1945).

1819 Broadway, Room 1922,
New York, N.Y.

Saturday, May 9th, 1931

Dear Miss Berry:

Famous Features Syndicate, a newspaper syndicate, has approached me with an offer to obtain for them a series of interviews with the women recently selected as America's most distinguished by the "Good Housekeeping" jury. I told the gentlemen of the syndicate that I would try, and I hoped for success. However, I am just sailing for Europe for a little vacation after a rather strenuous winter, and it will be impossible for me to see you personally, as I had hoped. Perhaps within the near future you would be able to write a little article for me along the lines I suggest below.

As you well know there has been tremendous interest in the selection by the "Good Housekeeping" jury. I must admit that despite my poor qualifications I am flattered and happy to be associated with a group of women who have done so much for humanity. And I am sure the women of the nation would like to know more of the work and ideas of this representative group, and derive inspiration from them.

I have the happiest memory of my visit to your school. The thought of those bright faces has been like sunshine all through the years in my dark world.

A little article by you describing your work and hopes would be inspiring to all of us, for your work is appreciated not only for its practical value, but also as a symbol of womanly devotion. You are a pioneer of America's new social conscience.

I do not pretend to set up any special subject, but I am sure there is some specific subject near your heart which you would like to write about for this little series.

I think about 1,200 to 1,500 words would fulfill the requirements.

I feel guilty in making such a request, for I know the demands on your time and energies are many and great; but I feel that your article would be of tremendous benefit to newspaper readers all over the country, and I am tremendously interested in making this series available to them.

With cordial regards,

Helen Keller

Miss Martha Berry
Mount Berry, Georgia.

Helen Adams Keller, a U.S. writer and lecturer, was blind and deaf from birth and was taught to speak and read.

Battle Creek Mich.,
May 13th 1931.

My dear Miss Berry:

According to my promise of last winter I am writing to a Mr. Benson of New Hampshire to find out if I can get a pair of white swans for you.

Will let you know as soon as I hear from him.

Do you have an express office near you or how are the birds to be sent and where?

Sincerely yours,

Carrie Staines Kellogg

The writer was married to W. K. Kellogg, founder of the Kellogg Company.

THE BERRY SCHOOLS

INCORPORATED ESTABLISHED 1902

MARTHA BERRY, FOUNDER AND DIRECTOR

CHRISTIAN INDUSTRIAL SCHOOLS FOR COUNTRY BOYS AND GIRLS

EXPRESSS AND TELEGRAPH OFFICE: ROME, GEORGIA

MOUNT BERRY, GEORGIA

June 17, 1931

Mr. W.K. Kellogg,
Kellogg Bird Sanctuary,
Augusta, Michigan.

Dear Mr. Kellogg:-

I am delighted with the Swans and they are admired by every one at Berry. You can see groups of boys every afternoon walking by the lake and commenting on them. It is a most valuable gift and I cannot tell you how much we do appreciate it. The man in charge is taking great care of them.

I think you are doing a great work in the preservation of wild life. I am trying to do in a small way what you have been doing for so long in a big way. I hope to see you and Mrs. Kellogg the next time I come to Battle Creek, and I do hope you visit Berry when you can. We would be delighted to entertain you and Mrs. Kellogg any time.

Again with grateful and appreciative thanks,

Faithfully yours,

Martha Berry

Mrs. James Roosevelt
HYDE PARK, N.Y.
TELEGRAPH POUGHKEEPSIE

Nov. 10 1931

My dear Miss Berry

I am sending you $100 for it seems to me you may have greater trouble than usual this year to keep up your great work. I only wish I could help more. If I ever go to Warm Springs, Georgia again to see my dear son when he goes for a week or two, I shall certainly go to see you.

Very sincerely yours

Sara Delano Roosevelt

Sara Delano Roosevelt was the mother of Franklin Delano Roosevelt, thirty-second president of the United States.

March 16, 1932

Dear Friends:

Another wonderful year is drawing to a close at Berry. Commencement and our Alumni Banquet are just ahead. We have a splendid graduating class one hundred strong. This year will live in Berry's history because it witnesses the first college graduating class to receive degrees. About twenty outstanding young men and women will receive senior college diplomas.* They are the charter members of Berry College and I am sure their lives and their work will introduce this newest and highest Berry institution to the world in a fitting manner.

May I call your attention to the splendid work of Percy Pentecost, our new Alumni Secretary? As rapidly as possible, he is getting in touch with every former Berry student. During the winter months, he has been re-organizing the Alumni Clubs and his efforts have met with a most enthusiastic response. Mr. Pentecost has also successfully established a Bureau of Appointments which will be of great assistance to all Berry Alumni in helping them secure positions and promotions. Write Mr. Pentecost about this. He will do everything possible for you.

My last word is, "be sure to come back to us for Commencement." You will want to see the beauties of our campus again. You will want to shake hands with old Berry friends. Your hearts will be warmed and your lives will be made brighter. But, most of all, we need your sympathetic and cheering words of greeting, we need to know and hear you say that you would make any sacrifice for Berry's sake, we need to feel that you remember us in your daily prayers.

Hoping to see you in larger numbers than ever before, the first week in May, I remain,

Most cordially and sincerely your friend,

G. LELAND GREEN

The Berry Alumni Quarterly, March 1932, Vol. 14, No. 3.
**Note: 17 students graduated ("Commencement," The Berry Alumni Quarterly, May 1932, Vol. 14, No. 4.)*

RICHARD B. RUSSELL, CHIEF JUSTICE
MARCUS W. BECK,
SAML. C. ATKINSON,
H. WARNER HILL,
S. PRICE GILBERT,
JAMES K. HINES,
ASSOCIATE JUSTICES

State of Georgia,
Supreme Court,
Atlanta.

GEO. W. STEVENS, REPORTER.
JOHN M. GRAHAM, ASST. REPORTER.
Z. D. HARRISON, CLERK.
K. C. BLECKLEY, DEPUTY CLERK.

March 31st, 1932.

Miss Martha Berry,
Rome, Ga.

Dear Miss Berry:-

Excuse me, please, for intruding upon the precious time of one who is engaged in important matters specially affecting the supervision of one of the greatest institutions in the country, and permit me to ask your help in a matter so small that it would generally be handled by some of your subordinates.

I am thinking of two fatherless and helpless girls. I am thinking hopefully of you as one who may be able to take them into the circle of your benign charity and your beautiful influence, for I feel that to these two girls, to touch even the hem of your garment will be a benediction. I appeal to your great charitable heart, for the nature of its impulses and the unselfish sweetness of its humanitarianism is known of all men. I appeal to you because I, myself, am helpless to do for these worthy children of Georgia anything substantial or lasting.

The two girls to whom I refer are the daughters of Mr. W. E. Talley, who was the first deputy clerk of the Court of Appeals as well as deputy clerk of the Supreme Court. As you know, the salaries in the judicial department have never been excessively large. Mr. Talley's compensation as a mere deputy was not large. Nevertheless, after a few months he was extremely competent. I doubt if there is a member of the bar in the State who had business in either court, that will not gladly bear witness to the fact that he never met a clerical officer more devoted to his duty, more patient, more courteous, or more obliging, than Mr. Talley. When he died some eighteen months ago he left an indebtedness upon his home, and the depression had cut the value of the property to less than half the price at which he had originally purchased it. Consequently, the loan company sold the home, and in a short time Mrs. Talley had consumed the small amount of insurance left after paying a few other debts, in renting a home for herself and children. She is now absolutely penniless, and a dispossessory warrant has been taken out, and she would have nowhere to place her furniture but for the kindness of one of Mr. Talley's lawyer friends, who will move her belongings and store them without cost in the cellar of his home. The two girls have been taken temporarily by a friend, and several of us have agreed to raise thirty dollars a month for Mrs. Talley, who is in feeble health, until we can see if it is possible for her to get any kind of employment.

Without my going into other details, you can see that the thirty dollars per month for a few months will make no permanent provision for these two girls, will really be insufficient to provide shelter for them all and leave enough over to feed the children, who have been going to school. I am reliably informed that both of the girls are well behaved, intelligent, and amiable. With Ned Talley's blood in them, I believe if they could have a home and receive an education in your matchless institution, that they would receive a training which, even if I should be disappointed as to their mental brightness, would enable them to become worthy citizens of value to the State, and at least foster that independence and consciousness of true ideals which will enable them to honorably support themselves.

You know so much more about these questions than I do, your life has been so much broader in the great field of humanity, and so much more unselfish than mine, that I can say no more than that if you can help them you will add to the admiration which I, in common with all other thoughtful Georgians entertain for you, the liveliest gratitude of

Your respectful friend,

RBR-cmh

Richard B. Russell

Richard B. Russell was father of Richard B. Russell, Jr., Governor of Georgia and U.S. Senator.

THE BERRY SCHOOLS

INCORPORATED ESTABLISHED 1902

MARTHA BERRY, FOUNDER AND DIRECTOR

CHRISTIAN INDUSTRIAL SCHOOLS FOR COUNTRY BOYS AND GIRLS

EXPRESSS AND TELEGRAPH OFFICE: ROME, GEORGIA

MOUNT BERRY, GEORGIA

April 5, 1932.

Judge Richard B. Russell,
State Capitol,
Atlanta, Georgia.

My dear Judge Russell:-

I have had to refer your letter, with regard to the children of Mr. Talley, to our principal and he will advise what can be done about the matter. You understand, of course, that with the waiting list we have at Berry the schools are filled for the next term long before the spring term closes.

This seems to be a very worthy as well as appealing case, and I wish it were possible for me to make a place for all the worthy and appealing cases that come to us. However, I have to leave the matter of accepting students entirely in the hands of our principal, and, in order to take care of the many applications, it is necessary for him to insist upon certain requirements - preference being given to boys and girls of rural districts.

I thank you for your letter and your appreciation of the work that we are trying to do at Berry. I feel sure you will understand that taking care of a few of the many applicants is all we can hope to do.

We so enjoyed having Mrs. Russell with us for the little visit, and I trust that you will be able to come next time as we certainly expect to have Governor Russell and his mother with us again.

Very truly yours,

Martha Berry

CORRA HARRIS
IN THE VALLEY
RYDAL, GEORGIA

June 29, 1932

Dear Dr. Berry:

My visit to you was a delightful experience. The hostess was a heroine who has written so much of her life in beauty and goodness. The company was gay, with that kind of clear minded happiness men and women have who earn their own peace with honor and service. The food was more than refreshing. It was sedately served and had that flavor imparted by the high standards in the oldest of human arts, that of cooking.

What one accomplishes depends upon the quality of the material with which one works and the methods used. I suppose this is true, even of the good God, who has had us in school for ages and a lot of dunces among us still. But this is certain, you have laid about you the scenes of happy days for a hundred years to come, with a gallant spirit and with the grace and imagination of a very fine lady. I have long known that you are an autocrat, the most willful of crusaders, but now I perceive that, true to your breeding and quality, you are really a romanticist in education. This is something to say for a woman who has dealt for so many years with the very Irish potato of daily expenses and with many of the most primitive least imaginative elements of human nature.

The scene in your weaving room was not an epic, except in your power to project it through others, it was a pastoral from old days. Those girls were not only learning one of the fine arts, they were acquiring practice in patience, beauty and high standards.

When we grow old and tired, and a little depressed at the thought that we also must die merely in sight of the Promised Land of our dreams, it is a comfort to be praised a little, even by those who cannot know the wilderness of mind and hardships through which one has passed to this last place. So I am writing you this letter, not for publicity, but as the offering of one woman to another woman.

I send you my respect and admiration.

Faithfully yours,

Corra Harris

CH/BR

Corra Harris was a Georgia author.

Executive Department
Atlanta

Eugene Talmadge
GOVERNOR

CHICAGO EXPOSITION

A CENTURY OF PROGRESS
CHICAGO, ILLINOIS

Tom Linder
SECRETARY EXECUTIVE DEPARTMENT

GEORGIA COMMISSION
SCOTT W. ALLEN, CHAIRMAN
ROY LECRAW, VICE-CHAIRMAN
J. C. ROBINSON, DIRECTOR

March 29, 1933

Miss Martha Berry,
% Martha Berry School,
Rome, Georgia.

Dear Miss Berry:

As you know, the Georgia Century of Progress Commission is preparing an Exhibit representing the State of Georgia at the World's Fair to be held in Chicago beginning June 1 to November 1.

The aim of the Commission in preparing this Exhibit is to have one that represents no special interests in the State, but presents Georgia as a whole, outlining our commercial, manufacturing, agricultural, and recreational advantages and also stressing the importance of our natural resources and the opportunities we have for their development to the prospective citizens who are looking for an opportunity to succeed.

As Governor of this State, I feel that this is the one opportunity that Georgia has had to sell herself to the world and be in a position to take advantage of the prosperity and share in the development of the South that is bound to come in the future.

Our Exhibit space at the Fair, will consist of 2400 sq. ft., with a ceiling height of 28 ft. It is the desire of the Commission to portray, by mural oil paintings or enlarged colored photographs, that will be placed in panels ranging from 12′ x 12′ to 12′ x 8′, our present advantages, natural resources, and otherwise.

Since the Berry School is one of the most outstanding schools of its kind in the United States and one of the most prominent educational schools in the South, we wish to portray to these people this school. We have selected you, as founder of the Berry Schools, to allow us to prepare a mural design as outlined above covering the school, or any part of it you may wish, and place this painting on our walls at the Exhibit in Chicago.

We have made investigations and naturally the preparation, maintaining, and illumination of this painting will incur some expense and our only request to you is that you pay for this.

Millions of people will attend our Exhibit and this really offers you an opportunity to do something for Georgia and at the same time make contacts that could be had in no other way, regardless of the price. I would appreciate it personally if you would advise me of your interest in this matter and it will be my pleasure to have a representative of the Commission to call upon you at once to go into this matter in detail.

With kindest regards and thanking you in advance for your favorable consideration and help in making Georgia's Exhibit a success, I am

Yours very truly,

Eugene Talmadge

Eugene Talmadge,
Governor of Georgia.

T
:
C

Eugene Talmadge served as Georgia Commissioner of Agriculture prior to his service as Governor. He was the father of Herman Talmadge, Governor of Georgia and U.S. Senator.

Seminole Lodge
FORT MYERS, FLORIDA

May 9th, 1933

Miss Martha Berry
Berry School
Mount Berry, Georgia

Dear Miss Berry:

I have just received word that the two Love Birds that I shipped you on the 2nd have been lost.

A copy of the letter which was received is enclosed for your information.

I regret this loss very much indeed for these birds were raised on our place here and I wanted you to have them.

Very sincerely,

Mina M Edison

Mrs. Thomas A. Edison

Mina M. Edison was married to inventor Thomas A. Edison.

THE BERRY SCHOOLS

INCORPORATED ESTABLISHED 1902

MARTHA BERRY, FOUNDER AND DIRECTOR

CHRISTIAN INDUSTRIAL SCHOOLS FOR COUNTRY BOYS AND GIRLS

EXPRESSS AND TELEGRAPH OFFICE: ROME, GEORGIA

MOUNT BERRY, GEORGIA

May 7, 1936.

Mrs. Henry Ford,
Fair Lane,
Dearborn, Michigan.

Dear Mrs. Ford:

Thank you so much for the peaches and the squash seed. I am having a wonderful time showing the peaches to all the Home Economics people. They are all admiring them very much and I know they would like to eat them. I am not going to let anybody eat them, though, as they are really just too pretty to be eaten.

Today we had some very important visitors in the Ford Dining Room to luncheon, and I wish you could have heard all the lovely things they said about the buildings there. They said it was the nicest dining room and kitchen they had ever seen anywhere. One of the men had won a Rhodes Scholarship and had studied for a long time in England. He said there was nothing so beautiful in England as the Ford Buildings.

All our guests agree with me that the only thing we needed to make the dining room complete was a portrait of Mr. Ford. I do hope we may have one. I remember when I visited you, last summer, you almost promised to send us a portrait. You said if the one you were having painted was good and if it pleased you perhaps you might send it to us. It would mean so much to us to have it. So many of the boys and girls have asked why we did not have a portrait of Mr. Ford in the dining room. They all love your portrait in Clara. I just wish you knew how much it is admired and appreciated.

I cannot tell you what a great disappointment it was to all of us not to have you and Mr. Ford stop and see us this Spring. We had really looked forward to your visit so long that we just could not get over not having you with us. I do hope that you will stop next time on your way down. I am glad that we are on your route and I do hope that you will come by and see us when you come this way.

I am so interested in your place in Savannah and was delighted to see the plans and to get the picture in my mind. We think of you every day, at Berry, and we wish you could see the Ford Buildings this Spring. They are more beautiful than ever and the shrubbery around has grown so that the buildings appear to have more age. The stone looks very mellow and lovely.

Just to thank you for the peaches and squash seed, and to send admiration and love from the thousand boys and girls, and your sincere friend, Martha Berry,

Faithfully yours,

Martha Berry

Clara Ford and her husband Henry were long-time friends of Martha Berry and benefactors of the schools. Clara Hall is named in her honor.

THE UNIVERSITY OF WISCONSIN
MADISON

OFFICE OF THE PRESIDENT

April 13, 1937

My dear Miss Berry,

The Faculty and the Regents of the University of Wisconsin direct me to present their compliments and to say that the University has the honor to renew its invitation to you to receive at its hands the Honorary Degree of Doctor of Laws in recognition of your distinguished services in the field of education.

The Commencement ceremonies will take place early Monday morning, June twenty-first, so that it will be necessary for recipients of Honorary Degrees to arrive in Madison on Sunday, which, as you know, can easily be done by taking a morning train from Chicago.

I shall look forward to hearing from you that you will be able to be with us to receive this degree.

May I, in conclusion, draw your attention to two matters: In the first place, the Honorary Degrees of the University are conferred only upon individuals who attend the Commencement exercises; secondly, the University desires to be in position to be the first to announce to the public the names of the distinguished persons who are to receive these degrees at Commencement time. This invitation must be, therefore, in a sense, confidential.

Yours very truly,

G.C. Sellery

G.C. Sellery
Acting President

Miss Martha McChesney Berry
Berry Schools
Mount Berry, Georgia

THE BERRY SCHOOLS

INCORPORATED ESTABLISHED 1902

MARTHA BERRY, FOUNDER AND DIRECTOR

CHRISTIAN INDUSTRIAL SCHOOLS FOR COUNTRY BOYS AND GIRLS

EXPRESSS AND TELEGRAPH OFFICE: ROME, GEORGIA

MOUNT BERRY, GEORGIA

April 19, 1937.

Dr. G. C. Sellery,
Office of the President,
The University of Wisconsin,
Madison, Wisconsin.

Dear Dr. Sellery:

Your kind invitation to receive the Honorary Degree of Doctor of Laws, from The University of Wisconsin, has just reached me. I cannot tell you how much I appreciate this invitation, and I shall be so happy to be with you June twenty-first to receive the degree.

I was deeply grieved and disappointed not to be able to attend the Commencement three years ago, but I shall look forward to being with you in June. Please express my sincere thanks to the Faculty and Regents of The University of Wisconsin, and tell them I greatly appreciate this honor.

Again thanking you, and looking forward to seeing you in June,

Faithfully yours,

Martha Berry

United States Senate

COMMITTEE ON
PRIVILEGES AND ELECTIONS

Vienna, Georgia
September 18, 1937

Miss Martha Berry
The Berry Schools
Rome, Georgia

Dear Miss Berry:

You will let me acknowledge your wire received today.

I shall be happy to urge the President to visit the Berry Schools on his next visit to Georgia.

It would be most helpful if you would visit the President and urge him to accept. It is difficult to say when he will be in Washington in view of the fact that on his return to Washington he expects to leave immediately on his Western trip. It is not known exactly when he will return to Washington. I have endeavored to see the President on other matters and believe the foregoing statements are correct.

With best wishes, I am

Sincerely yours,

Walter F. George

Walter F. George was a long-time U.S. Senator from Georgia.

MRS. LAURENCE S. ROCKEFELLER
115 EAST 67TH STREET
NEW YORK CITY

Dear Miss Berry:

I am very glad to send you again one hundred and fifty dollars for the work of your school.

We enjoyed so much seeing you on your last visit to New York and having a chance to show you our baby. She has grown so much now that I am sure you would hardly recognize her.

Wishing you every success.

Sincerely

Mary T. Rockefeller

November 26th, 1937

Mary T. Rockefeller's husband was a son of John D. Rockefeller, founder of Standard Oil Co.

Executive Department
Atlanta

E. D. RIVERS
GOVERNOR

August 15, 1938

Miss Martha Berry
Founder and Director
The Berry Schools
Mount Berry, Georgia

Dear Miss Berry:

I remember with pleasure my visit to Berry last year, and hope to be able to drop in on you again this fall.

I have discussed the other portion of your letter with Dr. Collins, and hope something will be able to be worked out. At any rate, I feel confident he will get in touch with you in regard to same. You know of my deep love for the schools, and especially an institution which renders such a noble service as the Berry Schools. I hope to see and talk with you sometime in the early fall.

With kind regards and every good wish, I remain

Sincerely yours,

E. D. Rivers

Governor

EDR/hfb

Governor E. D. Rivers initiated free textbooks for Georgia school children. Dr. Collins was state school superintendent.

TWENTY-FIRST STREET AND LEHIGH AVENUE

September 26, 1938

Miss Martha Berry,
The Berry Schools,
Mount Berry, Georgia.

My dear Miss Berry:

Was very nice of you to drop me a line inviting me to your school. You can be assured that it would be a great pleasure for me to visit your school and will do so at the first opportunity that I have.

In the meantime will try to arrange to send some baseball material. May not be able to send any but some used baseballs, but will do the best I can in this respect.

Trust that you are enjoying the best of health.

Respectfully yours,

CONNIE MACK
PRESIDENT

CM:P

Connie Mack was long-time manager of Philadelphia Athletics, a major league baseball team.

THE BERRY SCHOOLS

ESTABLISHED 1902 INCORPORATED 1903

MARTHA BERRY, Founder and Director

CHRISTIAN INDUSTRIAL SCHOOLS FOR COUNTRY BOYS AND GIRLS

EXPRESS AND TELEGRAPH OFFICE: ROME, GEORGIA

MOUNT BERRY, GEORGIA

January 24, 1939

Rev. Mr. Peter Marshall,
New York Avenue Presbyterian,
Washington, D.C.

Dear Peter Marshall,

I hope that you have not been so busy up there that you have forgotten us down here in Mount Berry. I think of you so often, and the lovely inspiration I received from your talks and the sermons you gave.

The students still talk of your last commencement address, and when Mrs. Carlisle was here recently she spoke of her pleasant memories of you.

We have our commencement this year on May 21 and 22, and I am hoping so you might give us our baccalaureate sermon again. I have been so ill for the past year I can not travel, and am begging old friends to come to see me, since I cannot go to them, and I pray you will be able to come.

Times are really very bad with us, as letters fail to bring the response the spoken voice does, and our gifts have fallen far off. However I have great faith in God, and in the knowledge we are in His hands always. I pray He bless you and yours this New Year,

Faithfully yours,

Martha Berry

Peter Marshall served as chaplain of the United States Senate.

NEW YORK AVENUE PRESBYTERIAN CHURCH
WASHINGTON, D. C.

MINISTERS
PETER MARSHALL
ALBERT EVANS

January 28, 1939.

Miss Martha Berry
The Berry Schools
Mount Berry, Georgia

My dear Miss Berry:

I was very glad to hear from you, but sorry to know of your indisposition. Somehow you have always looked so well and have travelled so much and been such a source of strength and inspiration to all those around you, one just doesn't think of you not being at your best.

What a joy it would be to drive down in May and visit you in your delightful home and be with the boys and girls on the campus. Nothing, I believe, would be more attractive, but I know it is impossible. I cannot get away on a Sunday. I have even had to decline an invitation to preach the baccalaureate sermon for Agnes Scott, simply because it came on Sunday. There is no possibility of my getting away and I am truly sorry for I would love to come.

Every now and then I run across a Berry graduate. There are several here in Washington and I met Raymond Forrest at the Westminster Choir College in New Jersey. What lovely things he had to say of you and of the Berry Schools!

Even though I cannot come to you, I shall constantly remember you and your great Cause in prayer and in fondest affection.

Sincerely yours,

Peter Marshall

Peter Marshall

PM:mj

Washington, D.C.
March 16, 1939

My dear Miss Berry,

When Mr. Marshall and I returned home last Saturday after a two week's trip to Florida and New Orleans, we found the lovely flowers waiting for us. The church secretary had opened the package and put them in vases all over the house, so that it was literally like a breath of springtime.

I can't tell you how much we appreciate them and what is more—your thinking of us and remembering us. I can't think of anything we would rather do than spend a few days on the Berry Campus, and you may be sure we shall if we get down to Georgia at all.

You and your work have a very warm place in our hearts and we pray God's continued guidance and blessings on it. Thank you for the flowers more than we can tell you—and with every best wish from both of us.

Sincerely,

Catherine Marshall
(Mrs Peter Marshall)

Catherine Marshall was an author.

THE BERRY SCHOOLS

ESTABLISHED 1902 INCORPORATED 1903

MARTHA BERRY, FOUNDER AND DIRECTOR

CHRISTIAN INDUSTRIAL SCHOOLS FOR COUNTRY BOYS AND GIRLS

EXPRESS AND TELEGRAPH OFFICE: ROME, GEORGIA

MOUNT BERRY, GEORGIA

Sept. 14, 1939

Dr. G. Leland Green,
President
Berry College.

Dear Dr. Green,

Next term we must try to have half pay and half work students.

Please bear this in mind in making any new selections. The students and the South must be required to pay a greater share of the operating costs of Berry, for our expenses are great, and our old friends are falling by the wayside.

Ten years ago the students' cash tuition was $27,000. Last year it was practically $20,000 less.

Please make your plans for this next term and for next year very definitely in the direction of having half pay and half work students.

Yours faithfully,

Martha Berry

THE BERRY SCHOOLS

ESTABLISHED 1902 INCORPORATED 1903

MARTHA BERRY, FOUNDER AND DIRECTOR

CHRISTIAN INDUSTRIAL SCHOOLS FOR COUNTRY BOYS AND GIRLS

EXPRESS AND TELEGRAPH OFFICE: ROME, GEORGIA

MOUNT BERRY, GEORGIA

September 15, 1939

Miss Martha Berry, Founder & Director,
The Berry Schools,
Mount Berry, Georgia.

Dear Miss Berry:

I acknowledge receipt of your letter to the effect that we must work at once toward getting half pay students and half work students. We shall take definite steps toward achieving this result next term. The goal should be fully realized by next fall.

As I said in our recent conversation, it is impossible to get half pay students for the high schools. If we get half pay students for the high schools, it will be necessary to develop them into preparatory schools with a wealthier class of people for patrons.

There are public high schools within reach of practically all boys and girls today. Most of these are consolidated schools where there is no charge for tuition or bus fare.

Assuring you of my full cooperation in this matter, I am,

Sincerely yours,

G. Leland Green

G. Leland Green,
President.

MARGARET MITCHELL

Atlanta, Georgia
November 7, 1939

My dear Miss Berry:

Thank you so much for your letter of October 31st and its cordial invitation to meet with you and the faculty and students of the Berry Schools. I am greatly honored to have such an invitation from you and I am sincerely sorry that I cannot accept. My reason is one which you can understand and, I hope, sympathize with probably better than anyone else in Georgia.

Since the week "Gone With the Wind" was published in 1936, I have made no speeches, talks or formal visits anywhere. With the many demands that are made on you, you can understand the situation in which I was placed as a result of the popularity of my novel. It brought, and still brings, me many invitations to visit schools and other institutions and to speak before organizations of every kind—so many, in fact, it would be humanly impossible for me to accept them all. You can appreciate the dilemma in which I was placed. I am most humbly grateful for the amazing kindness people everywhere have shown my book and me, but I could not possibly accept all the invitations. If I had attempted to pick and choose, I would have been in the position of slighting many kind people while favoring others. So, I had to adopt the policy of declining all the invitations. This has not been a happy situation for me. It has cut me out of a great deal of pleasure in meeting with good friends and making new friends, but there seemed no other course for me to take.

I may seem to be contradicting everything in the above when I say that I did visit the Berry Schools this past summer. I was one of your guests at the dinner you gave the Georgia Press Association, and enjoyed it very, very much—everything about it, in fact, except that you were unable to be present. Everyone missed you.

That visit was not contradictory to the policy I have outlined, for I was not at the editors' meeting as a special guest but as one who has been attending the conventions for nearly twenty years. I am a former newspaper reporter; my husband is a member of the Press Association, and attending the conventions was our regular custom long before I became an author. I still attend them because the editors permit me to come as my husband's wife, and not as "Margaret Mitchell, Author." They are my old friends and I consider it the highest proof of their friendship that they let me meet with them on the same informal basis as in the past. This has been a source of great happiness to me, for their meetings are almost the only ones I can attend these days as myself, and not as the author of a book that happened to sell a great many copies.

Could I come to see you very informally some day? My husband and I are great admirers of you and, like all other Georgians, we feel an intense personal pride in the Berry Schools and all that you have done. Some time when we are in your neighborhood, we would consider it a great honor if you would permit us to call. I know how busy you are and I promise that we will not take up too much of your time if you will give us this great pleasure.

If my circumstances were different, if I could go and do as I pleased, I would have gladly accepted the invitation you extended, for I know of no place I would rather visit than the Berry Schools. It is a real inspiration just to see your students and I would enjoy meeting and talking with them. The brightness in their eyes, the freshness in their faces, their charming manners, their simple naturalness, their sturdiness and calm, all show that you are building men and women as well as educating children. I would like to know them better and I am truly sorry it is not possible now. But, if you will permit me, I want to slip in quietly some day for a little visit with you on your beautiful campus. It would be a great privilege if I could tell you personally of my admiration for your wonderful work, and I know that I would benefit if I could talk for even a few minutes with someone who has shown herself truly great, as you have done.

Sincerely yours,

Margaret Mitchell Marsh
(Mrs. John R. Marsh)

Margaret Mitchell was a famous Georgia journalist and author of the novel Gone With the Wind.

ICHAUWAY PLANTATION NEWTON, GEORGIA

January 3, 1940

Dear Miss Berry:

Thank you so much for that beautiful, handwoven tie, which you sent me at Christmas. It was mighty sweet of you and I appreciate the tie and your remembering me a very great deal.

I hope that you are keeping well and happy and that you and your school have a most successful year ahead of you.

With my very best regards, I am

Yours sincerely

R W Woodruff

Miss Martha Berry
Mount Berry
Georgia

Robert W. Woodruff, long-time chief executive and major owner of The Coca-Cola Company, was a noted philanthropist.

DEPARTMENT OF BUSINESS ADMINISTRATION

BERRY COLLEGE

MOUNT BERRY, GEORGIA

April 18, 1940

Miss Sophie Payne Alston
Mount Berry, Georgia

Dear Miss Alston:

One of the accounting classes, Business Administration 21, has been invited to observe the business office of the Tubize-Chatillon Corporation Saturday Morning, April 20.

Two of your young ladies, Florence Coker and Alowene Paulk, are members of the class and should be included in this group. The observation class is an integral part of our work, and I shall appreciate it if you can arrange for the young ladies to have permission to go. I am sure they, too, will thank you for your kindness.

Yours respectfully:

Ralph Farmer

Friday A.M. [Handwritten note to president from dean of women]:

Dear Dr. Green,

Will you please let me know what you think about this. The girls have never gone on field trips off campus.

Sincerely,
S.P. Alston

Sophie Payne Alston was long-time dean of women at Berry. Ralph Farmer, Berry graduate, was long-time head of Berry's business administration department.

ERWIN A. HOLT
BURLINGTON
NORTH CAROLINA

SAT.
April 20, 1940.

Dr. G. Leland Green,
The Berry Schools,
Mount Berry, Ga.

My dear Dr. Green:-

I also want to write you a few lines to accompany our birthday greeting and extend our very best wishes, hoping this finds you well and to wish you an unusually happy birthday.

Our last trip to BERRY was unusually pleasant and in spite of the rain (part of Sunday) and it feels like every last is always the best.

Was especially glad that Mrs. Holt could become better acquainted and begin to realize more and more what it is etc.

She certainly was more and more impressed.

Naturally, I have thought of dear MISS BERRY most often and especially yesterday when she was to receive her AWARD and wondered whether or not she got to DALLAS and this I will know very soon from the papers, CROWELL'S and others.

By the way, I am hoping they will be here a few days en route the Mountains and in that way take it easy and see this immediate section, DUKE University (where they know one of the instructors) etc. etc.

In making a book order to HARPERS to-day, I ordered 50 copies of "I WILL LIFT UP MINE EYES TO THE HILLS" sent you to pass around and would suggest that one copy be left on the table in the GUEST COTTAGE and would also suggest that the three booklets of GRACE NOLL CROWELL and if you have any more left to include "INSPIRATION & IDEALS".

It seems Dean Alston did not get a copy of the latter.

Would also like to see Mrs. Crowell's photo in the GUEST COTTAGE before so very long.

Please excuse so many suggestions and wishes.

Was sorry not to see you again, and to miss Mrs. Green and hope she had a nice trip North and of course delighted with her grand son.

Would also like to see a COPY of "POEM WITH POWER TO STRENGTHEN THE SOUL" in the GUEST COTTAGE and is likely I may order some more and send you some as well as some of Rev. F. W. Boreham's and will know later what I will do.

As it is getting late and I am still in a rush will close for this time.

Again extending our heartiest birthday greetings and wishing you many more, I am,

Most sincerely,

P.S. Think I told you that you were born on the 4th. Sunday after EASTER as EASTER was the 25th. of March that year and I never will remember [sic] that deep snow of 12". If this had not been leap year this EASTER would have been on same date and there was snow here this EASTER having snowed about all day and some 6" deep.

Erwin Hart, textile industrialist, was a long-time friend of Martha Berry and supporter of the institution.

UPTON SINCLAIR
STATION A, PASADENA
CALIFORNIA

February 13, 1941

Martha Berry,
Berry College and Berry Schools,
Mount Berry, Ga.

Dear Mrs. Berry:

I am glad to have your friendly letter, and I send you a copy of "World's End" and also some pamphlets and recent circulars. I will not autograph the book, because painful experience has proved that it is better not to do this with books intended for a library. They have a way of disappearing.

Sincerely,

Upton Sinclair was a famous American author and reformer.

Fair Lane
Dearborn, Michigan

May 17th [1947]

Dear Inez,

Thanks for your two kind notes. First I want to thank you for all that was done for us at Berry, and the good things you put on the car when we came away. The turkey, we had for dinner on Monday night, the night Mr. Ford passed away. He enjoyed his dinner very much.

The flowers were fresh when we got home. The little chickens, we had for dinner on the way home, and the ginger snaps were so very much, and we both spoke of it a number of times. It looked so good in every way, just as good as when Miss Berry was there. I am so happy to think Mr. Ford saw it again.

Monday, April the 7th was a wonderful day for Mr. Ford, read most of the morning, and after lunch he said he would go down to the power house, in the basement of the garage, to see if he could help do something to help get the electricity going. It was all under water. Then he went all through the Greenfield Village to see if the water had done damage to the old houses. Then he went to the Rouge plant, drove all through it. When he got back, I said, "You have been gone a long time." He said, "Yes, and you must come with me soon. The plant is so interesting." I said I would. He rested until dinner time. Then we listened to a program on the radio, then tried to read by candlelight. The electric lights were out. We did not like reading by candlelight, so thought we might as well go to bed. We went upstairs, he to his dressing room, me to mine. Shortly I heard him coughing and wheezing. He was sitting up in bed. I went to him and tried to help him, but could not stop the cough, so I sent for the doctor, thinking he could give him something to stop the cough. It eased up a little, and I eased him back on his pillow. He stopped coughing, and was very quiet, just said put out the light. I did, then put it on again, but he was gone. I think he must have stooped to take off his shoes, and caused the hemorrhage in his brain.

I still cannot believe he is gone, he was so well, and in such good spirits. His passing could not have been more peaceful.

I am glad you could come to the funeral. Please tell Mr. Keown and Dr. Lindsay I am glad that they could be here, and that you were all taken care of.

Thank you for the program, and pictures taken at Berry. I have mislaid the pictures. Could you send me another set? They want to put one in the *Farm and Garden Magazine*. If you come to Michigan, do come to see me.

Sincerely,

Clara Ford

Inez Henry, graduate of the girls' high school, served as assistant to Martha Berry and to Berry presidents.

Part V

Additional Reading about Martha Berry and Her Schools

Books

Biographical Directories

Book Sections

Articles

New York Times

Unpublished Manuscripts

Berry College Archives: Selective Collections

Books

Bassett, Ruth (writer) and Ken Hawkins (new photography). *Berry College: Building Upon the Miracle.* Atlanta: Corporate Stories, Ltd., 1996.

Berry, Martha. *I Wish't You'd of Come Sooner.* Mount Berry: Berry Schools, 1935.

Blackburn, Joyce. *Martha Berry, Little Woman with a Big Dream.* New York: J. B. Lippincott Company, 1968.

Blackburn, Joyce. *Martha Berry, A Woman of Courageous Spirit and Bold Dreams.* Nashville: Rutledge Hill Press, 1986.

Byers, Tracy. *For the Glory of Young Manhood and Womanhood—Yesterday, Today and Tomorrow.* Mount Berry: Berry Schools, Vol. 1, 1963; Vol.2, 1964.

Byers, Tracy. *Martha Berry, the Sunday Lady of Possum Trot.* New York: Putnam, 1932.

Byers, Tracy. *Martha Berry's Living Glory.* Mount Berry: Berry College, 1967.

Cook, S. H. *Half Century at Berry.* Mount Berry: Berry College, 1961.

Dickey, Ouida and Herman Higgins, eds. *Berry Trails: An Historic and Contemporary Guide to Berry College, Centennial Edition.* Mount Berry: Berry College, 2001.

Kane, Harnett T. *Miracle in the Mountains.* Garden City: Doubleday, 1956.

Myers, Elisabeth P. *Angel of Appalachia: Martha Berry.* New York: J. Messner, 1968.

Pendley, Evelyn Hoge. *A Lady I Loved.* Mount Berry: Berry College, 1966.

Pendley, Evelyn Hoge. *A Berry Cavalcade.* Mount Berry: Berry College, 1981.

Pendley, Evelyn Hoge. *Education for Service: An Account of the Administrations of the Berry Schools from 1902–1979.* Mount Berry: Berry College, Vol. 1, 1963; Vol. 2, 1977; Vol. 3, 1985.

Phelan, Mary K. *Martha Berry.* New York: Thomas Y. Crowell Company, 1972.

BIOGRAPHICAL DIRECTORIES

The American People's Encyclopedia. Vol. 3. Chicago: Spencer Press, 1948. 3-4.

Biographical Dictionary of American Educators. Vol. 1. Westport: Greenwood Press, 1978. 119-120.

Compton's Pictured Encyclopedia. Vol. 2. Chicago: F. E. Compton & Co., 1960. 144-145.

Current Biography. New York: H. W. Wilson, 1940. 80-81.

Current Biography. New York: H. W. Wilson, 1942. 79.

Dictionary of American Biography (supplement three). New York: Scribner's 1941-1945. 62-64.

Encyclopedia of American Biography. Vol. 2. New York: American Historical Society, 1934. 150-151.

Herringshaw's American Blue Book of Biography. Chicago: American Publishers Association, 1915. 110.

Leaders in Education. Vol. 2. New York: Science Press, 1941. 78.

MacDonald, Victoria-Maria. "Martha McChesney Berry." *American National Biography.* Vol. 2. New York: Oxford University Press, 1999. 689-690.

The National Cyclopedia of American Biography. Vol. C. New York: James T. White, 1930. 49-50.

The New Century Cyclopedia of Names. Vol. 1. New York: Appleton-Century-Crofts, 1954. 483.

Notable American Women, 1607-1950. Vol. 1. Cambridge: Belknap, 1971. 137-138.

Webster's Biographical Dictionary. Springfield: Merriam, 1943. 145.

Who Was Who 1941-1950. Vol. IV. London: Adam & Charles Black, ca 1967. 94.

Who Was Who in America 1943-1950. Vol. 2, 4th ed. Chicago: Marquis, 1963. 94.

Who's Who 1935. London: Adam & Charles Black, 1935. 258.

Who's Who 1937. London: Adam & Charles Black, 1937. 260.

Who's Who 1941. London: Adam & Charles Black, 1941. 245.

Who's Who and Why, 1940. New York: H. W. Wilson Company, 1940. 80- 81.

Who's Who in America, Vol. XI Chicago: Marquis, 1920-1921. 240.

Who's Who in America, Vol. XXII Chicago: Marquis, 1942-1943. 313.

Woman's Who's Who of America. New York: The American Commonwealth Co., 1914-1915. 97.

Book Sections

Abbott, Lawrence F., ed. *The Letters of Archie Butt.* Garden City: Doubleday, Page and Company, 1924. 267-269.

Ashenhurst, J.O. *The Day of the Church.* New York: Funk and Wagnalls, 1910. 91-92.

Bartlett, Robert Merrill. *Builders of a New World.* New York: Friendship Press, 1933. 145-146.

Bartlett, Robert Merrill. *They Dared To Live.* New York: Association Press, 1937. 7-10.

Boogher, Wm. F. *The Lineage of Miss Martha Berry.* Washington D. C., 1910. 7.

Burgess, Mary W. *Education: Contributions of Women.* Minneapolis: Dillon Press, 1975. 46-69.

Cooney, Loraine M. *Garden History of Georgia—1722-1933: Georgia Bicentennial Edition.* Ed. Hattie C. Rainwater. Atlanta: The Peachtree Garden Club, 1933. 447-452.

Dean, Vera T. "The Dream of Martha Berry." *A North Georgia Journal of History.* Ed. Olin Jackson. Woodstock: Legacy Communications, 1989. 56-61.

Fenner, Mildred Sandison, and Eleanor C. Fishburn. *Pioneer American Educators.* Washington: National Education Association, 1944. 145-152.

Forsee, Alyesa. *Women Who Reached for Tomorrow.* Philadelphia: Macrae Smith Company, 1960. 178-202.

Hillinger, Charles. *America People and Places in all Fifty States.* Santa Barbara: Capra, 1996. 89-93.

Howell, Clark. *History of Georgia.* Vol.2. Atlanta: S. J. Clarke Publishing Co. 1926. 408–413.

Huff, Warren, and Edna Lenore Webb Huff, eds. *Famous Americans Second Series.* Los Angeles: Charles Webb and Co., 1941. 41-54.

Kelly, Fred, and Ella Ratcliffe, *College Projects for Aiding Students.* United States Office of Education. Washington: GPO, 1938, 49-53.

Knight, Lucien Lamar. *Georgia's Bi-Centennial Memoirs and Memories.* Vol. 2. Atlanta: Knight, 1932. 62-91.

Knight, Lucien Lamar. *Georgia's Landmarks, Memorials, and Legends.* Vol. 1. Atlanta: Byrd, 1913. 250-261.

Knight, Lucien Lamar. *A Standard History of Georgia and Georgians.* Vol. 2. Chicago: Lewis, 1917. 1034.

Kulkin, Mary-Ellen. *Her Way, Biographies of Women for Young People.* Chicago: American Library Association, 1976. 33-34+.

Leipold, L. E. *Famous American Teachers.* Minneapolis: T. S. Denison, 1972. 51-58.

Main, Mildred Miles, and Samuel H. Thompson. *Footprints.* Austin: Steck-Vaughn, 1957. 218-226.

Mears, Louise Wilhelmina. *They Come and Go.* Boston: Christopher Publishing House, 1955. 51-53.

Morgan, Angela. *Angela Morgan's Recitals.* Philadelphia: Penn Publishing Co., 1913. 79-81.

Morgan, Angela. *Silver Clothes.* New York: Dodd, Mead and Company, 1926. 144-145.

Nevin, James B., ed. *Prominent Women of Georgia.* Atlanta: The National Biographical Publishers, 1928. 14-15.

Nevins, Allan, and Frank Ernest Hill. *Ford Expansion and Challenge, 1915-1933.* New York: Scribner's, 1957. 497-498+.

Proceedings of the Ninth Conference for Education in the South. Richmond: Richmond College, 1906. 82-91.

Scott, Anne Firor. *World Book Encyclopedia.* Vol. 2. Chicago: World Book, Inc., 1994. 272.

Steed, Hal A. *Georgia: Unfinished State.* New York: Alfred A. Knopf, 1942. 242 –253.

Stidger, William L. *The Human Side of Greatness.* New York: Harper, 1940. 162-175.

Strawhorn, John C. *Returning to South Carolina: Growing Up in the Rural South in the Early 20th Century.* Fredericksburg: BookCrafters, 1998. 171-234.

Articles

Armes, Ethel. "Roosevelt's Trail." *The Sunday Constitution Magazine* 3 May 1925: 3+.

Atkins, Jonathan M. "Philanthropy in the Mountains: Martha Berry and the Early Years of the Berry Schools." *Georgia Historical Quarterly* Winter 1998: 854-876.

Ayers, Mary Frances. "Martha Berry: Her Heritage and Her Achievements Part I." *Georgia Journal* August/September 1983: 37-38.

Ayers, Mary Frances. "Martha Berry: Her Heritage and Her Achievements Part II." *Georgia Journal* October/November 1983: 26+.

Basso, Hamilton. "About the Berry Schools, an Open Letter to Miss Martha Berry." *The New Republic* 4 April 1934: 206-208.

Bellamy, Francis R. "Martha Berry." *Good Housekeeping* October 1921: 21-22+.

Berry, Martha. "Address." *National Education Association Proceedings and Addresses* 1929: 337-340.

Berry, Martha. "Corner Stone in Child Training." *Junior Home for Parent and Child* August 1932: 6-7.

Berry, Martha. "The Evolution of a Sunday School." *Charities and the Commons* November 1906: 195-200.

Berry, Martha. "Growth of the Berry School Idea." *Survey* 16 December 1911: 140+.

Berry, Martha. "A School in the Woods." *Outlook* 6 August 1904: 838-841.

Berry, Martha. "The Story of the Berry Schools." *The Southern Highlander* December 1915: 176-186. April 1916: 3-21. June 1916: 53-71.

Berry, Martha. "To 1934 Graduates." *Progressive Farmer* May 1934: 31.

Berry, Martha. "Uplifting Backwoods Boys in Georgia." *World's Work* July 1904: 4986-4992.

"The Berry Schools." *Dixie Highway* September 1917: 8.

Booth, Alice. "America's Twelve Greatest Women: Martha Berry." *Good Housekeeping* August 1931: 50-51+.

Booth, Alice. "America's Twelve Greatest Women." *Literary Digest* 5 September 1931: 21-22.

Boyce, Faith. "Berry—The Living School." *Woman Citizen* 21 March, 1925: 11-12+.

Byers, Tracy. "The Berry Schools of Georgia." *The Missionary Review of the World* January 1933: 33-36.

Childers, James Saxon. "The Sunday Lady of Possum Trot." *Reader's Digest* July 1954: 55-58.

Childers, James Saxon. "The Sunday Lady of Possum Trot." *Town and Country* July 1954: 68-69+.

Cooper, Walter G. "Notable Constructive Work." Atlanta: The Georgia College Placement Office, 1925. 4-7.

Cooper, Walter G. "The Wonderful Work of Miss Martha Berry." *The City Builder.* May 1925: 8-9+.

Crawford, W. A. "Berry Schools, Near Rome, Georgia, Unique Educational Institution." *Central of Georgia Magazine* June 1931: 6-7.

Dickey, Charles H. "Martha Berry." *Christian Herald* June 1934: 4+.

"Died." *Time* 9 March 1942: 42.

"A Distinguished Citizen of Georgia." *School and Society* 5 September 1931: 314-315.

Doremus, Harnette V. A. "The Gate of Opportunity." *Young People's Friend* 29 January 1939: 1.

Dowdle, Lois P. "Martha Berry and Her Schools." *Progressive Farmer* March 1933: 5.

Edmonds, Richard Woods. "The Berry Schools." *Manufacturer's Record* 7 July 1927: 77-81.

Edwards, Harry Stillwell. "Epic of the Berry Schools." *The Atlanta Journal* 14 January 1932: 8.

Gardner, Maude. "Martha Berry's Labor of Love." *School Arts Magazine* May 1926: 519-526.

Gaston, Joel. "Centennial for Lady of Possum Trot." *The Atlanta Journal and Constitution Magazine* 2 October 1966: 24-28+.

"Georgians of the Century." *Georgia Trend* January 2000: 50.

Glover, Katherine. "Working for an Education in a Southern School." *Craftsman* March 1909: 707-717.

Goldman, R. L. "The Sunday Lady." *Shrine Magazine* June 1926: 7-11+. July 1926: 20-23+.

Hagedorn, Hermann. "A Pilgrimage to the Berry Schools." *Outlook* 10 June 1925: 214-216.

Hammond, Emily V. "Will You Go 'Berry-ing'?" *Commerce and Finance* 1926: 881.

"Have You Named Your Great Women?" *Good Housekeeping* December 1930: 82-83.

Hay, James Jr. "Lifters, Not Leaners." *American Motorist* September 1929: 13.

Heck, W. H. "Educational Uplift in the South." *World's Work* June 1904: 5026.

Henry, Inez. "Famous Georgia Women: Martha Berry." *Georgia Life* Autumn 1979: 30-32.

Hill, W. C. "What One Woman Has Done." *Inspiration News* May 1930: 83-87.

Hoehler, Fred K. "Martha Berry—Her School and Her Forest." *American Forests* July 1925: 400-401+.

Hoehler, F. K. "Sunday Lady of Possum Trot." *Success* November 1923: 54-58.

Howard, Annie H. "Home of Martha Berry." *Georgia Homes and Landmarks* Atlanta: Southern Features Syndicate, 1929: 97-98.

"Humanitarianism Award to Teacher." *Christian Science Monitor.* 19 February 1940. 19.

Hunt, Frazier. "Martha Berry." *College Humor* October 1932: 32-33+.

Kane, Harnett T. with Inez Henry. "Miracle in the Mountains." *The Atlanta Journal Constitution Magazine* 14 October 1956: 10-11+.

Kelly, F. J., and E. B. Ratcliffe. "Self-Help Colleges: Berry College." *U. S. Office of Education Bulletin.* 1938: 49-53.

King, Barrington. "To Walk in the Light." *American Forests* July 1961: 16-19.

Klingelhoffer, George H. "Berry School Methods in Carpentry and Construction." *Manual Training* November 1915: 184-189.

Lewis, Ann E. "Martha Berry—Her Heirs and Legacies." *Georgia Magazine* October/November 1966: 18-20.

"Long-Running Ford." Editorial. *Rome News-Tribune* 25 January 2001: 4.

Lord, Russell. "In Quest of Another Lincoln." *Country Home* January 1933: 14-15.

"Martha Berry Opened a Gate to Opportunity." *Southern Living* October 1985: 4+.

"Martha Berry's Vision." Editorial. *Rome News Tribune.* 25 January 2001: 4.

"Martha Berry Portrait." *Spur* August 1934: 42.

"Martha McC. Berry." *Survey* 7 March 1942: 81.

"Martha McChesney Berry." *School and Society* 2 March 1940: 274. 7 March 1942: 269.

Matthews, John L. "The Sunday Lady of Possum Trot." *Everybody's Magazine* December 1908: 723-732.

"Miss Martha Berry." *High School Quarterly* October 1928: 3.

"Miss Martha McChesney Berry." *Etude* April 1942: 220.

"Most Worthy Institution." *Rome News-Tribune* 12 January 1902.

Mullett, Mary B. "21 Years of Begging—for Other People." *American Magazine* April 1923: 68-69.

"New Honors Come to Martha Berry for Her Heroic Work for Rural Mountain Children." *Southern Cultivator* 15 November 1928: 4.

Newton, Louie D. "Making Dreams Come True." *The City Builder* August 1924: 11-13+.

North, Eleanor B. "Martha Berry...Pioneer in 'Different' Education." *The Delta Kappa Gamma Bulletin* Fall 1957: 13-19.

"Obituary." *Etude* 1942: 220.

"Obituary." *School and Society* April 1942: 269.

"Obituary." *Survey* 7 March 1942: 81.

"Obituary." *Time* 9 March 1942: 42.

"One Woman's Vision." *American Forests* February 1954: 14-15.

Parkhurst, Genevieve. "The Sunday Lady of Possum Trot." *Pictorial Review* January 1929: 14-15+.

Parton, Mary Field. "We-uns Has Come. Larn Us." *The World Review* 13 May 1929: 218-219.

"Portrait." *American Forests* February 1954: 12.

"Portrait." *Good Housekeeping* December 1930: 82.

"Portrait." *Outlook* 29 April 1925: 640.

"Portrait." *World's Work* June 1907: 9017.

Reese, J. C. "Martha Berry." *American Magazine* December 1910: 182-185.

Reply to letter of Don West. *The New Republic* 25 October 1933: 292.

Roberts, Harvey. "The Berry Schools of Georgia." *The Georgia Review* Summer 1955: 179-189.

Roberts, Sarah Elizabeth. "The Berry Schools." *Saint Nicholas* September 1925: 1140-1143.

"The Roosevelt Medals." *Outlook* 29 April 1925: 640.

Ross, Ishbell. "Opportunity Gate on the Dixie Highway." *New York Herald-Tribune Magazine* 10 May 1925: 5.

"Schools for the Mountains." *The New Republic* 4 April 1934: 202-203.

"Selected to Receive the Second Annual Humanitarian Award of the Variety Clubs of America." *School and Society* 2 March 1940: 274.

Senate Journal of the Georgia General Assembly Atlanta: Stein, 1924: 214.

Shaw, Albert. "Martha Berry and Her Patriotic Work." *The American Review of Reviews* June 1925: 593-597.

Springer, Lois. "Some Illustrious Bell Collectors: Martha Berry's Bells." *Hobbies* April 1955: 34-35.

Stuart, Jim. "From the Kentucky Hills." *The New Republic* 3 January 1934: 228.

" 'Sunday Lady' Honored, Variety Clubs Award Plaque to Berry Schools' Founder."*Newsweek* 2 April 1940: 37-38.

"The Sunday Lady of Possum Trot." *Literary Digest* 5 September 1931: 21-22.

"The Sunshine Lady." *National Education Association Journal* April 1942: A54+.

"Supersalesman." *Entrepreneur Spirit* 1 August 1974: 49-52.

Swain, John D. "In Tune With Our Times." *Red Book Magazine* June 1932: 44-52.

Tally, Alma. "Floyd Woman Devotes Life, Wealth to Education of Southern Mountain Folk at Berry Schools." *Rome News-Tribune* 26 November 1930: 4.

Tarbell, Ida M. "When Roosevelt Was Here." *Red Cross Magazine* October 1920: 15-20.

Tate, W. K. "A Visit to the Berry School." *Journal of Education* 8 April 1915: 375-381.

"Thanks for Miss Berry." *Life* 24 October 1955: 91-92+.

Van Ness, James. "Martha Berry and Her Mountain School." *The Mentor* August 1928: 18-20.

West, Don. Letter. "Sweatshops in the Schools." *The New Republic* 4 October 1933: 216.

New York Times

Berry, Martha. Letter. "A Mountain School." *New York Times* 30 December 1915: 12.

Berry, Martha. Letter. "Berry School's Loss." *New York Times* 10 May 1926: 20.

"Berry Schools Need Help." Letter. *New York Times* 2 May 1926. sec. E: 8.

"Chase to Be Berry Speaker." *New York Times* 2 December 1936: 10.

"Coolidge Presents Roosevelt Medals." *New York Times* 16 May 1925: 23.

Davis, Lloyd D. Letter. "Concerning the Berry Schools." *New York Times* 1 January 1916: 10.

"Dr. Berry Honored by Kappa Delta Pi: Woman Founder of Georgia School Made Fraternity Member—28 Others Also Inducted." *New York Times* 6 December 1936: 50.

"Educators Study School in Georgia." *New York Times* 11 November 1956: 130.

Kelly, Florence Finch. "The Founder of the Berry Schools." Rev. of *Martha Berry, The Sunday Lady of Possum Trot,* by Tracy Byers. *New York Times* 8 May 1932, sec. 4: 11.

"Left Family Home to Berry Schools." *New York Times* 6 March 1942: 14.

"Martha Berry Asks Aid for Berry Schools in Training Poor." *New York Times* 19 Nov. 1930: 23.

"Martha Berry Gets Patriotism Medal for Work in the South." *New York Times* 24 February 1933: 14.

"Martha Berry Gets Town Hall Medal." *New York Times* 20 November 1931: 25.

"Martha Berry Wins Town Hall Medal." *New York Times* 14 May 1931: 2.

"Martha M'C. Berry, Educator, Is Dead." *New York Times* 27 February 1942: 17.

"Miss Berry and Her School." *New York Times* 2 November 1928: 26.

"Miss Berry's School." *New York Times* 1 January 1912: 12.

"Miss Berry Chosen '39 Humanitarian." *New York Times* 18 February 1940: 5.

"Miss Berry Honored by 850 at Dinner." *New York Times* 29 November 1935, sec. 18: 17.

"Miss Earhart Gets Oglethorpe Degree: Flier is Honored With Eleven Other Outstanding Women by Georgia University." *New York Times* 27 May 1935: 10.

"More Roosevelt Medalists." *New York Times* 20 April 1925: 16.

Pope, Virginia. "Bringing Light to the Mountaineers." *New York Times Magazine* 10 May 1925, sec. 4: 4.

"Roosevelt Holds, People Back Him." *New York Times* 24 November 1933: 1.

"Roosevelt Medal for Three Pioneers." *New York Times* 20 April 1925: 19.

"Schools Founder Feted: Miss Martha Berry Honor Guest at Reception in Quebec." *New York Times* 10 August 1933: 14.

"Seeks $1,000,000 for Hill Children." *New York Times* 16 September 1928, sec. 2: 20.

"Southern Editors Adopt Ethics Code." *New York Times* 8 July 1925: 5.

"Three Get Medals in Social Sciences." *New York Times* 11 May 1939: 25.

"To Be Honored for 'Service to Humanity'." *New York Times* 7 May 1939, sec. 3: 5.

"Topics of the Times: Georgia Public Schools." *New York Times* 4 March 1942: 18. 19 November 1930: 23.

"Twelve Women Declared Nation's Greatest." *New York Times* 24 February 1931: 18.

Unpublished Manuscripts

Asbury, Susan. "The Berry Family: An Evolution of a Southern Family Living in the Reconstruction and New South Eras." Paper submitted for graduate credit in History 788 at the University of South Carolina, Columbia, December 2, 1997.

Asbury, Susan. "History of the Oak Hill Home: Historic Analysis for a Planned Historic Structure Report." Rome, Georgia, August 7, 1997.

Asbury, Susan. "Mr. Ford's Car and Martha Berry's Buggy." Presented at Founder's Day, Berry College, January 18, 2001.

Marks, Paul. "Berry College Intercollegiate Athletics: A History from 1946." Mount Berry, Georgia, February 6, 1993.

Peterson, Charles E. "Dr. Martha Berry: An Investigation into the Academic Honors Bestowed on a Remarkable Woman." Rome, Georgia, November 1997.

Pirkle, Willis Nathaniel. "Lectures and Historical Perspectives of the Berry Schools." Mount Berry, Georgia, 1992.

Berry College Archives: Selective Collections

Berry Alumni Quarterly. 1914-1966, 1973-1980.

Berry Alumni Quarterly Southern Highlander. 1966-1973.

Berry Chronicle. 1995-present.

Berry College Catalog. 1973-present.

Berry College Graduate Catalog. 1972-present.

Berry Dispatch. 1985-present.

The Berry News. 1921-1924.

Berry Quarterly. 1980-1985.

The Berry School News. 1912-1921.

Berry Schools Bulletin. 1904-1973.

Cabin Log. 1935-present.

Campus Carrier. 1960-present.

G. Leland Green Correspondence, Berry Schools Office of the Principal, Record Group 2, Berry College Archives, Memorial Library, Berry College.

Information Weekly. 1969-1985.

John R. Bertrand Papers. Record Group 4, Berry College Archives, Memorial Library, Berry College, 1956-1979.

Martha Berry Papers. Record Group 1, Berry College Archives, Memorial Library, Berry College, 1902-1942.

The Mount Berry News. 1924-1960.

Robert H. Adams Letters Received, Berry Schools Office of the Principal, Record Group 2, Berry College Archives, Memorial Library, Berry College.

The Southern Highlander. 1907-1966.